By Holli Rovenger, M.B.A., R.D./L.D. and Alexa Bosshardt, M.P.S., R.D./L.D.

Cover Design: *Brian Fein*

Photograph on back cover: *Chet J. Auerbach*
taken at Cafe Arugula, Lighthouse Point, Fla.

Typesetting: *FIU Publications*

Printing: *McNaughton and Gunn*

Copyright © 1991 by Nutritional Marketing Services, Inc.
All rights reserved. Printed in the United States of America.
Library of Congress Catalog Card Number: 91-90523
ISBN: 0-9630382-0-6

Published and Distributed by:
Nutritional Marketing Services, Inc.
1131 N.W. 99 Ave.   260 Hibiscus Ave.
Plantation, FL 33322   Lauderdale-by-the Sea, FL 33308

Any questions regarding purchasing: 305-472-9649
                                         305-772-6872

ABOUT THE AUTHORS:

Holli Rovenger, M.B.A., R.D./L.D. is in Private Practice - a consultant dietitian to individuals referred by physicians and others in the community. She also consults for restaurants and newspapers - such as the Miami Herald; and teaches wellness programs for groups and corporations, including "Heart Healthy" cooking classes. A graduate of Syracuse University and Florida International University, Holli is also an Adjunct Professor with the Florida International University Department of Dietetics and Nutrition. She is a member of the American Dietetic Association, the Broward County Dietetic Association, Dietitians/Nutritionists in Private Practice and Sports and Cardiovascular Nutritionists.

Alexa Bosshardt, M.P.S., R.D./L.D. is a Menu Development Manager for Arby's, Inc. in Miami Beach. A graduate of the Cornell University School of Hotel Administration, Alexa is also an Adjunct Professor with the Florida International University Department of Dietetics and Nutrition and teaches continuing education classes in nutrition for the Chef Association of Greater Ft. Lauderdale. She is an active member of the American Dietetic Association, The Broward County Dietetic Association and the American Culinary Federation, and directs a restaurant review committee for the Broward County Chapter of the American Heart Association. Alexa was named the 1990 "Culinarian of the Year" by the Chef Association of Greater Ft. Lauderdale.

Holli and Alexa are principals of Nutritional Marketing Services, Inc.

Acknowledgements

This book is dedicated to my Mom, Elaine Stein, who gave me the opportunity to go to school, and instilled in me the belief that you can be, and do, anything you set out to!

I would like to thank my husband, Scott, for his patience, opinions and help on this project; and my wonderful children, Dani and Josh, who repeatedly asked the questions - "Are you on the phone/cooking again???"

Holli

This book is dedicated to my Mom, Valerie Hart, with whom I have stood back to back in the kitchen through countless gourmet dinner parties and family gatherings.

Special thanks to my husband, Kurt, who had to endure hours of recipe testing but, at least, didn't have to type this manuscript as he did my graduate monograph!

Alexa

Thanks to our Recipe and taste Testers who helped with our overflow:

Janis Altman
Barbara Bianchi
Lori Eisenberg
Paulette Gruskin
Linda Hale
Valerie Hart
Michelle Isaacson
Jane Matzkin
Debra Rubin
Lori Stern
Ina Witlin

A special thanks to Valerie Hart, Scott Rovenger and Ina Witlin for their editorial help!

TABLE OF CONTENTS

Main Dish Salads

Side Sauces/Dressings

Side Dishes/Vegetable Dishes

Breads

Seafood -

Poultry

7

Beef/Veal/Lamb/Pork

Associations and Abbreviations Featured in Today's Specials

References

Order Forms

PREFACE

Today's Specials is a cookbook that features heart healthy recipes from popular chefs and restaurants throughout Florida. Recipes submitted to us represent a range of traditional and ethnic influences. Many feature New World cuisine, a creative combination of fresh tropical foods that's gaining a national reputation. These recipes were analyzed for nutritional content and are printed as submitted, or modified if necessary, so that they now meet dietary guidelines recommended by major health organizations. Each recipe has been tested in several home kitchens and adapted, as needed, so the finalized recipe is suitable for quick and easy, as well as nutritious preparation. Each recipe includes nutritional information per serving. The modified or adapted recipe is as flavorful as the original or classical recipe. Registered and licensed dietitians applied proven food science techniques to ensure successful results.

Today's Specials also serves as a guide to popular restaurants around the state. Most recipes are prefaced with background and anecdotal information about the chef or establishment. In addition, the text includes nutrition information, preparation and cooking tips, and information about "healthful" Florida food products, such as tropical fruits and vegetables, the "Skinniest Six" cuts of beef and native seafood.

FOREWORD

Many restaurants today are making an effort to "lighten" up their menu offerings. Many chefs are reducing or omitting the amount of cream and butter they were taught to use in favor of the natural flavors of foods, a light touch of infused vinegars and oils, and fresh herbs. They are using more stock reductions and vegetable purees instead of roux to thicken sauces. Today's Specials focuses on the heightened health consciousness of restaurants and chefs all over the state of Florida.

We hope to show you how good nutrition and the pleasure of cooking and eating can go hand in hand. You will find recipes that are creative, gourmet and easy to follow! Consider the following guidelines while reading and experimenting with any recipe:

1. Be flexible with some ingredients, whether due to unavailablility (seasonality) of a given fruit or vegetable or the dislike of a particular herb or spice.

2. Don't be afraid to substitute a similar ingredient, such as dried herbs for fresh, or use a frozen product, such as an IQF (individually quick frozen) form, instead of fresh.

3. Feel free to increase the portion size of any vegetable or grain accompaniment. We have tried to illustrate this throughout the book.

4. For those of you who are not fish lovers, we urge you to try some of the more eclectic dishes such as "Tea Smoked Scallops with Pistachio Pesto," as they may convert you! In addition, many recipes that call for fish can be prepared with chicken instead, and vice versa.

5. Many sauces can be mixed and matched as we have noted with a "♥" after the recipe.

6. Author's suggestions throughout the book are noted with a "♥". Don't be afraid to experiment and have fun with Today's Specials. After all, this is how chefs create!

All recipes have been tested in home kitchens and comply with dietary guidelines promoted by leading professional organizations. Each recipe features the nutritional information today's health-conscious consumers are looking for, including fat, cholesterol and sodium. Meat, poultry, or fish protein portions are based on a 6 oz. raw weight or 4 to 5 oz. cooked portion, unless otherwise noted. However, if you would like to have a larger portion, do so; just note the nutrient values will also increase, reflecting your modification.

PLEASE BE AWARE that in order to translate "heart healthy" nutritional information into practice, we have had to modify (decrease fat or salt content, substitute ingredients, etc.) many of the original recipes that were submitted to us. Some of the recipes by the same name featured in this publication **may** be prepared and served differently in the actual restaurant. Also, the chefs and restaurants featured were working where indicated at the time we received their recipes.

We would like to thank all the chefs and restaurants who have been so creative and cooperative. It has been a real pleasure working with them!

Note:
We are on a mission to promote the creative abilities of chefs and restaurateurs to cater to today's more healthful lifestyle! We apologize if we have unintentionally missed one of your favorites. Please contact us if you or your favorite chef or restaurant anywhere in the country would like to participate in our next publication.

Please send in the form below and we will send you Today's Specials information A.S.A.P.

Chef (Restauranteur) _____

Rèstaurant_____

Type of Cuisine _____

Address_____

Phone #_____

DIETARY GUIDELINES FOR AMERICANS

What are some of the things we hear about our diets? We hear that the "typical" American's diet is too high in sugar, fat, sodium and cholesterol and too low in complex carbohydrates and fiber! We are told we don't eat enough of a variety of fresh fruits and vegetables! We indulge in too much ground beef and too many eggs! We hear that too many children are substituting nutrient-rich milk with nutrient-empty colas and other sweetened carbonated beverages. In addition, we spend too much time in front of the television eating high fat and high sodium snack foods!

Heart disease and cancer are, respectively, the number one and number two killers in this country. Our diet, among other factors, such as heredity, a smoking habit, and a sedentary lifestyle, may play an important role in reducing the risk for these and other chronic diseases. We have summarized below some of the dietary guidelines promoted by many professional health organizations:

Eat a nutritionally adequate diet consisting of a variety of foods.
There is no "perfect food". No food by itself provides all the essential nutrients our bodies need. A variety of foods must be consumed to provide the body with an adequate and balanced amount of those nutrients . Use the "Basic 4 Food Groups" as a guide, with an emphasis on foods from the Bread/Cereal and Fruit/Vegetable groups.

Achieve and maintain a healthy body weight.
Determining a "healthy" body weight takes into consideration the height and body frame type of the individual, as well as his or her activity level. Exercise is an important component in achieving a healthy body. One can be over fat without necessarily being overweight. Remember that muscle weighs more than fat. The more fit the body is and the greater the amount of lean muscle tissue to fat, the more the body may weigh. Health risks increase with being either overweight or underweight; both overnutrition and undernutrition are forms of malnutrition.

Control fat consumption, especially saturated fat and cholesterol.
The American Heart Association and other organizations recommend that total fat intake be less than 30% of calories. In addition, many recommend controlling the amount of saturated fat in the diet. They also recommend that dietary cholesterol intake not exceed 300 mg per day. Today's Specials guidelines were to keep the fat content to within 30-35% of total calories for each of the recipes featured and to

keep the cholesterol content to approximately 100 mg or less per recipe. Our recipes focus on the use of monunsaturated oils, such as olive oil or polyunsaturated oils, such as corn oil. Soft tub margarines are preferred over stick margarines.

Cholesterol is an important constituent of cells and body fluids. Yet, excessive cholesterol in the blood may deposit along the walls of the arteries, creating fatty streaks and narrowing the passageway for blood to flow through. This, in turn, may increase one's risk for heart and other cardiovascular diseases, such as a heart attack or a stroke. Avoiding too much dietary fat, especially saturated fat and cholesterol may help reduce your risk.

Egg yolks are the number one contributor of cholesterol to the American diet, with one large egg containing approximately 213 mg cholesterol. The American Heart Association recommends limiting whole eggs to 3-4 per week. This includes egg yolks used in recipe preparation, as well as those consumed for meals. Most meat, fish and poultry portions contain between about 20-30 mg cholesterol per ounce cooked weight. All animal-based foods contribute cholesterol to the diet. Liver and other organ meats are especially high in cholesterol and should only be consumed occasionally . No plant foods contain cholesterol, though, so don't be fooled by certain brands of vegetable oils claiming "no cholesterol!" All oils, however, derive 100% of their calories from fat.

It is the saturated fats (ie; the fats found in dairy products, meats, butter and "tropical oils," such as coconut, palm oil and cocoa butter) that elevate **BLOOD** cholesterol levels. This is where most consumers are confused. Many products are advertised "low cholesterol" or "no cholesterol", which may very well be true, but if you investigate further (read the label), you may see that the product is loaded with fat, especially saturated fat. Please be aware of this and become an educated consumer!

Choose foods that are high in complex carbohydrates and fibers.
To insure a healthful mix of both soluble and insoluble fiber, include a variety of fresh fruits, vegetables, legumes and grains. The National Cancer Institute recommends increasing fiber intake to 20-30 g per day, with an upper limit of 35 g. To meet these guidelines, consume at least five servings per day of raw or lightly cooked fruits and vegetables and a variety of legumes and whole grains. Carbohydrates should make up at least 55% - 60% of the total daily calories. In recipes that call for white, enriched rice or other grains, such as breads or pastas, substitute a whole

grain variety to increase the fiber content of the meal. Be sure to check package directions for the preparation of different grains.

Use sugars only in moderation.

Most Americans derive too many of their carbohydrate calories from refined sugars, leading to dental caries. Sugar, by any other name, is sugar. Sucrose, glucose, fructose, dextrose, levulose, maltose, lactose, high fructose corn syrup, corn syrup, corn sugar, dextrin, molasses, honey, most jams and jellies, and syrups all have distinct flavors of their own and different sweetening powers. However, they all provide "empty" calories; virtually no nutritional value.

Consume salt and sodium in moderation.

Sodium is one of many minerals referred to as "electrolytes," which play a role in regulating fluid balance and acid/base balance in the body. Sodium also assists in nerve impulse transmission. Sodium chloride, or table salt, is 40% sodium and 60% chloride. One teaspoon (1 teaspoon = about 5 g) of salt contains approximately 2000 mg of sodium. Although sodium is vital to life, most of us consume much more than we need to. The most recent Recommended Daily Allowances (1989) established an Estimated Minimum Requirement (EMR: what your body physiologically needs) for sodium to be just 500 mg/day. The average American consumes about 10-15 g of salt per day; the equivalent of about 4,000 - 6,000 mg of sodium. A high sodium intake is one of many factors correlated with hypertension, a sustained elevation of blood pressure. Hypertension is a risk factor for heart disease, stroke and kidney disease.

The National Research Council suggests limiting salt (sodium chloride) intake to 6 grams or less per day; approximately 2,400 mg of sodium. Shaking just a 1/4 teaspoon of salt on your food will add approximately 500 mg sodium to your daily intake. Today's Specials guidelines were to keep the sodium content to approximately 1000 mg or less per recipe.

If you consume alcohol, do so in moderation.

What is moderation? One "drink" is considered to be the equivalent of a 4 oz. glass of wine, a 12-oz. beer, or 1 oz. of "hard" liquor, such as vodka, gin or scotch. "Moderate" consumption has been defined as no more than 1 drink per day for females, no more than 2 drinks per day for males or that no more than 10% of the total calories consumed per day be alcohol calories. In addition, pregnant women, children and adolescents should abstain.

Adapted from Nutrition and Your Health - Dietary Guidelines for Americans, U.S. Dept. of Agriculture, U.S. Dept. of Health and Human Services, 3rd Ed, 1990.

TIPS FOR MORE HEALTHFUL CUISINE

If you take away most of the fat and salt from a recipe, what do you have? Usually, a pretty bland and boring item. So, how do you create a nutritious and healthful version of an original or classical recipe that looks and tastes as good? The first thing to do is look at each of the ingredients in the recipe. Fruits and fruit juices, vegetables, broths, wine and other spirits, and herbs and spices can all be used to help "pep" up a modified recipe. Different combinations of chopped or pureed fruits and vegetables can help make your dishes a hit by offering a wonderful contrast of flavors, textures and colors.

Explore the vegetable and fruit purees and the cornstarch and arrowroot-thickened variations on the "classical" sauces illustrated throughout. See how surprisingly "creamy" a sauce prepared with evaporated milk instead of heavy cream can be!

So, don't just say "gravy" or "sauce," say "salsa," "coulis," and "concasse!"

How Quickly Fat and Calories Add Up

Many cooks are surprised to find that even recipes they've attempted to "lighten up" still derive too many of their calories from fat!

How can that be when you've made every effort to grill instead of fry and to substitute margarine, olive oil or canola oil for butter? Well, the fact of the matter is that the *type* of fat or oil you choose in preparation is only half the battle; the other half is controlling the *total* amount of fat in the recipe.

In addition, many foods are sources of what is called, "hidden fat;" fat that is not as obvious to see or taste in the food. In the chart below, each of the indicated portions of the foods listed provides approximately 5 grams of fat (1 teaspoon fat) and approximately 45 fat calories:

Avocado	1/8 medium
Butter*	1 teaspoon
Margarine	1 teaspoon
"Diet" margarine	1 tablespoon

17

Bacon*	1 slice
Coconut, shredded*	2 tablespoons
Cream (light)*	2 tablespoons
Cream, Sour*	2 tablespoons
Cream, Heavy Whipping*	1 tablespoon
Cream Cheese*	1 tablespoon
Coffee Whitener, powder**	4 teaspoons
Coffee Whitener, liquid**	2 tablespoons
Mayonnaise, regular	1 teaspoon
Mayonnaise, reduced calorie	1 tablespoon
Nuts: Almonds, dry-roasted	6 whole
Cashews	1 tablespoon
Pecans	2 whole
Peanuts	10 large or 20 small
Walnuts	2 whole
Pumpkin seeds	2 teaspoons
Sunflower seeds (shelled)	1 tablespoon
Pine nuts	1 tablespoon
Oil	1 teaspoon
Olives	5 large or 10 small
Salad dressing - oil based	1 tablespoon
Reduced calorie	2 tablespoons
Mayonnaise based	2 teaspoons
Reduced calorie	1 tablespoon
Chocolate	1/2 oz.

*   High in saturated fats.
**   Non dairy creamers may not contain the cholesterol that their dairy counterparts do, and the newer products on the market may not contain the saturated fats from the "tropical oils" they used to, but they still derive a high percentage of their calories from fat.

Fat is more than *twice* as calorically dense as either protein or carbohydrate. Fat furnishes about 9 calories/g versus 4 calories/g for protein or carbohydrate.

Try some of these substitutions to control the amount or type of fat in a recipe:

Instead of:	Try:
Cottage cheese, 4% milkfat	Cottage cheese, 1% milkfat
Regular hard cheeses	Lowfat cheeses
Cream cheese	Neufchatel cheese, marketed as light cream cheese
Heavy Cream, 36%fat	Evaporated skim milk/Evaporated whole milk*
Mayonnaise or Sour Cream	Reduced fat mayonnaise or Plain Nonfat Yogurt**
Milk, whole, 3.5% fat	Milk, skim, less than 1% fat
Bacon	Canadian Bacon
Unsweetened chocolate (1 oz.)	3 tablespoons Unsweetened cocoa + 1 tablespoon polyunsaturated oil
Ice Cream	Frozen non-fat yogurt, ice milk
Whole eggs (each) or fresh	1/4 cup egg substitute products, egg whites
Butter	Soft tub margarine, vegetable oils, vegetable oil cooking sprays

* When substituting evaporated milk for cream in recipes containing alcohol, use an evaporated milk/cornstarch mixture for additional thickness. Less alcohol than the amount called for in the recipe will be needed to provide the same flavor.

A combination of evaporated whole/skim milk and plain lowfat yogurt can be substituted in some recipes for heavy cream - see "Strawberry Bavarian," Primavera Restaurant.

** When substituting yogurt for cream in hot sauces, add yogurt just before serving and do not let the sauce boil, otherwise, the sauce may curdle. Yogurt added to "cream" soups, such as tomato soup, may curdle, anyway, because of the chemical reaction between the acidity of the tomatoes and the protein of the yogurt. For acidic sauces and soups try serving a dollop of yogurt on top of each sauce or soup portion at the table. Mixing 1 tablespoon flour per cup of yogurt also helps stabilize a hot sauce; remove sauce from heat as it reaches the boiling point.

***   Egg whites may be substituted in part or in full for whole eggs, depending on the recipe. Egg substitutes can be used successfully for breading foods, for omelettes and in waffle and pancake batters.

Low fat cooking:

Lowfat methods of cooking include baking, roasting, grilling, pan broiling and stir steaming. In order to keep the item you are cooking moist and keep the fat content low at the same time, try any of the following:

1.   Add stock or broth. Chicken, vegetable, beef, fish stock, or even bottled clam juice create steam during the cooking process which helps cook the food and adds moisture. To have homemade stock on hand at all times, freeze stock in ice cube trays and "flip out" cubes, as needed. One average ice cube will yield approximately one - two tablespoons stock.

2.   Saute in a minimal amount of fat in a non-stick pan; try using a spray or two of a vegetable oil cooking spray. This is a good product to have on hand - a 2.5 second spray adds only approximately 6 calories. You can also lightly saute the item on the stove top, then, finish cooking by either tranferring the item onto an ovenproof dish or by putting the whole pan in the oven. Caution: Make sure the pan is ovenproof and be sure not to touch the pan handle without a thick, dry potholder when removing it from the oven.

3.   Cover chicken and fish with foil when baking to keep it from drying out.

Preparing foods en papillote, using parchment paper, brown bags, or edible wrappings, such as cabbage or grape leaves helps retain the natural juices of the food and makes a great plate presentation that is low in fat.

Phyllo (Filo) dough is a low-fat alternative to pastry; an "en croute" alternative for meats or for vegetables. Try lining muffin tins with a few layers of phyllo dough and filling with your favorite seasoned vegetable mix . You don't need to brush each layer with fat, just use a spray of a vegetable oil cooking spray. Encase vegetables with phyllo dough and bake for fast, yet fancy side dish.

How to Jazz up your "Oh, honey, chicken again?"

1.   Mix equal portions (or to taste) honey and dijon mustard together and brush chicken portions. Experiment with different flavored mustards and/or add curry powder, chopped shallots, or tarragon or tarragon vinegar to the mixture for variation.

2.   A few companies now sell no sugar added, natural fruit spreads in a variety of flavors, such as peach, orange, apricot and raspberry. Simply heat and glaze skinless chicken or skinless duck portions or spread on raw portions and bake.

The Sodium Shake-Up

Most of the sodium in our diet is from sodium-based additives used in the processing of food products. Salt is used as a preservative and flavor enhancer. In addition, sodium is used in leavening agents, emulsifiers, antioxidants, sequestrants, anticaking agents, dough conditioners and many other types of additives. Only a small amount of the sodium we consume comes from the sodium that foods naturally contain and discretionary salt use. We assume products like potato chips, salted peanuts, pretzels and other "salty" snack foods are high in sodium. But, what about soup and sauce bases, cheeses, frozen entrees and desserts, or canned vegetables and soups? Most highly processed foods are very high in sodium, even though they may not taste salty. The following chart illustrates the increase in the sodium content of selected foods the more processed they become:

Sodium Content of Selected Foods: (Approximate values)

Food, Portion	Sodium
Pork Loin, fresh,1 oz.	15 mg
Pork Sausage link, 1 oz.	349 mg
Ham, lunchmeat, 1 oz.	405 mg

Crab, Dungeoness, 3 1/2 oz.	299 mg
Surimi (imitation crabmeat), 3 1/2 oz.	834 mg
Cheddar Cheese, 1 oz.	176 mg
Processed American Cheese, 1 oz.	406 mg
Corn, 1 ear	1 mg
Corn flakes, 1 oz.	282 mg
Rolled Oats, regular/1 minute, 3/4 cup cooked	2 mg
Instant Oatmeal, packets, 3/4 cup cooked	254 mg
Apple, 1 average	1 mg
Apple Pie, 1/8 pie	208 mg
Potato, 1 med.	5 mg
Potato (Instant mashed), 1/2 cup	243 mg
Potato, (Canned), 1 cup	753 mg
Tomato, 1 average	11 mg
Tomato Puree, 1 cup	49 mg
Tomato Ketchup, 1 tablespoon	202 mg
Tomato Juice, 1/2 cup	439 mg
Tomato Sauce, home recipe, 1 cup	517 mg
Tomato Sauce, canned, 1 cup	1481 mg
Tuna, 3 oz	50 mg
Tuna (Canned), 3 oz	384 mg
Sherry, 1/2 cup	10 mg
Sherry Cooking Wine, 1/2 cup	370 mg
Cucumber, 7 slices	2 mg
Dill Pickle, 1 slice	928 mg

Source: Pennington & Church, <u>Food Values of Portions Commonly Used</u>, 14th Ed. and ESHA Research Food Processor II System and Nutritionist III database

Creating a meal that meets the dietary guidelines for sodium often means more than just hiding the salt shaker. Try following these suggestions to become more aware of and to lower the sodium content of the diet:

1.   Learn to read food labels. Foods that make a health claim MUST explain that claim on the nutrition information panel and include sodium information. The Food and Drug Administration (FDA) established sodium labeling guidelines for food manufacturers in the mid 1980's. They stipulate the following for food products:

"Sodium free"	Less than 5 mg sodium per serving
"Very Low Sodium"	Less than 35 mg sodium per serving
"Low Sodium"	Less than 140 mg sodium per serving
"Reduced Sodium"	Sodium content reduced by 75%
"No Salt Added" or "Unsalted"	No salt added in processing; sodium content may vary

2.   Learn to identify those ingredients and condiments that are high in sodium and use them sparingly.

Use the following in moderation:

	Sodium values per Tablespoon:
Barbeque Sauce	128 mg
Chili sauce	228 mg
Ketchup	202 mg
Mustard (prepared)	195 mg
Olives: Green, pitted, each	93 mg
Ripe, large, each	39 mg
Pickle relish	107 mg
Soy Sauce	1029 mg
Tabasco sauce	101 mg
Teriyaki sauce	690 mg
Worcestershire Sauce	146 mg

3.   Do not salt water when cooking rice, pasta, or vegetables.

4. Make up a bulk batch of a "signature" blend of herbs and spices that are sodium free. Try a mix of onion powder, dried mustard powder, basil, thyme, oregano and dried parsley on steamed vegetables, such as cauliflower and broccoli. Add a dash or two of Tabasco or any other brand of hot sauce for added "zing."

Use any of the following "sodium free" flavorings and seasonings in recipe development:

Allspice, Anise, Basil, Bay Leaf, Caraway, Cardamon, Celery seed, Chervil, Chives, Cinnamon, Cloves, Coriander, Cumin Seed, Curry, Dill, Dry Mustard, Fennel, Garlic, Ginger, Mace, Marjoram, Mustard Powder, Nutmeg, Onion Powder, Oregano, Paprika, Pepper, Parsley, Poppy seed, Pumpkin Pie spice, Rosemary, Saffron, Sage, Saffron, Tarragon, Thyme, Vinegar.

Mint and most flavored extracts are also sodium free.

When using dried herbs or spices instead of fresh, use only 1/3 the amount called for in the recipe.

"Blackening" blends are generally a mixture of red, white and black pepper with (salt and) other seasonings and can add a burst of fat-free flavor to meats, fish and vegetables. The following mix is from South Seas Plantation in Captiva Island:

Blackened Seasoning Mix

1 tablespoon sweet paprika
(2 1/2 teaspoons salt)
1 teaspoon onion powder
1 teaspoon garlic powder
1 teaspoon cayenne pepper
3/4 teaspoon white pepper
3/4 teaspoon black pepper
1/2 teaspoon dried thyme leaves
1/2 teaspoon dried oregano leaves

5.   Use homemade , reduced salt, or "no salt added" varieties of condiments, sauces and stocks. In recipes calling for tomato sauce, feel free to increase the amount per portion when using a homemade, unsalted sauce.

6.   Use lemon, lime and other fruits, peppers and flavored vinegars to flavor and season food.

7.   Don't be afraid to make LIKE substitutions, if a particular ingredient is unavailable or if you prefer a particular seasoning more so than the one called for. For instance, parsley for cilantro, etc.

How to Become A Recipe Detective

In recipe development, if one starts with a high fat and/or high cholesterol food as the center-of-the plate item, of course, a greater effort must be made to complement that item with foods that are either no or low-fat /cholesterol to achieve a total plate presentation that is, indeed, more healthful.

Let's look at a recipe that, on first glance, appears to be "light" and low in fat:

"Cajun Chicken Pasta"

6 oz. boneless, chicken breast with skin

3 tablespoons olive oil

1/4 oz. (1/2 tablespoon) blackening seasoning

1 oz. green pepper strips

1 oz. red pepper strips

2 oz. snow pea pods

6 oz. ckd. pasta

2 tablespoons grated parmesan cheese

You may be surprised to find that 55% of the calories in this dish come from fat! 66% of the fat in the recipe comes from the olive oil alone. Another 25% comes from the chicken. Let's see how we can apply some low-fat cooking techniques to bring the fat content within dietary guidelines and below 30% of total calories:

1. Use no more than 1 tablespoon of fat or oil in the "stir-fry" process. If you have ever measured out 1 tablespoon of oil, you will probably agree it doesn't look like much in the pan! To further coat the pan, try adding a spray or two of a vegetable oil cooking spray.

A rule of thumb to remember is that butter, stick margarine and any type of oil all contain virtually the same amount of calories, and all of those calories are from fat.

2. Start with a skinless portion of chicken. A 6 oz. raw weight portion of chicken with the skin contains about 16 g of fat and 295 calories, 49% of which come from fat. The same portion of skinless chicken contains 188 calories and 1.24 g fat - only 10% fat. A six ounce raw weight portion becomes approximately 4-5 ounces, cooked. All the chicken recipes featured in this book call for skinless boneless, chicken breasts.

3. Stir-"steam" instead of "fry." Use a bit of water or (unsalted) chicken stock or broth as the method of heat transfer, instead of or in addition to the fat, and cover your wok or pan. Fat calories really add up: The original recipe contains approximately 1000 calories; the modified version with only 1 tablespoon of oil and skinless chicken breast contains approximately 660 calories, only 29% of which come from fat.

In summary, remember that there are no "good" foods or "bad" foods. What counts is how a specific food contributes with other foods to the total diet. With this in mind, the key words for nutritional balance are "moderation" and "variety." Plan a recipe with no more than a 6 oz. raw portion of skinless chicken or fish or lean meats, such as beef top round or eye round, or beef or pork tenderloin. Although you may prefer the use of a monounsaturated oil, such as olive oil or canola oil, or a polyunsaturated oil, such as corn oil or safflower oil, you really have to watch how *much* of the oil you include in the recipe. **If you are watching your weight**, do not hesitate to try to cut down the fat and, thus, calories, even further from the recipes. Remember, we decreased the fat only where necessary to meet general health guidelines! A tiny drop is usually all you need for flavor. If you are watching your sodium intake, remember, fresh is best!

An A to Z Guide to Food Preparation Tips

We hope the following recipes will teach you new preparation techniques, in addition to exposing you to new and exciting grains, legumes, native foods and spices. Different terminology is used throughout the book to describe the way a particular food should be cut or processed for the proper preparation of the recipe. The definitions below should help you determine what the resulting appearance and texture of these various processes will be:

Arrowroot - A starch with a fine powdery texture extracted from several tropical plants. Arrowroot should be mixed first with cold liquid and should never be boiled. It produces a sauce with a slight glaze or shine and is best for hot sauces to be served immediately.

Arrowroot can be used in place of flour or cornstarch. Substitute 1 1/2 teaspoons arrowroot for each 1 tablespoon of flour called for in a recipe. Omit the fat the flour is usually mixed with (to make a "roux") and instead, dissolve arrowroot in a bit of cold liquid, such as water or stock.

Blanch - To partially cook a food in boiling water, often to prepare it for further processing. Foods that are blanched are then, typically, plunged in iced water to stop the cooking process. Blanching removes strong odors and flavors from vegetables such as cauliflower and onions, facilitates the peeling of tomatoes, and increases the digestibility of all fruits and vegetables.

Boil - To cook in water, stock, etc. at 212 F. (water) with continuous bubbles breaking the surface.

Broil - To cook with dry heat; with radiant heat from above. Grilling is the same process as broiling, except the heat source is below the food. The source of heat may be electric, gas, or charcoal.

Chiffonade - To cut into ribbon-like strips; often used as a garnish.

Chop - To cut a food into small pieces, generally with a knife. A food can be coarsely or finely chopped, depending on the recipe.

Chutney - A sweet and sour mixture of chopped or pureed fruits and/or vegetables, usually cooked with vinegar, sugar and spices.

Concasser - A French term meaning to chop or pound a substance, either coarsely or finely. When a skinned and seeded tomato is finely chopped it is often referred to as a "tomato concasse." The term may also be used to apply to other fruits or vegetables or, even, to fresh herbs or meats that have been chopped as such.

To peel and seed a fresh tomato:

1. Pierce the skin with an "X", using a sharp knife, across either the top or the bottom
2. Put in boiling water for 20-30 seconds
3. Plunge in an ice water bath
4. Peel
5. Gently squeeze out seeds
6. Dice flesh

To roast a pepper:

1. Preheat oven to 500 F. or broiler to hot
2. Place peppers on a rack 4-6 inches from the heat
3. Roast, turning frequently, until skin is charred and blistering
4. Place hot peppers in a brown paper bag and roll up tightly or into a pot with a fitted lid and let steam until cool to the touch
5. Peel off skin

Cornstarch - A starch that produces a sauce with a high sheen, characteristic of Oriental sauces and fruit pie fillings. It should be mixed with cold liquid before heating and reaches optimum thickness when boiled.

A rule of thumb is that 1 tablespoon of cornstarch will adequately thicken 1 cup of liquid. Cornstarch must be brought to the boiling point to be used as a thickening agent and will give sauces and dressings a glossy shine.

Substituting a water/cornstarch mixture for some or all of the oil in a salad dressing may produce an acceptable product, and give the original yield, but the salad should be consumed as soon as it is tossed with the dressing. Be sure to mix cornstarch with cold liquid first, bring liquid to a boil to thicken, then cool and mix with remaining dressing ingredients. [Note - if less than the indicated quantity of water/cornstarch mixture is used in any of the recipes, you will have a more concentrated dressing, but the yield will be decreased]. The dressing will keep for 3-5 days in the refrigerator. Shake well to blend when ready to use. This type of "modified" dressing can not be successfully used for marinated salads.

Court Bouillon - A flavored liquid generally used for cooking fish and other seafood. The liquid may contain a mixture of fresh and dried herbs and vegetables, as well as some wine, vinegar, or lemon.

Deglaze - To add liquid to a hot skillet or baking pan after the sauteing or roasting process, while scraping the sides and bottom of a skillet to loosen browned bits and to mix the liquid in, creating a sauce.

Dice - To cut into uniformed sized cubes, generally about 1/2 " square.

Flambe - To ignite an alcohol containing mixture to burn off the alcohol.

Fumet - A concentrated stock made with wine and herbs.

Gelatin - A gelling substance used for making jellies and numerous cold or iced desserts. One "packet," 1 tablespoon of granular, unflavored gelatin will gel approximatley 2 cups of liquid. Gelatin must be dissolved in cold liquid, first, before heating.

Grate - The process of rubbing foods over a utensil with a rough surface and holes of different sizes and shapes to produce shreds of different thicknesses.

Grill - See "Broil." Meat, fish, poultry and many vegetables can be grilled to impart a unique flavor. Be careful not to char food!

Herbs de Provence - Refers to a classical mixture of herbs, generally consisting of thyme, rosemary, bay, basil and savory, although variations are available.

Julienne - To cut into thin, match-like strips. Fresh basil, cooked and cooled meats and vegetables, such as carrots, onions and celery all julienne well.

Marinate - To soak a food in a flavored liquid for a period of time to infuse flavor and help tenderize (meats). A basic marinade consists of an acid, such as lemon juice, tomato juice or wine, and herbs and seasonings. Although many marinades call for oil, generally to impart a unique flavor and "coat" the food, all but a small amount of the oil can be omitted. Poke holes in chicken or beef before adding marinade to infuse the most flavor.

Mince - To finely chop; a process successfully performed by quickly turning on and off a food processor.

Poach - To cook in simmering liquid, such as stock or water, at a temperature just below the boiling point. The food may be either partially or fully immersed in the liquid.

Puree - To process in a food processor or a blender or by pressing through a sieve to obtain a creamy, smooth consistency. Many vegetables and legumes can be pureed to thicken sauces or soups. Cooked fruit purees, served either hot or cold, may be served with meats or as dessert accompaniments.

Reduce - To concentrate or thicken a sauce, stock, or other liquid mixture by gently boiling it to evaporate some of the volume.

Roux - An equal mixture of heated fat and flour cooked together as a base for thickened sauces, soups, etc.

Salsa - A chunky mixture of fruits and/or vegetables. Traditionally a Mexican offering of tomatoes and peppers, salsas now are made from a variety of tropical fruits and vegetables and are typically low in fat or fat free.

Sauté - To cook food quickly in a small amount of fat in a skillet or sauté pan over direct heat.

Simmer - The cooking of a food in a liquid at a temperature just below the boiling point; hot enough so that small bubbles rise to the surface occasionally; approximately 185 F.

Slice - To cut into pieces of different thicknesses, depending on the recipe.

Slurry - A blend of cornstarch, arrowroot, or flour and a cold liquid. This is then added to a hot liquid and heated until thickened.

Smoke - A traditional method of preserving food, generally including salt in the process and drying the food to a certain extent, smoking is now often used to refer to imparting a unique flavor to meats, fish, and even, vegetables. The smoking process may take anywhere from 20 minutes to days, depending on the food and smoking medium.

Steam - To cook above a simmering or boiling liquid, often in a perforated container. Steaming food helps retain nutrients that might, otherwise, be lost by submerging the food in the liquid, such as in the boiling or poaching process. Steam is also a leavening agent released by liquids in baked goods during the baking process.

Zest - To remove the outer, colored portion of citrus skin in thin strips, either with a grater or, a vegetable peeler, or a zester. The zest does not include the white, bitter part under the skin. The zest of 1/2 fresh orange yields about 1/2 teaspoon and is the equivalent of approximately 1/6 teaspoon dried zest.

Other preparation tips

Fruits and Vegetables:

In recipes calling for frozen berries, add berries while still frozen; do not defrost first!

In recipes calling for spinach, drain cooked spinach well, making sure all water is squeezed out.

In recipes calling for sun-dried tomatoes use the plain, dried form, not the type packed in oil. Rehydrate dried tomatoes by simmering them in water for 2-3 minutes.

Experiment with adding other dried fruits, such as cherries, cranberries or raisins, to plain brown sauces or to turkey or chicken salads. Plump dried fruits to be used in cold salads in hot water. Drain and chill before adding to other cold ingredients.

Fish Cooking Chart
Compliments of Chick Fuller
The Fish Peddler, Inc. Lincoln Park West, 7794 N.W.44th St., Sunrise (305)741-1933

Species		Bake	Broil	Grill	Saute
Bluefish	Temperature	350 F	High	Med.High	Med.Heat
	Time	15-20 Min.	8-10 Min.	10 Min.:	8-10 Min.:
				Flesh side down	Turn once
SUBSTITUTES - Mackerel; King Fish					
Cod Fillet	Temperature	350 F	High	Med.High	Med.Heat
Scrod	Time	20 Min.	8-10 Min.	15 Min.:	8-10 Min.:
Cod Steak				Wrap in foil	Turn once
SUBSTITUTES - Haddock; Hake; Pollack					
Dolphin	Temperature	350 F	High	Med.High	Med.Heat
	Time	15 Min.	8-10 Min.	4-5 Min./side	8-10 Min.:
					Turn once
SUBSTITUTES - King Fish; Spanish Mackerel					
Flounder	Temperature	350 F	High	Not	Med.Heat
	Time	10 Min.	6 Min.	Recommended	6-8 Min.
Note: all times should be adjusted to the thickness of fish (cooks quickly) ie, 1" or less - 10-12 min.; 1-3" - 20-25 min.					
SUBSTITUTES - Lemon Sole; Grey Sole					
Grouper	Temperature	350 F	High	Med.High	Med.Heat
	Time	15-20 Min.	10 Min.	4-6 Min./side	8-10 Min.:
					Turn once
SUBSTITUTES - Snapper; Orange Roughy					
Halibut	Temperature	350 F	High	Med.High	Med.Heat
	Time	15-20 Min.	6 Min./side	5-6 Min./side	8-10 Min.:
					Turn once
SUBSTITUTES- None					
Ocean	Temperature	350 F	High	Med.High	Med.Heat
Perch	Time	10-15 Min.	8 Min.	8 Min.:	6-8 Min.:
				Flesh side down	Turn once
SUBSTITUTES - Snapper; Orange Roughy					

Species		Bake	Broil	Grill	Saute
Orange Roughy	Temperature Time	350 F 15 Min.	High 8 Min.	Med.High 4 Min./side	Med. Heat 8-10 Min.: Turn once

SUBSTITUTES - Snapper; Grouper

Pompano	Temperature Time	350 F 15 Min.	High 8 Min.	Med.High 8 Min.: Flesh side down	Med.Heat 6 Min.: Flesh side down

SUBSTITUTES- None

Rainbow Trout	Temperature Time	350 F 12-15 Min.	High 8 Min.	Med.High 8-10 Min.: Flesh side down	Med.Heat 8-10 Min. Turn once

SUBSTITUTES - Brook Trout

Salmon Fillets	Temperature Time	350 F 15 Min.	High 10-12 Min.	Med.High 5 Min./side	Not Recommended: May poach 10 Min.
Salmon Steaks		15-20 Min.	High 10-12 Min.	Med. High 6 Min./ side	" " "

SUBSTITUTES - Trouts

Snapper	Temperature Time	350 F 10-12 Min.	High 6-8 Min	Med.High 6-8 Min.: Flesh side down	Med.Heat 8-18 Min.: Turn once

SUBSTITUTES - Grouper; Orange Roughy

Spanish Mackerel	Temperature Time	350 F 15 Min.	High 10 Min.	Med.High 10 Min.: Flesh side down	Med.Heat 8-10 Min.: Turn once

SUBSTITUTES - King Fish

Swordfish	Temperature Time	350 F 15 Min., then 2 Min. under broiler	High 5 Min./ side	Med.High 5 Min./ side	Med.Heat 8-10 Min.: Turn once

SUBSTITUTES - Tuna

Species		Bake	Broil	Grill	Saute
Tuna	Temperature	350 F	High	Med.High	Med.Heat
	Time	10-12 Min.	4 Min./ side	4 Min./ side	4 Min./ side

Note - Tuna can be pink or red inside - rare or med.
SUBSTITUTES - Swordfish

SHELLFISH

Species		Bake	Broil	Grill	Saute
Bay Scallops	Temperature	350 F	High	Not	Med.Heat
	Time	10 Min.	4-6 Min.	Recommended	4-6 Min.

Note - Cooks very quickly.

Species		Bake	Broil	Grill	Saute
Sea Scallops		10-15 Min.; longer for larger scallop	8-10 Min.: Turn once	Med.High 4-6 Min./ side	8-10 Min.: Turn once
Blue Crab	Temperature	350 F	High	Not	Med.Heat
	Time	Only to heat	Only to heat	Recommended	Only to heat

Note - Crabmeat is a cooked product, further cooking is only for heating.

Species		Bake	Broil	Grill	Saute
King Crab	Temperature	Not	Split and	Not	Not
	Time	Recommended	Broil to heat	Recommended	Recommended

Note - Frozen and cooked; drop crab in a pot of boiling water, turn off heat and let stand for 10 Min.

Species		Bake	Broil	Grill	Saute
Shrimp	Temperature	350 F	High	Med.High	Med.Heat
	Time	10-15 Min.: longer for large shrimp	4-6 Min.: Turn once	4-6 Min.: Turn once	4-6 Min.: Turn once
Snow Crab	Temperature	Not	Not	Not	Not
	Time	Recommended	Recommended	Recommended	Recommended

Note - Drop crab in a pot of boiling water, turn off heat and let stand 5 Min. and serve.

Ingredient Chemistry

Many health-conscious people wonder how they can make a dessert recipe better fit today's low-fat and high-fiber dietary guidelines. Can we really have our cake and eat it, too? This chapter explores...

"The Anatomy of a Cake"

Some recipes, especially those in the baked goods and breads category, are successful because of the delicate chemical interaction of their ingredients. Randomly substituting or eliminating ingredients will affect the chemical balance of the recipe and the final results can be less than desirable! Let's look at the anatomy of an old-fashioned chocolate cake recipe, dissect each of its ingredients and discuss how we can modify those of concern.

Old-Fashioned Chocolate Cake

Yield: 12 servings
1 3/4 cups all-purpose flour
2 teaspoons baking powder
1/2 teaspoon salt
1/2 cup butter
1 1/2 cups sugar
4 eggs
1/2 cup sour cream
1 teaspoon vanilla extract
3 oz. (3 squares) baking chocolate

Nutritional info. per serving:

Calories	313	
Protein	5	g
Carbohydrate	50	g
Fat	43	%
Sodium	237	mg
Cholesterol	96	mg
Fiber	.5	g

Flour: Flours are labeled for use according to certain properties; in particular, their protein content and the milling process they have undergone. The higher the protein content the greater the gluten development of the flour and, thus, the stronger the texture.

Cake flour has a low protein content and a soft texture, which helps produce a cake with a fine crumb. Bread flour, or gluten flour, has a higher protein content and a harder, coarser texture, which helps produce a strong and chewy yeast bread. The chemical make-up of All-Purpose Flour falls somewhere in between cake flour and bread flour and is fine for most biscuit, muffin, pancake, waffle and tea bread recipes.

Flour in any baked good recipe adds structure. Only whole grain, unrefined flours, though, contain the germ of the grain, which contains some polyunsaturated fat and the fiber-rich bran portion of the grain.

Nutritionally, one may want to substitute a whole grain flour for a refined flour in a given recipe to add more fiber to the recipe. In most recipes, some or all of the flour called for can be substituted. However, whole grain flours are heavier and will lack the gluten development of refined flours. Thus, the more whole grain flour you use, the more dense the texture of the baked good will be.

Baking Powder: Baking Powder and baking soda are leavening agents; they help make baked goods light. Baking powder contains approximately 450 mg sodium per teaspoon. Baking soda (sodium bicarbonate) contains approximately 820 mg sodium per teaspoon. Both baking powder and baking soda release carbon dioxide for their leavening power.

Two other leavening agents which do not contain any sodium are air and steam. Thoroughly creaming the fat and sugar ingredients together and whipping, then gently folding egg whites into a batter, introduce air, which helps make the baked good lighter. Liquid ingredients, including milk or water, create steam during the baking process. Although carbon dioxide typically makes the most significant leavening contribution to cakes and tea breads, an acceptable product can result without their use. Some cakes, such as angel food cake, depend solely on air and steam for their leavening. However, some baked goods, such as biscuits

and some muffins, may be too heavy without added leavening agents.
Note that self-rising flours contain as much as 1400 mg sodium per cup, because of the baking powder added to them. The fat and sodium content of a biscuit recipe calling for a mixture of 1 cup whole milk and 4 teaspoons baking powder can be reduced by substituting 1 cup of skim milk + 1 tablespoon of lemon juice or white vinegar for the milk and 1/2 teaspoon baking soda + 2 teaspoons baking powder for the baking powder.

Salt: Salt adds flavor to baked goods, but also affects the chemical reaction of flours in the baking process. Salt can be effectively eliminated in baked goods that are not yeast-leavened. Yeast-raised breads prepared without salt tend to have a different and, sometimes, undesirable grain and texture.

Butter: Both butter and stick margarines contain the same number of calories per tablespoon. An equal measure of margarine can be successfully substituted for butter to reduce the cholesterol content of the recipe and to improve the polyunsaturated to saturated fat ratio (P:S ratio) in virtually all baked goods. The exception would be those products, such as danish and puff pastry, that depend on a high quality butter with good "plasticity" to make a flaky and not a mealy pastry product. In many bread and cake recipes, the total amount of fat can also be reduced by using a few tablespoons less fat than the recipe calls for. At approximately 100 calories per tablespoon, you can really save a lot of fat calories by experimenting with decreasing the fat content of selected recipes. Note that many of the "fat free" baked goods on the market derive their fattening, cake-like "mouthfeel" from a high proportion of sugar and com-mercially available gums and stabilizers.

Sugar: Aside from adding a desirable and characteristic sweetness to baked goods, sugar acts as a tenderizing ingredient, especially in cakes. Sugar also aids in incorporating air into a batter when it is creamed with fat, and, thus, contributes to the leavening process. Substituting honey or brown sugar for white sugar in recipes will affect the taste and texture of the final product, but not the nutritional profile. Honey and brown sugar actually contain *more* calories than white sugar and only trace amounts of nutrients. Blackstrap molasses is a good source of some nutrients, particularly iron, calcium and potassium, but is not an acceptable substitute for granulated sugar in most recipes. Reducing the amount of sugar called for in a recipe will affect the sweetness of the baked good and may also affect the color of the final product, since it is the caramelization of the sugar during the baking process that helps create a nice golden brown color in many cakes and breads. Adding small amounts of canned or dried fruits, such as pineapple and raisins, can help add sweetness to some baked goods, thus allowing you to decrease the amount of sugar called for in the recipe.

Eggs: Eggs add structure to baked goods. All the fat in an egg is in the yolk. Egg substitutes contain less fat and cholesterol than whole shell eggs. Egg substitutes can be successfully substituted for whole shell eggs in many baked good recipes. However, since the egg yolk contains a natural emulsifier, lecithin, make sure to incorporate the substitute product well into the batter to ensure even distribution. Many recipes calling for whole eggs can also be prepared using 1 whole egg + 1-2 egg whites, stiffly beaten and folded in for every 2 eggs called for. Beating the white helps to incorporate air into the batter and results in a lighter baked good.

Vanilla: Vanilla and other extracts add flavor, but contain virtually no nutritional value. They can be used as called for.

Sour Cream: Sour Cream or heavy cream add liquid, fat, flavor and texture to baked goods. Milk and other liquids also help create steam, and, thus, leavening, during the baking process. Substitute plain or vanilla flavored nonfat yogurt for heavy cream or sour cream. Substitute skim milk or non-fat dry milk solids mixed with water for whole milk called for in recipes. In some cases, soured skim milk ("buttermilk" produced by acidifying each cup of milk with 1 tablespoon lemon juice or white vinegar) can be substituted for sour cream or heavy cream.

Chocolate: 1 average ounce of semi-sweet chocolate contains 10 g fat and 140 calories. 64 % of its calories come from fat. Sweet, semi-sweet and bittersweet chocolate all contain a combination of chocolate liquor, sugar, cocoa butter and vanilla or other flavors. Unsweetened baking chocolate generally does not contain added sugar or flavoring. To make cocoa powder, the chocolate liquor is pressurized and most of the cocoa butter (the fat) is pressed out. Chocoholics who are watching their fat intake should explore dessert recipes that feature cocoa instead of other forms of chocolate. Modifying a chocolate recipe to a cocoa recipe may require modifying the sugar and liquid ingredients called for. Cake recipes may be especially tricky!

Modified or "New"- Fashioned Chocolate Cake:
Yield: 12 servings

1/2 cup + 1 tablespoon cocoa
1 3/4 cups all-purpose flour
1 1/2 teaspoons baking powder
(1/4 teaspoon salt)
1/2 cup margarine
2 cups sugar
2 whole eggs + 2 egg whites
1/2 cup non-fat plain yogurt (skim milk will work)
1/2 cup boiling water

Nutritional info. per serving:

Calories	297	
Protein	5	g
Carbohydrate	50	g
Fat	27	%
Sodium	204	mg
Cholesterol	36	mg
Fiber	.5	g

Fortunately, the authors of this book are chocoholics and have provided three additional chocolate recipes for your enjoyment!

Chocolate Custard
Yields: 4 servings (2 cups total)

Scant 1/2 cup sugar
2 cups 2% milk (reserve 1/4 cup cold to mix with cornstarch)
1 envelope plain gelatin
1 1/2 tablespoons cornstarch
1 egg yolk
1/4 teaspoon vanilla extract
1/3 cup cocoa powder, sifted

In small saucepan mix sugar, milk and gelatin and heat over low heat to simmer, stirring.

Mix cornstarch and reserved milk together. Whip in egg yolk and stir into above mixture. Continue to heat, stirring, until thickened. Remove from heat and stir in vanilla and cocoa until well blended.

Pour custard into serving dishes and chill before serving.

Serving suggestion: Chill custard to room temperature. Pour into prepared meringue shells and top with fresh fruit or a fruit puree sauce.

Nutritional info. per serving:

Calories	175	
Protein	7	g
Carbohydrate	28	g
Fat	24	%
Sodium	66	mg
Cholesterol	64	mg
Fiber	2	g

Raspberry Chocolate Chip Cake
Yield: 15 servings

2 1/2 cups all-purpose flour
1 1/2 cups sugar
1/3 teaspoon baking powder
1 3/4 teaspoons baking soda
1/3 cup safflower oil
2/3 cup cocoa
1 cup water
1 egg
2 egg whites
1 teaspoon vanilla
1 tablespoon Raspberry Liqueur
1/2 cup semi-sweet chocolate chips
1 cup raspberries
1 tablespoon powdered sugar

Pre-heat oven to 350 F.

Spray 9"x13" baking pan with a vegetable oil cooking spray. Sift together flour, sugar, baking powder and baking soda into large bowl. Add oil, cocoa and 2/3 cups of water; beat a few minutes. Add remaining 1/3 cup water, egg, egg whites, vanilla, raspberry liqueur; beat until smooth. Mix in chocolate chips. Pour into pan and sprinkle raspberries evenly over top.

Bake in oven for 30-35 minutes or until tester inserted in center comes out clean. Sprinkle powdered sugar over when cool.

Nutritional info. per serving

Calories	304	
Protein	4	g
Carbohydrate	54	g
Fat	25	%
Sodium	151	mg
Cholesterol	14	mg
Fiber	1	g

Cappucino Chip Brownies
Yield: 16 servings

1 3/4 cups brown sugar (can use 3/4 cup light and 1 cup dark)
3/4 cup margarine, soft tub
2 teaspoons vanilla
2 eggs
2 egg whites
1 tablespoon instant coffee dissolved in 1 tablespoon water
10 tablespoons (1/2 cup + 2 tablespoons) Hershey's cocoa
1 1/4 cups all-purpose flour
1 teaspoon baking powder
1/2 cup semi-sweet chocolate chips
Cinnamon sugar: Mix together 1 teaspoon cinnamon and 1
    tablespoon granulated sugar

Preheat oven to 325 F.

Spray 9"x 13" pan with vegetable oil cooking spray. In large bowl, beat sugar, margarine and vanilla until smooth. Add eggs and whites, 1 at a time, beating well after each addition. Mix in coffee and cocoa. Sift together flour and baking powder and mix in. Stir in chocolate chips.

Pour in pan and bake for 10 minutes. Sprinkle cinnamon and sugar mix over top. Take a knife and gently swirl into top of batter. Bake an additional 25 minutes or until tester inserted into center comes out clean.

Nutritional info. per serving

Calories	293	
Protein	3	g
Carbohydrate	45	g
Fat	35	%
Sodium	190	mg
Cholesterol	27	mg
Fiber	--	

The Case of the Missing Ingredient

Many of the recipes in this book feature unusual ingredients, which can be found in a well-stocked supermarket or in most specialty gourmet stores and markets, health food stores, or Oriental and other ethnic markets. Most stores are very cooperative and, if possible, will order specialty items for you. All you have to do is ask!

The following ingredients are featured in Today's Specials:

Arborio Rice: Short-grained, Italian rice that cooks up "starchy."

Ancho/Poblano Chiles: Heart-shaped with pointed tip peppers that are green and generally mild in flavor.

Boniato: A light-fleshed, chestnut flavored sweet potato, also known as a Cuban sweet potato.

Carambola: A typically yellow-fleshed fruit with a "mixed fruit" taste; also known as "Star fruit" because it forms a star shape when sliced.

Chayote Squash: Also known as a vegetable pear or mirliton.

*Chili Paste with Garlic: Chinese preparation made of hot peppers, salt and garlic; also known as "Szechwan Paste."

Cilantro: Coriander is the dried seeds of the plant, whose flowery leaves, when fresh have a unique flavor. Although also known as Chinese or Mexican parsley, cilantro's aroma and flavor is much different than parsley.

Couscous: A traditional north African grain, made of hard wheat semolina.

Daikon radish: Typically a white carrot-shaped Japanese radish that has a crisp, mild taste.

Jicama: A crunchy white tuber, with a texture like water chestnuts.

Kirbies: Small, pale green cucumbers.

Malanga: A tuber that is closely related to taro and has a shaggy brown, yam-like appearance. Its skin color may be beige to brown to reddish-brown and, when cooked, it has a nutty flavor.

*Mirin: Sweet Japanese Sake mainly used for cooking.

*Oyster Sauce: An Oriental sauce made from oysters.

Passion fruit: Colors range from deep purple to purple-brown, reddish or gold, with a tart, yellow pulp.

Rhubarb: Pink to green stalks and very sour; usually used to make pies or compotes. Available fresh or IQF (individually quick frozen).

*Soba Noodles: Thin Japanese noodles made from buckwheat and wheat flours.

Tahini: Sesame paste.

Wheat berries: Whole grains of wheat that are first soaked and then cooked in recipe preparation.

Also:

    Chilpotle in Adobo
    Sun-dried tomatoes (not packed in oil)
    Different flavored oils and vinegars
    Fresh and exotic flavored pastas
    Edible flowers
    Unusual flours, such as rice flour and semolina or durum wheat flour
    *Chinese black tea leaves
    *Oriental mushroom soy sauce
    *Tamari
    *Black sesame seeds
    *Chinese 5-spice powder
    *Pickled ginger
    Unusual grains such as polenta and *rice noodles
    Wood chips for smoking and flavoring, such as mesquite, oak or cherry

    *Oriental products.

NUTRITIONAL ANALYSIS OF RECIPES:

We have included nutritional data per serving with each recipe for your information to illustrate how gourmet can be translated into "heart healthy!"

Please note that the nutritional values indicated for sodium, calories, etc. **may** be different than what you will actually realize in some instances. Nutritional analysis is not an exact science; the evaporation of liquids, including alcohol, the form of the food used and chemical reactions between foods all affect the actual nutritional content. Different brand name foods and comparable foods used in calculation may have similar, but not exact nutrient profiles.

Some recipes include a starch accompaniment, such as rice, potatoes, or pasta as part of the analysis, either because the chef intended it as part of the recipe or because we added it to reduce the total fat content of the recipe. Feel free to increase the suggested amount of any starch or substitute one starch for another (ie; potatoes for pasta).

Using homemade stocks and sauces or low sodium commercially available varieties of soups, sauces, condiments, or cheeses will lower the analyzed sodium content of the recipe. Note that all the recipes (with the exception of breads and muffins) were tested and analyzed without the addition of table salt even though the chefs **may** have included salt in their submitted recipes. If necessary, a pinch or two of salt per portion may be added for flavor, provided you are not on a sodium-restricted diet.

Since shellfish, such as shrimp and lobster, are both popular and low in fat, they are also included in many of the recipes. However, because of the cholesterol content of some shellfish, you will note the small portion sizes recommended in some of the recipes. If you are not following a cholesterol-restricted diet, you may want to increase the suggested portion size in these recipes to 4-5 oz. Please note that squid and veal are higher in cholesterol than most other meat/fish/poultry items.

We did not include the polyunsaturated to saturated ratio (P:S ratio) with each recipe. A good P:S ratio in the diet is 1:1 or slightly, better, in favor of polyunsaturated fat. Although our recipes conform to the maximum 30-35% total fat guideline, please be aware that recipes calling for veal, cheese, duck, pork, ground turkey, or beef will be higher in saturated fat than those recipes calling for most types of seafood or skinless chicken breast.

The software programs used to analyze each recipe were the Nutritionist III and The Food Processor II.

Values for foods not available in the software programs were obtained through research, from the manufacturers of the specific food, or from analysis of comparable foods. Recipes, unless otherwise indicated, were analyzed using the nutritional information available for:

Regular canned tomato sauce
Regular canned chicken broth or beef broth
Bottled clam juice (instead of homemade fish stock)
Kikkoman "Lite" soy sauce or regular Tamari
Regular L & P Worcestershire sauce
Hershey's cocoa

Unless otherwise noted, pasta and rice have been analyzed without having salt or fat added during cooking process.

If you must follow a particular diet for medical reasons, you may want to consult a Registered Dietitian to see how the recipes featured can fit into your meal plan. Some recipes may have to be further modified to meet your individual dietary guidelines.

A CULINARY TOUR OF THE SUNSHINE STATE

NORTH

Grayton Beach

Destin

Jacksonville

Panama City Beach

Pensacola

Tallahassee

St. Augustine

Gainesville

CENTRAL

Deland

Cocoa Beach

Melbourne

Maitland

Orlando and Lake Buena Vista Village

S O U T H W E S T

S O U T H E A S T

*Denotes Florida Restaurant Association members (see page 323)

NORTH

H·A·R·B·O·R

D·O·C·K·S

LA PARISIENNE
Restaurant

24
—MIRAMAR—

Jamie's
FRENCH·RESTAURANT

ANDREWS
upstairs
A BAR AND GRILLE

SLIDERS
CAFE
JACKSONVILLE, FLORIDA

Le Pavillon
45 San Marco Avenue
St. Augustine, Florida 32084

Criolla's
Grayton Beach (904)267-1267

Johnny Earles, the Chef/Owner, began working in restaurants at age 14. He went to Louisiana State University for 3 years, then moved to Grayton Beach to open a place called Paradise Cafe. After 5 years of operation, he and his partner split and he opened Criollas in Feb. 1989.

Most memorable meal - during his stay at Restaurant Lafayette in New York City this past winter (he spent a month working in Manhattan Restaurants). He finished work early both Thursdays he was there, and enjoyed Chef Jean-Georges Vongerichten's tasting menu. Each time, the chef and his staff prepared seven courses and four desserts, all a "lesson in beautifully prepared, ingeniously uncomplicated food." Each course was very different from the next as were the desserts he had. The wait staff brought different wines to taste and he finished the meals with a cup of espresso! Johnny's mentor - Jeremiah Tower.

♥ Pan-Seared Tuna with Costa Rican Broth
Yield: 2 servings

Pico de Gallo:
Yield: 2 cups
2 cups fresh tomatoes, chopped 1/4" cubes
3 tablespoons diced onion
2 serrano chiles, finely chopped
2 tablespoons chopped cilantro
Juice of 1/2 lime

Mix all ingredients together and set aside.

Costa Rican Broth:
3 cups chicken stock
1/4 cup chopped green onion
1/2 cup cooked Anasazi beans (pinto beans can be substituted)
1/3 cup cooked fresh corn
1/3 cup julienned spinach
1/4 lime
1/4 cup chopped fresh cilantro
1/3 cup Pico de Gallo

In a skillet bring stock to a boil, add green onions, beans, corn and spinach, reduce by 1/3. Squeeze juice from lime into skillet, add entire lime and cilantro; remove from heat. Add pico de gallo.

2- 6 oz. (2 in. thick) tuna steaks
1 3/4 tablespoons olive oil
1 teaspoon ancho chile paste (ancho chile pepper seeded, roasted
   in low oven, and pureed into a paste)*
2 teaspoons chopped garlic
1 teaspoon chopped parsley
Lime
Chives
2 dinner rolls (or grain of your choice)

Preheat oven to 350 F.
   Mix olive oil, chili paste, garlic and parsley and coat tuna steaks with mixture. Heat skillet on medium high heat, sear tuna steaks for one minute, turn, sear other side for one minute and place in oven, five minutes for medium rare, nine for medium. Remove from pan and place each in colorful bowl with half of the broth (approx. 1 " broth in bowl). Garnish with lime and whole chives.
Serve with 1 dinner roll (or grain of choice) per serving.

Nutritional info. per serving

Calories	583	
Protein	49	g
Carbohydrate	46	g
Fat	35	%
Sodium	1019	mg
Cholesterol	57	mg
Fiber	6	g

* ♥ Can use chili paste, from a jar, found in Oriental markets.

Harbor Docks
538 Highway 98, Destin (904)837-2506

Charles Vicknair graduated from a restaurant management school and has worked in New Orleans and Ft. Walton Beach.
Most memorable meal - stuffed Pork Loin with Green Peppercorn Sauce, that was served the first time he prepared the dish. Everyone loved it!
His mentor - Dennis Hutley, the Head Chef at Versailles Restaurant in New Orleans.

♥ Grilled Whole Oysters with Ginger Lime Sauce
Yield: 8 servings

24 oysters, unshucked

Sauce:
1/2 cup Japanese radish (daikon), minced
3/4 cup fresh lime juice
3/4 cup rice vinegar
2 tablespoons fresh grated ginger
2 tablespoons lite soy sauce

Mix together sauce ingredients and set aside.
Grill oysters on grill until they open. Serve on platter with the sauce for dipping.

Nutritional info. per serving

Calories	81	
Protein	9	g
Carbohydrate	7	g
Fat	22	%
Sodium	242	mg
Cholesterol	184	mg
Fiber	-	

24 Miramar\Sliders Cafe

446 Hendricks Avenue\9810-3 Baymeadows Road
Jacksonville (904)448-2424\645-7777

Tim Felver, Corporate Executive Chef, Sliders Cafe, Inc. is a C.I.A. graduate. Previously, he worked in numerous French restaurants and with Wolfgang Puck in Los Angeles.
Most memorable meal - cooking during a special party for Baron Phillipe Rothchild, Rudolph Nureyev and Robert Mondavi when they came out with "Opus."
Tim's mentor - Wolfgang Puck (Spago and Chinoise on Main in Los Angeles).

♥ California Chicken Salad
Yield: 4 servings

4 - 4 oz. chicken breasts, skinless, boneless
1 tablespoon mushroom soy sauce (Chinese)
1 tablespoon Japanese soy sauce
1 oz. Mirin

Marinate chicken in above for 15 minutes. Grill chicken and slice.

Dressing:
Scant 1/4 cup peanut oil
1/4 cup rice vinegar
1/2 teaspoon sesame oil
3 teaspoons sugar
2 teaspoons lemon juice
Pinch white pepper
Scant 1/2 cup water/cornstarch mixture (optional, see preparation tips)

Place all dressing ingredients in a blender and blend.

8 cups mixed greens: romaine, arugula, curly endive, boston lettuce
4 tablespoons diced mango
4 tablespoons diced pineapple
4 tablespoons diced tomato
4 teaspoons diced red pepper
4 tablespoons diced apples
8 tablespoons pickled ginger
2 shallots, diced
Cilantro to taste

1 teaspoon black sesame seeds
4 pita bread pockets (or grain of your choice)

In large salad bowl, toss greens with dressing and divide among four plates. In separate bowl mix mango, pineapple, tomatoes, peppers, apples, pickled ginger, shallots and cilantro. Sprinkle on top of greens.

Place sliced chicken on top; sprinkle with sesame seeds. Serve with 1 pita (or grain of choice) per serving.

Nutritional info. per serving

Calories	445	
Protein	34	g
Carbohydrate	37	g
Fat	35	%
Sodium	801	mg
Cholesterol	72	mg
Fiber	4	g

Captain Anderson

5551 N. Lagoon Drive, Panama City Beach (904)234-6800

John Patronis, Owner.

♥ Grilled Scamp
Yield: 1 Serving

6 oz. Scamp (a member of the grouper family called "The Fisherman's Fish")
1 tablespoon margarine
1 1/2 oz. lump crabmeat (cooked)
1 teaspoon fresh lemon juice or to taste
3/4 cup cooked brown rice (or grain of your choice)

Bake Scamp in 350 F. oven, or grill. Heat margarine in small pan and saute lump crabmeat until heated. Add lemon juice and serve over scamp, with rice (or grain of choice).

Nutritional info. per serving

Calories	408	
Protein	40	g
Carbohydrate	34	g
Fat	26	%
Sodium	620	mg
Cholesterol	76	mg
Fiber	3	g

Jamies

424 East Zarragozza Street, Pensacola(904) 434-2911

Anthony Karl Redfield is a graduate of the A.C.F. apprentice program in Montgomery, Alabama and is currently working on being certified as a working chef with the A.C.F. He has cooked in the South for over 13 years with experience in offshore work in Louisiana, hotel work in Alabama, and fine dining experience in Florida and Alabama. Anthony plans on living in his hometown, Pensacola, the rest of his life!

Most memorable meal - in order to graduate from school, the students had to plan a seven course dinner including making the menus (in French), cook, and serve it to the local chefs and their wives. It was very intimidating to cook for all the people they respected so much, but they pulled it off and received many accolades.

Anthony's mentor - Chef Dale Schulman, who was the first chef he actually had a chance to work under. Chef Dale got Anthony interested in school to expand his career, and showed him the artistic side of cooking.

♥ Supreme De Volaille Aux Salsa
Chicken Breast with Pineapple Salsa and Rice Pilaf
Yield: 4 servings

4 - 6 oz. chicken breasts, skinless, boneless
2 tablespoons olive oil
1 teaspoon garlic powder
1 tablespoon dried basil leaves
Pepper to taste

Lightly brush chicken breast with olive oil and season with garlic powder, basil and pepper. Place on charbroiler and cook on both sides. Make sure not to overcook.

Rice Pilaf:
2 cups chicken stock
1 stalk celery, diced
1/2 yellow onion, diced
1/2 green bell pepper, diced
3 oz. fresh mushrooms, sliced
1 cup white rice
1 tablespoon chopped fresh parsley
Pepper to taste

To prepare rice, heat chicken stock in large sauce pan and add celery, onion, green bell pepper and mushrooms. Bring to a boil, add rice and turn down to a simmer and cover pot tightly. Cook for 20 minutes without removing lid. When done, add parsley and pepper to taste. Keep warm.

Salsa:
1 cup fresh pineapple, medium diced (canned in juice can be substituted)
1/2 cup diced red bell pepper
1/3 cup diced bermuda onion
1/4 cup chopped scallions
2 tablespoons chopped fresh parsley

In a bowl combine pineapple, red bell pepper, bermuda onion, scallions and parsley. Mix well and set aside.

To serve: Spoon rice on plate, place chicken on top of rice and cover with a generous portion of pineapple salsa.

Nutritional info. per serving

Calories	487	
Protein	43	g
Carbohydrate	49	g
Fat	23	%
Sodium	485	mg
Cholesterol	97	mg
Fiber	2	g

Andrews Upstairs

228 S. Adams St., Tallahassee (904)222-3446

Andrew Reiss, Owner, and Chef Wayne Papka. Andrew grew up doing every job at The Carillon Hotel in Miami Beach, where his father was the Food and Beverage Director. He graduated from Florida State University's Hotel and Restaurant Management School. After graduation, he married and went to Europe to work. From there he worked in Aspen at The Wienerstube, and on to San Francisco. He came to Tallahassee and opened: The Deli in '73; Andrews Second Act in '75; Maxins in '77; Tutto Bene in '79; Epicurean Catering in '81; and in '85 Tutto Bene and Maxin's merged to form Andrews Upstairs. In '90 he opened Trio!

Andrew feels "you're only as good as your last meal." He serves state celebrities often. Andrew's mentor - his dad who was "the greatest front man ever!"

♥ Andrew's Pasta

Yield: 1 serving

5 oz. chicken breast, skinless, boneless
1 tablespoon olive oil
1 tablespoon fresh garlic, minced
2 teaspoons fresh chopped thyme
1/2 cup chopped green onions
1 1/2 cups sliced mushrooms
1 tablespoon pecan halves
1/2 cup red pepper, julienned
1 oz. canadian bacon, cut in slivers
1 artichoke heart, cut in 4's
4 tablespoons chicken broth
2 cups cooked linguini, cooked al dente
Pepper to taste
Parsley

Grill chicken breast. Heat olive oil in medium skillet and saute garlic, thyme, green onions, mushrooms, pecans, red pepper and canadian bacon for 2 minutes. Don't burn the garlic!

Add chicken broth and artichoke heart pieces.   Simmer another minute. Add cooked linguini and pepper; toss until hot. Arrange sliced chicken breast on top. Garnish with parsley.

Nutritional info. per serving

Calories	779	
Protein	54	g
Carbohydrate	83	g
Fat	31	%
Sodium	732	mg
Cholesterol	101	mg
Fiber	8	g

Chef's note: Serve with parmesan cheese sprinkled over top, if desired.

La Parisienne
60 Hypolita Street,St. Augustine (904)829-0055

Marianne Poncet went to an 8 month cooking school for the basics and then had 10 years working experience in different famous French restaurants: "L'Hostellerie du Palais" - French Riviera; "Les Trois Marches" - Versailles; "Le Potager du Roy"- Versailles; "Le Restaurant d' Olympe" - Paris and "L'Auberge de Noves" - French Riviera.
Every meal is a memorable one for Marianne, "when she knows that her customers enjoyed and are pleased with their lunch and/or dinner."
Her mentors - 2 famous French chefs: Henri Chapiron, "L'Hostellerie du Palais" and Gerard Vie, "Les Trois Marches."

♥ Grouper in Curry
Yield: 2 servings

1/2 apple, diced
1 banana, diced
1/2 mango, diced
Pinch curry powder or to taste
3 tablespoons evaporated skim milk
2 teaspoons olive oil
12 oz. grouper, cut in 2 oz. pieces
1/4 oz. pinenuts, roasted

In saute pan, cook diced fruit for 2 minutes with evaporated skim milk and a pinch of curry powder. Stir to mix well, and reserve. In another pan, heat olive oil and saute pieces of fish until cooked.

To serve: Place the mixture of fruit in the middle of a plate and display the pieces of fish around it. Use roasted pinenuts for decoration.

Nutritional info. per serving

Calories	317	
Protein	32	g
Carbohydrate	31	g
Fat	23	%
Sodium	89	mg
Cholesterol	54	mg
Fiber	3	g

Note: Fish could be cooked without the oil - poached or steamed to decrease the fat and calorie content.

Le Pavillon

45 San Marco Ave., St. Augustine (904)824-6202

Claudio Sinatsch, Executive Chef/Owner, started his culinary career by completing a 3 year formal apprenticeship at The Palace Hotel in Montreaux, Switzerland. In the U.S., before opening Le Pavillon, he worked in Connecticut, Massachusetts, New York and Rhode Island. In 1990, he was inducted into The American Academy of Chefs (A.A.C.), one of this country's most prestigious honorary culinary circles.

♥ Chicken Curry
Yield: 4 servings

4 - 6 oz. chicken breasts, skinless
Scant 3 tablespoons margarine
4 oz. (1 small) onion, chopped
1 1/2 apples, sliced
2 teaspoons curry powder or to taste
1 1/2 cups chicken stock
1 tablespoon cornstarch dissolved in 1/4 cup cold water or stock
4 oz. evaporated skim milk
2 1/2 teaspoons lemon juice

Garnish with:
4 tablespoons chopped onion
2 egg whites, hard-cooked, chopped
4 tablespoons diced pepper (red or green)
4 tablespoons diced pineapple
4 tablespoons raisins
4 tablespoons sliced bananas
4 tablespoons mango chutney

(Preheat oven to 350 F).
Heat margarine in large saute pan and saute chicken. Add chopped onions and sliced apple, and continue sautéeing. Dust with curry powder and add enough chicken stock so that the chicken is just covered by the liquid.

Braise covered for 20-25 minutes until the chicken meat is tender (or bake covered in oven). Remove chicken pieces from the stock. Thicken stock with cornstarch dissolved in water/stock. Add the evaporated skim milk and lemon juice. Reduce the liquid to a smooth sauce. Strain (or leave chunky if desired). Place chicken back in the sauce and keep warm. Serve with garnishes.

Nutritional info. per serving

Calories	444	
Protein	43	g
Carbohydrate	38	g
Fat	28	%
Sodium	553	mg
Cholesterol	98	mg
Fiber	3	g

Chef's serving suggestion: Serve with rice creole.

♥ Try adding all garnishes, except chutney, into the sauce.

Toby's Corner

101 S.E. Second Place, Gainesville (904)375-7620

John Cook, Executive Chef, went to The University of Florida. He has worked for all types of establishments: hotels, a country club, a private club and an institutional facility.
Most memorable meal - the night he cooked for, and got to meet "two of baseball's greats: Roger Maris and Mickey Mantle."
John's mentor - he has "been greatly influenced by both Jacques Pepin and Jeff Smith (Frugal Gourmet)."

♥ Grouper with Tomato, Lobster and Fennel
Yield: 4 Servings

4 - 6 oz. grouper fillets
1 teaspoon oil
1 small onion, diced
3 ribs celery, diced
1 tablespoon fennel seeds
2 tablespoons minced garlic
14 oz. can plum tomatoes, drained and crushed
4 oz. red wine
8 oz. lobster meat (or 2 Florida Lobster tails)
Pepper to taste

Preheat oven to 350 F.
Spray a baking sheet with a vegetable oil cooking spray and bake grouper in oven for 15-20 minutes.
Heat oil in medium size saucepan and saute onions, celery, fennel and garlic. Add crushed tomatoes and wine and simmer, covered, 10 minutes. Add lobster and cook approximately 5 minutes; remove lobster meat from shell, slice and add back to sauce. Spoon on baked fillet.

Nutritional info. per serving

Calories	257	
Protein	39	g
Carbohydrate	12	g
Fat	12	%
Sodium	433	mg
Cholesterol	84	mg
Fiber	2	g

Chef's suggestion: Try with Orange Roughy or Tuna.

CENTRAL

Chalet **Suzanne**®
Restaurant and Country Inn

La Normandie
authentic french gourmet restaurant

Jordan's grove

PORTOBELLO
YACHT CLUB

PREMIER CRUISE LINES
The Official Cruise Line of Walt Disney World®

Pondos

1915 Old New York Avenue, Deland (904)734-1995

Curtis Cunningham, Chef.
Doug Fisher and his wife Sylvia have owned and operated Pondos since 1980. Located in a historic building, built in 1921, Pondos features homemade pastas, desserts and breads.

♥ Duck Breast with Orange Amaretto Sauce
Served on a Saged Bread Dressing
Yield: 4 servings

4 - 6 oz. duck breasts, skinless, boneless
2 tablespoons fresh rosemary
2 stalks celery, cut in half
2 peeled carrots, cut in half
1 medium onion, cut in half
1/2 cup orange juice

Preheat oven to 350 F.

Season duck with rosemary. Place equal amounts of carrot, celery and onion under duck breasts, and put in baking pan. Pour orange juice on top of duck.

Cover pan and bake in oven approx. 1/2 hour (until cooked). Remove vegetables, coarsely chop when cool, and set aside for the dressing. Keep duck refrigerated until ready to assemble.

Saged Bread Dressing:
1 1/2 cups chicken stock
2 cups stale bread, ground finely
1/2 teaspoon sage
1/4 teaspoon white pepper
Coarsely chopped vegetables from the ducks

In saucepan heat chicken stock to a boil, then reduce heat. Stir in crumbs, sage, white pepper and vegetables.

Place in refrigerator until cool. After cool, if not quite stiff enough, you may add more breadcrumbs.

Orange Sauce:
1 cup orange juice
1/4 cup light brown sugar
1/2 teaspoon cinnamon
1/4 teaspoon Amaretto or almond extract
1 tablespoon low calorie margarine
1 tablespoon cornstarch diluted in 1/4 cup cold water

In a small saucepan combine all ingredients except cornstarch mixture. Bring to a boil, stirring, making sure all ingredients are blended.

Stir cornstarch mixture in and bring to boiling point again. Lower heat to simmer or cool and refrigerate.

To assemble: Spray vegetable oil cooking spray on a flat baking sheet.

Preheat oven to 400 F.

Place 4 equal amounts of stuffing on sheet. Form into flat rectangular shapes being sure to leave space for all four duck breasts. Place ducks over stuffing.

Place in hot oven for 12-15 minutes, covered. Carefully place on plate and top with warm orange sauce.

Note: Ducks and stuffing (keep separate) can be prepared and refrigerated for 2 days in advance.

Nutritional info. per serving

Calories	450	
Protein	32	g
Carbohydrate	44	g
Fat	32	%
Sodium	551	mg
Cholesterol	102	mg
Fiber	4	g

♥ Try with chicken too!

Bernard's Surf

2 South Atlantic Ave., Cocoa Beach (407)783-2401

Charles D. Ragland, General Manager, attended the University of Houston. He was previously with The Piccadilly Cafeteria chain for 13 years, and has been at Bernard's Surf for 18 years! Most memorable meal - "the dinner Bernard's Surf held for the cosmonauts and astronauts in 1975," what an impressive list of guests!

♥ Seafood Cream Sauce
Yield: 4 servings (on fish)

1 tablespoon margarine
1/2 oz. onion
1 tablespoon white flour
1/2 cup clam stock (juice)
3/8 cup evaporated milk *
3/8 cup evaporated skim milk
1/8 teaspoon cayenne pepper (or blackening mix)
3 oz. shrimp
2 oz. crab (use imitation, if desired)
3 oz. scallops
1 tablespoon cornstarch diluted in 1/4 cup cold water

Heat margarine in pan and saute onions; add flour and lightly brown. Add clam juice and mix well. Add both milks, pepper, shrimp, crabmeat (no shells) and scallops and mix lightly until cooked.

Add cornstarch mixture to sauce, and thicken as desired.

Nutritional info. per serving

Calories	129	
Protein	12	g
Carbohydrate	10	g
Fat	31	%
Sodium	330	mg
Cholesterol	46	mg
Fiber	-	

♥ Can be used as a sauce on pasta, for 2 servings.

* Entire recipe can be prepared with evaporated skim milk, which will also decrease the fat content.

Nannie Lee's Strawberry Mansion

1218 E. New Haven Ave., Melbourne (407)724-8627

Pete Wynkoop, Chef/Owner, is a C.I.A. graduate. He has previously worked at "Poor Richards Inn" in Melbourne Beach; "The Mouse Trap" in Cocoa Beach; and "The Red Tailed Hawk" in Fort Pierce.

♥ Crabcakes
Yield: 6 servings

1 tablespoon olive oil
1/2 cup celery, diced
1/2 cup onion, diced
1/2 cup green pepper, diced
1 oz. sherry wine
1 1/2 cups seasoned bread crumbs
1 egg
1-2 egg whites
1 tablespoon lite mayonnaise
1 tablespoon Dijon mustard (such as Grey Poupon)
1/2 teaspoon Worcestershire sauce
1/2 teaspoon lemon juice
Dash white pepper
1 lb. lump crabmeat precooked - lay out and remove any shells
    carefully. Imitation crabmeat may be substituted.
2 oz. romano cheese
Paprika
2/3 tablespoon margarine, melted
1/3 tablespoon white wine
Dash dill

Preheat oven to 350 F.
   Heat olive oil in medium pan and saute celery, onion and green pepper. When cooked, add sherry and then cool.
   In a large bowl, mix all remaining ingredients except crab, romano cheese, paprika, margarine, wine and dill. Add crab carefully and portion out crabcakes onto baking pan. Sprinkle romano cheese and paprika over crabcakes. Mix white wine, margarine and dill, and sprinkle over crabcakes.

Bake in oven, until hot, for 8-10 minutes.

Nutritional info. per serving

Calories	280	
Protein	17	g
Carbohydrate	29	g
Fat	31	%
Sodium	1012	mg*
Cholesterol	61	mg
Fiber	1	g

* Analyzed with imitation crabmeat. Please note that if lump crabmeat is used the sodium content will decrease but, the cholesterol content will increase.

Chef's suggestion: Serve with cocktail sauce, if desired.

Jordan's Grove

1300 South Orlando Ave., Maitland (407)628-0020

Clair L. Epting Jr., Executive Chef, has "worked in Maine, New Orleans, (under Paul Prudhomme), Maryland and Florida establishing a rich background in seafood styles." Clair has 27 years of kitchen experience, including time at The Dallas Playboy Club.
Most memorable meal - Summer of 1985 in Kennebunkport, Maine. He was the sole chef for Vice President Bush and 11 of his staff, for breakfast and lunch, during a meeting at the restaurant he was working at.
Clair's mentor - his grandmother who "did so much with so little."

♥ Seared Sea Scallops
Served with a Black and White Bean Vinaigrette
Yield: 1 serving

1 oz. each of black and navy beans, precooked and rinsed
2 oz. cucumber, seedless, cubed
1/2 oz. (approx. 1 tablespoon) bell pepper (red or yellow), diced
3/4 tablespoon olive oil
1/2 tablespoon lemon juice
Dash Louisiana hot sauce
1 tablespoon chopped cilantro

6 oz. cleaned and drained sea scallops

Combine navy and black beans in a bowl. Add all other ingredients except scallops and let stand for 20 minutes. Serve over seared scallops.

To sear scallops: Using a non-stick pan you can quickly sear the scallops golden brown if the pan is almost smoking hot (and no oil is needed), and the scallops are thin and patted dry. You can also cook scallops in a pan, sprayed with a vegetable oil cooking spray, over medium heat.

Nutritional info. per serving

Calories	325	
Protein	34	g
Carbohydrate	20	g
Fat	33	%
Sodium	282	mg
Cholesterol	56	mg
Fiber	4	g

The Bubble Room Restaurants
1531 South Orlando Ave., Maitland (407)628-3331
15001 Captiva Dr., Captiva Island (813) 472-5558
4320 North Tamiami Trail, Naples (813) 263-3434

Jeff Scavo, General Manager, Maitland location, grew up in Cincinnati, Ohio, and graduated from Miami University, majoring in Economics and Political Science. Jeff's Bubble Room experience started in 1985 as a waiter at the "Little Bubble Room" Ashville, N.C. (now closed). In February, 1986, he transferred to Captiva Island and was made manager of the Captiva Bubble Room in June of that year. As the restaurant group expands, Jeff spends time in management between the Captiva, Naples and Orlando locations. Two of Jeff's brothers, Mike and Jay, also serve in management postitions with the restaurants.
Memorable meal - Bubble Room Restaurant, Spring Break 1985 - "A huge Bubble Room Prime Rib dinner hooked me on the zany Bubble Room and the restaurant business!"
Jeff's mentor - Jamie Farquharson, original owner of the Bubble Room. "Jamie taught me how to cook, to always strive for perfection and to be an ambitious hard worker."

♥ Teahouse Of The August Moon
Yield: 1 serving

Orange Ginger Glaze:
Yields: 20 oz.; approx.10 servings
25 oz. orange marmalade
1 oz. lite soy sauce
1 oz. fresh ginger, grated
3 oz. Rose's lime juice
2 oz. orange juice

To prepare glaze, combine all ingredients in a sauce pan. Cook over low heat for 8-10 minutes until hot to touch.

6 oz. fillet of red snapper, cut into 3 or 4 strips lengthwise
3 oz. broccoli florets
3 oz. baby carrots, peeled
3 oz. yellow squash, sliced
3 oz. cauliflower florets
3 oz. snow pea pods
3 oz. button mushrooms
3 oz. red pepper, sliced
Paprika
Lime
Clean and prepare all vegetables. Place fillet of snapper in the middle of

a 9" diameter round bamboo steamer basket. Place vegetables, except red pepper, around outside edge and lay 3 strips of red pepper across the fillet. Place uncovered steamer basket in activated steamer. Steam basket for approximately 8-10 minutes until fish is white throughout and contains no translucent areas.

Ladle 2 oz. of orange glaze over snapper fillet only. Lightly sprinkle with paprika and garnish with a lime. Serve covered in bamboo steamer.

Nutritional info. per serving

Calories	555	
Protein	48	g
Carbohydrate	88	g
Fat	7	%
Sodium	239	mg
Cholesterol	67	mg
Fiber	13	g

♥ The glaze is wonderful for chicken too.

Arthurs 27

Buena Vista Palace in The Walt Disney World Village Hotel Plaza
Lake Buena Vista (407)827-3450

Bruno Wehren, Executive Chef, is a native of Switzerland, who knew at a very young age his life-long goal was to study and perfect recipes native to countries all over the world. After completing his apprenticeship in French cuisine in 1967, he began immediately to pursue this goal by joining a luxury passenger cruise line which took him on several trips around the world. Upon arriving at each country, he sought out the best chefs and carefully studied the art of their native cuisines. He then utilized his collection of culinary specialties in first-class hotels and restaurants.
Most memorable "assignments" - "have varied from the creation of a multi-tiered traditional English fruitcake rising 10' high with a 6' base for the wedding of the Zambian President's son, to a melon carving featuring the "Irma La Douce" movie theme for Shirley McLaine." Chef Bruno and his wife, Betty, grew quite fond of the former Queen Mother of Siam who often took tea in his hotel, located near the Queen Mother's Palace. In Thailand, his cuisine became the favorite of the movie cast on location for "The Man With The Golden Gun."

♥ Mango Apricot Stuffing
Yield: 1 large loaf or 2 regular loaves - 20 servings

1 oz. (2 tablespoons) liquid margarine
3.5 oz. (1 cup) pine nuts
16 oz. (2 cups) fresh or canned mangoes, cubed
8 oz. (1 cup) fresh or canned apricots, halved
6 oz. (7 stalks) celery, diced
6 oz. (1 large) onion, diced
1 oz. (2 tablespoons) garlic, finely chopped
26 oz. (26 slices) of (stale) bread, cut in 1" cubes
3.5 oz. (7/8 cup) walnut pieces
2 tablespoons fresh assorted herbs: basil, thyme, marjoram, oregano
4 tablespoons parsley, chopped
4 oz. (2/3 cup) raisins
10 oz. apricot juice or mango juice (or orange juice)
4 eggs
8 egg whites
1/8 oz. (1/4 tablespoon) hot sauce
1/4 oz. (1/2 tablespoon) Worcestershire sauce
Seasoning to taste

Preheat oven to 275 F.

Heat 1 tablespoon margarine in small pan and saute pine nuts until brown. Mix together all remaining ingredients in a large bowl until the bread cubes are thoroughly soaked.

Note: If using fresh apricots and mangoes, substitute orange juice for the apricot or mango juice.

Put in loaf pans, drizzle remainder of margarine on the top of the stuffing, and bake in oven for 1 1/2 hours.

Nutritional info. per serving

Calories	228	
Protein	9	g
Carbohydrate	31	g
Fat	34	%
Sodium	295	mg
Cholesterol	43	mg
Fiber	6	g

♥ Try Stuffed Vidalia onions for 4: Prepare 1/4 of recipe, with the exception of the bread - use 6 oz., and pack in large Vidalia onion shells (onions that have been scooped). Bake, covered, in pan that has been sprayed with vegetable oil cooking spray, following cooking instructions above!

♥ Court Bouillon for Fish and Seafood
Yield: 1 1/2 quarts

2 medium size carrots, sliced thin
White part of 1 leek, sliced thin
1 stalk of celery, sliced thin
4 or 5 green onions or
    1 medium size white onion, sliced thin
2 shallots, sliced thin
2 cups dry white wine
1 1/2 quarts of water
(1 tablespoon of coarse salt)
Seasonings:
5 thin slices of lemon peel
2 whole cloves of garlic, unpeeled

25 green peppercorns
Bouquet garni: 6 parsley sprigs, 1/2 bay leaf, a small piece of
  fresh fennel, a sprig of thyme and 1 clove

Heat a saucepan sprayed with a vegetable oil cooking spray over medium heat and cook the sliced vegetables, covered, for 5 minutes. Then add the wine, water, (salt) and the seasonings.

Simmer, covered, for 20 minutes. The vegetables should remain slightly firm if used in certain sauces that accompany fish and seafood dishes.

♥ Macadamia Chocolate Chip Cookies
Yield: 30 large

3 oz. margarine
3/4 cup light brown sugar
2/3 cup powdered sugar
1 egg
1 teaspoon vanilla
2 1/2 cups all purpose flour
1 teaspoon baking soda
1/3 cup semi-sweet chocolate chips
1/4 cup chopped macadamia nuts

Preheat oven to 325 F.
In large bowl, cream margarine and sugars. Add egg and vanilla and mix in. Add sifted dry ingredients and then the chopped nuts and chocolate chips; mix.

Roll dough (you may need to sprinkle with water) into tube ("slice and bake") shape and refrigerate one hour. Slice - 1/2" thick and place on baking sheet and bake in oven for approx. 10 minutes.

Nutritional Info. per serving

Calories	109	
Protein	1	g
Carbohydrate	17	g
Fat	35	%
Sodium	62	mg
Cholesterol	7	mg
Fiber	-	

♥ Crepes with Apples and Armagnac
Yield: 3 servings

6 crepes (recipe follows)
4 apples
1/2 lemon
2 tablespoons margarine
1/4 cup powdered sugar, sifted
3 apricots, peeled, halved, pitted
1 teaspoon vanilla
2 additional tablespoons powdered sugar, sifted
1/4 cup Apricot Liqueur
1/4 cup Armagnac

Make crepes. If prepared in advance, cover with plastic and refrigerate.

Preheat oven to 375 F.
Peel and core apples, cut into slices and rub with lemon.
Heat margarine in heavy-bottomed skillet over medium heat until it turns golden brown. Add apples and saute over medium high heat for about 3 minutes, until they start to color. Add 1/4 cup powdered sugar (to encourage browning) and apricot halves and cook for 5 minutes, stirring frequently. Mix in vanilla.
Stuff crepes with the apple-apricot filling, roll up and arrange seam-side down in a baking (or chafing) dish sprayed with a vegetable oil cooking spray.
Sprinkle crepes with 2 tablespoons of powdered sugar and pour on Apricot Liqueur and Armagnac. Bake in oven for 15 minutes before serving. If desired, add additional liqueur and flame. Serve very hot.

♥ Crepes
Yield: 5 servings, approx. 10 crepes

3 1/2 oz. (7/8 cup) flour
1 1/2 oz. (6 tablespoons) powdered sugar
1 egg
1 egg yolk
Finely grated peel of 1/2 orange
Scant 1/2 pint (1 cup) nonfat milk

1 1/2 oz. (3 tablespoons) margarine
Vegetable oil cooking spray

To prepare the batter: Blend the flour, sugar, whole egg, egg yolk and the orange peel in the blender, adding the milk gradually and continuing to blend until smooth.

Meanwhile, heat margarine in a small saucepan. When it turns golden and ceases to sizzle all the water in it has evaporated.

Add the margarine to the batter and blend well; allow to rest for 1/2 hour.

To cook the crepes: Spray the inside of a frying pan lightly with a vegetable oil cooking spray. Stir the crepe mixture thoroughly. Heat the pan over a medium heat, and when it is hot, ladle a small amount of the batter, about 2 1/2 tablespoons into the center, giving the pan a swift circular shake at the same time in order to spread the batter in a thin, even layer over the surface. Let the crepe cook for a minute to a light golden brown on each side, sliding a metal spatula carefully underneath to turn it. When it is done, slide the pancake from the pan and pile on to a plate. Follow the same process to make nine more crepes. You can use two pans to make two crepes at once, but you must work quite fast and efficiently.

Nutritional info. per serving

Calories	554	
Protein	6	g
Carbohydrate	78	g
Fat	25	%
Sodium	198	mg
Cholesterol	86	mg
Fiber	5	g

Atlantis
Stouffer Orlando Resort 6677 Sea Harbor Dr., Orlando (407)351-5555

Hiroshi Noguchi, a Master Chef specializing in Japanese and French cuisine, is a native of Japan. He apprenticed at Hotel Okura, the largest hotel in Tokyo, when he was 18. In the U.S., he has worked in Atlanta, Itasca, Il. and Chicago. Presently in Orlando, he orchestrates the operation of 3 restaurants highlighting French specialities and Chinese and American cuisines; a spectacular Sunday brunch; and sit down banquets of up to 1800 persons. He is "world renowned" for his award winning technique that won him several medals, "including the gold - at the Frankfurt Olympiad of Cooks." Hiroshi is a member of the ACF, Les Toques Blanches Chapter of Central Florida, and a member of Chaine des Rotisseurs.
Most memorable meal - A banquet for the opera in Orlando in honor of Pavorotti in concert, December 31, '88.
Hiroshi's mentor - his teacher, Chef Masakiche Ono of Japan.

♥ Pepper Vegetable Timbales
Yield: 2 servings

2 whole yellow or red peppers, tops cut off, seeded and set aside
1 carrot, chopped
1/4 head broccoli, chopped
1/4 head cauliflower, chopped
3 oz. (3) egg whites
1/4 teaspoon sugar
1/4 teaspoon cinnamon
1/4 teaspoon nutmeg
Pepper
2 pieces phyllo dough

Preheat oven to 400 F.
Steam each vegetable, except peppers, separately until tender. Put each vegetable, except peppers, one at a time in food processor and puree: carrot with sugar, 1 oz. egg white and pepper; broccoli with cinnamon, 1 oz. egg white and pepper; cauliflower with nutmeg, 1 oz. egg white and pepper. Layer vegetable purees inside each pepper, wrap peppers in plastic and steam 15 minutes. Let cool, take plastic off. Wrap in phyllo dough sprayed with a vegetable oil cooking spray, and bake in oven for approx. 7 - 10 minutes or until phyllo is a golden brown.

Nutritional info. per serving

Calories	147	
Protein	10	g
Carbohydrate	28	g
Fat	4	%
Sodium	184	mg
Cholesterol	-	
Fiber	5	g

♥ Dressing for Vegetables and Salads
Yield: 22 Tablespoons

1 teaspoon olive oil
1/4 cup sherry wine vinegar
1 teaspoon black pepper
1/2 cup tomato juice
1 whole tomato, diced
1/2 cup water/cornstarch mixture (optional, see preparation
   tips)

Mix together all ingredients.

Nutritional info. per tablespoon

Calories	7	
Protein	-	
Carbohydrate	1	g
Fat	28	%
Sodium	23	mg
Cholesterol	-	
Fiber	-	

Cascades

Hyatt Regency Grand Cypress One Grand Cypress Blvd., Orlando (407)239-1234

Marco Barbitta, The Executive Chef, is originally from Switzerland, where he attended the Hotel School in Lucerne. He is a member of Chaine des Rotisseurs and Toques Blanches. Marco has worked in Spain, Panama City, New Mexico, Puerto Rico, Kowloon Hong Kong and for Hyatt in California, Connecticut and now Orlando.
His mentor - Rene Mettler, Executive Chef Hyatt Regency Waikoloa, Hawaii.

♥ Breaded Snapper Cuisine Naturelle
Yield: 1 serving

Lentil Relish:
Yield: 10 servings
10 oz. cooked lentils
5 oz. red and green pepper, diced
4 tablespoons fresh herbs or 1 tablespoon herb seasoning blend
    of choice
1/8 teaspoon black pepper
Juice of 2 lemons
Juice of 2 limes
2 oz. white wine
2 oz. white vinegar

Toss all ingredients together. Use as filling for cucumber garnish (see below).

6 oz. snapper fillet
1 slice whole wheat toast
1/2 oz. shelled pistachio nuts, finely crushed
1 tablespoon fresh herbs or 1 teaspoon herb seasoning blend of
    choice
3/4 teaspoon olive oil
2 oz. corn off the cob
1/4 tomato, seeded and chopped
1 portion lentil relish

Garnish:
1/4 cucumber, inside scooped out
4 snow peas

Preheat oven to 350 F.
Crumb the whole wheat toast into fine breadcrumbs, toss with pistachio and fresh herbs. Pat crumb mixture onto snapper fillet. Spray pan with a vegetable oil cooking spray, add oil and heat. Pan fry snapper; put in oven, in pan if ovenproof or baking pan, to finish cooking.

To serve, place on left side of plate; place corn kernels in middle of plate and place tomato on top of corn. Spoon lentil relish into cucumber shell and place on right side of plate. Snow peas should fan out from tip of corn.

Nutritional info. per serving
Calories	450	
Protein	40	g
Carbohydrate	43	g
Fat	29	%
Sodium	245	mg
Cholesterol	53	mg
Fiber	12	g

♥ Try substituting crushed macadamia nuts for the pistachio nuts.

Disney Village Marketplace
Walt Disney World, Orlando

Certified Executive Chef Johnny Rivers, C.E.C., A.A.C., joined the Disney team in 1970 and has helped open each Disney hotel, including the Contemporary Resort, The Grand Floridian Resort and the Pleasure Island complex. Johnny is presently the Executive Chef - Research and Development - for Walt Disney World Resorts. Chef Rivers is National Secretary for the American Culinary Federation and has been a member of the American Academy of Chefs since 1975.
His most memorable meal - one he describes as "interesting" was a Father's Day meal his 15 year old daughter prepared for him.
Johnny's mentor - his mother, who worked "miracles" in the kitchen to feed his large family!

♥ Chicken Mediterranean
Yield: 4 servings

Tomato Sauce:
4 teaspoons olive oil
1 cup (1 medium) chopped onion
1 green pepper (about 6 oz.), chopped
6 tablespoons tomato paste
1 cup tomatoes, fresh or canned, diced
2 beef bouillon cubes
1 1/2 teaspoons sugar
1/2 tablespoon finely chopped fresh garlic
1 bay leaf
Oregano and black pepper to taste

Heat olive oil in 1-quart saucepan over medium heat. Add onions and green pepper; cook stirring, until onions are clear. Add tomato paste and cook for 30 seconds. Add all other ingredients and let simmer for 20 minutes.
Remove from heat and hold to add to chicken.

1 cup uncooked white or brown rice
4 - 6 oz. chicken breasts, skinless, boneless, sliced into strips
4 tablespoons flour
2 tablespoons olive oil
4 each large black (ripe) and green olives, sliced into slivers

Prepare rice according to package directions. Remember to allow a longer cooking time for brown rice.

Lightly dust chicken strips in flour.

Heat oil over medium high heat in large skillet with deep sides and tight-fitting lid, and saute chicken until 3/4 done, about 5 to 7 minutes. Add tomato sauce over chicken and reduce heat to simmer. Simmer, covered, until chicken is done, about 10 minutes longer. Add more water, as necessary, if sauce becomes too thick.

Place cooked rice in a serving dish; put chicken and sauce over top. Garnish with olive slivers.

Nutritional info. per serving

Calories	475	
Protein	44	g
Carbohydrate	38	g
Fat	30	%
Sodium	775	mg
Cholesterol	98	mg
Fiber	4	g

La Normandie
2021 East Colonial Dr., Orlando (407)896-9976

Claude Melchiorri, Chef/Owner, has worked at: "LeParc Relais," Lisieux, France; "Maxim's of Paris"; Navalship "Jeanne D'Arc," Switzerland; Connaught Hotel, London; Bermudian Hotel; "Le Camebert," "Rive Ganache," and "La Mere Duquesne," San Francisco.

♥ Grand Marnier Souffle
Yield: 8 servings

Base:
2 oz. (4 tablespoons) margarine
1/2 cup flour
1/2 qt. (2 cups) lowfat milk
1/2 cup sugar
Zest of 1/2 orange

Melt margarine in saucepan and stir in half of flour. In a bowl mix milk, sugar, orange zest and remaining flour; add to saucepan and bring to boil, stirring. Set aside, keeping warm in double boiler.

Mix:
4 egg yolks
4 oz. (1/2 cup) Grand Marnier
8 egg whites
1 tablespoon sugar

Preheat oven to 350 F.
Prepare 2 souffle dishes (1 quart each) by spraying each with a vegetable oil cooking spray. Sprinkle with sugar (prevents souffle from sticking).
Mix egg yolk and Grand Marnier, add to base. In a bowl, whip egg whites and 1 tablespoon sugar until they form a peak. With spatula, fold into base, mixing gently. Pour into prepared souffle dishes.

Place souffle dishes in large pan with water. Place in oven for 20 minutes or until puffed and golden brown. Serve immediately.

Nutritional info. per serving
Calories	259	
Protein	8	g
Carbohydrate	30	g
Fat	34	%
Sodium	153	mg
Cholesterol	112	mg
Fiber	-	

Portobello Yacht Club

Pleasure Island 1650 Buena Vista Dr., Lake Buena Vista (407)934-8888

Ron Pollack, Chef, came to Central Florida with The Levy Restaurants from Chicago. He was associated with the critically acclaimed Chestnut Street Grill in Chicago's Watertower Place.
Most memorable meals include: the night Bob Hope dined at The Portobello Yacht Club and when leaving received applause and a standing ovation; the night Alan Alda's laugh could be heard through the main dining room; catering Roy Disney's private jet; and preparing Tom Cruise's Bucatini All Amatriciana (a pasta dish).
Ron's mentors - Executive Chef Warren Dodge; Executive Chef de Cuisine James Blake; and "The Levy Restaurants' overall style and passion for excellence have been the driving force in his growth and development."

♥ Pesce Griglia Alla Portobello Yacht Club
Yield: 4 servings

4 - 6 oz. fish fillets (halibut, snapper, grouper or salmon)
1 oz. (2 tablespoons) Italian extra virgin olive oil
Pepper
1/2 oz. fresh basil leaves, thinly sliced chiffonade
4 plum tomatoes, peeled, seeded and diced
4 cups grilled vegetables such as zucchini, mushrooms, eggplant, and
    sweet peppers
2 cups cooked brown rice (or grain of your choice)

Brush fish fillets with 1/2 oz. oil. Season with pepper.
Place fish on well cleaned, hot grill surface, lightly sprayed with a vegetable oil cooking spray, skin side up. Turn fish fillet 45 degrees to form cross marks. Cook fish 4-6 minutes on each side, depending on thickness. Turn fillet and follow the same procedure to form cross marks. Be certain not to overcook. When done, turn fillet and remove the skin with spatula and tongs (it should come off easily).
Place fish on warm serving platter. Drizzle fillets with remainder of olive oil. Top with diced tomatoes, then chiffonade of fresh basil.

Serve with 1 cup fresh grilled vegetables and 1/2 cup cooked rice (or grain of choice) per serving.

Nutritional info. per serving

Calories	374	
Protein	35	g
Carbohydrate	33	g
Fat	27	%
Sodium	96	mg
Cholesterol	47	mg
Fiber	5	g

Chef Patrick Denis from Le Quercy Restaurant, which was on University Drive in Plantation, suggests another great tomato concasse to serve on grilled fish (Swordfish or Tuna steaks).

♥ Tomato (Vinaigrette) Concasse
Yield: 2 servings

1 medium tomato, peeled, seeded and diced
1 teaspoon olive oil
1 teaspoon Balsamic vinegar
2 teaspoons chopped fresh mint
1 teaspoon finely diced red onion
Crushed black pepper

Toss all ingredients and chill. Put in radicchio cup, or serve on top of fish.

While experimenting with different spices, wines and vinegars we came up with the following concasse:

♥ Tomato Concasse
Yield: 4 servings

2 large tomatoes, peeled, seeded and chopped
3/4 teaspoon oil
1 tablespoon chopped fresh basil

1 tablespoon dry white wine
1 teaspoon red wine vinegar
Black, red, and white peppers to taste

Mix all ingredients and season. You can serve chilled, or heat and reduce for several minutes.

Note: Also see the recipe - Tomato-Ginger Vinaigrette - from The Grand Cafe, Grand Bay Hotel for another great concasse to serve on/with fish.

Premier Cruise Lines
The Official Cruise Line of Walt Disney World ®
(407)783-5061

The original rice pudding recipe was modified for Premier Cruise Lines by Joyce Julien,M.S.,R.D./L.D. and Ronnie Julien,M.S.,R.D./L.D.

♥ Healthy Rice Pudding
Yield: 15 - 3 oz. servings

1/2 quart (2 cups) water
3/4 quart (3 cups) skim milk
3 1/2 oz. (1/2 cup + 2 tablespoons) **short** grain rice such
   as Arborio
Drop of vanilla extract
1/2 lb. (1 cup + 2 tablespoons) sugar
1/4 quart (1 cup) whipped cream (use pressurized or imitation)
4 oz. fruit, diced
Pinch cinnamon
1/2 oz.(1 tablespoon) Grand Marnier

In saucepan, bring the rice and the water to boil; cook until almost all the water is absorbed by the rice, do not let it dry too much. Add skim milk and vanilla, mix in. Lower the heat and watch carefully. The rice pudding can burn very fast if unattended (be patient). Add sugar towards the end. Pour into individual serving dishes.

Cool the pudding in refrigerator; when cold mix in the whipped cream, fruit, cinnamon and Grand Marnier.

Nutritional info. per serving

Calories	124	
Protein	2	g
Carbohydrate	27	g
Fat	8	%
Sodium	31	mg
Cholesterol	4	mg
Fiber - depends on the type of fruit		

Le Cordon Bleu

537 West Fairbanks Ave., Winter Park (407)647-7575

George Vogelbacher, Master Chef/Owner and Monique Vogelbacher travel to Switzerland to get new ideas!
One of George's most memorable meals was served in Switzerland at "Nussbaumer" in Baselland where he was served a fresh Grapeleaf salad.

♥ Chicken Napa Valley
Yield: 4 servings

1/2 lb. red seedless grapes
1/2 lb. white seedless grapes
1/4 lb. snow peas
4 artichoke hearts, halved
3-4 medium size tomatoes, peeled, seeded and diced
2 cups white wine such as Napa Valley Ingelnook
Pinch white pepper
4 - 6 oz. chicken breasts, skinless, boneless

In large saucepan, simmer all ingredients, except chicken, for 10 minutes.
Grill chicken until 70% cooked. Add chicken to poached vegetable mixture and finish cooking.

Nutritional info. per serving

Calories	391	
Protein	38	g
Carbohydrate	31	g
Fat	11	%
Sodium	182	mg
Cholesterol	96	mg
Fiber	4	g

Chef's serving suggestion: Serve over steamed rice and garnish with a Baked Tomato - tomato seasoned with herbs, bread crumbs, pepper, a tiny drop of olive oil, and baked.

Maison and Jardin

430 South Wymore Rd., Altamonte Springs (407)862-4410

Hans Spirig, Executive Chef, went to culinary school in St. Gallen, Switzerland. He has worked at "Schweizerhof," "Hote Metropole" and "Hotel Hecht Appenzelle," Switzerland; "Hotel Corfu Palace," Greece; "Hotel Queen Elizabeth," Canada; a private club in Bermuda; "Watergate Restaurant Washington, D.C.," Hotel Embassy Row, D.C.; "Williamsburg Inn," Virginia and "Continental Plaza," Illinois.

Most memorable meals- during the parties he served for Martha Mitchell in her apartment in Washington, D.C.. "The roving body of security guards around him drove Hans bananas! Martha tried to help too, but to no avail."

His mentor - Ernesto Schlegeel, Executive Chef at "The Ritz" in Barcelona, Spain, and at "Schweizerhof" in Switzerland.

♥ Bouillabaisse Maison
Yield: 4 servings

2 teaspoons olive oil
1 stalk celery, chopped
1 small leek, white part with some green, chopped
1 tablespoon tomato paste
1/2 cup white wine
10 threads saffron
1 teaspoon fennel seeds
10 branches thyme, chopped
1 bay leaf
4 cloves
1 teaspoon garlic, chopped
1 1/2 qts. seafood stock (or clam juice)
2 medium tomatoes, diced
1/2 oz.(1 tablespoon) Pernod
Pepper

Seafood:
2 oz. medium sea scallops
2 oz. shrimp
4 crab claws
4 mussels
4 clams
8 oz. fish (such as grouper or snapper)

4 oz. lobster meat

Heat olive oil in stock pot and saute leeks and celery for 5 minutes. Add tomato paste, saute another 3-5 minutes. Deglaze with white wine. Add all herbs plus garlic, then seafood stock.

Cook until vegetables are al dente. Add diced tomatoes and boil 5 minutes. Add Pernod and pepper to taste.

Add all seafood and cook until clams open and fish is cooked.

Nutritional info. per serving

Calories	241	
Protein	34	g
Carbohydrate	9	g
Fat	18	%
Sodium	1074	mg
Cholesterol	90	mg
Fiber	1	g

Chef's suggestion: Serve with garlic bread.

Chalet Suzanne

Lake Wales (813)676-6011

Carl Hinshaw, Executive Chef.
Most memorable meal - The Broiled Grapefruit has been served as the first course at The Chalet
Suzanne since 1931 and honored by the Florida Citrus Commission. It has been served to many
celebrities over the years, including Astronaut Colonel James Irwin of the Apollo Space Mission.
*   Chalet Suzanne is the "Home of Chalet Suzanne Gourmet Soups served aboard Apollo Flights*
to the moon!"
Carl's mentor - his mother Bertha Hinshaw.

♥ Broiled Grapefruit
Yield: 1 serving

3/4 oz. chicken liver
1 teaspoon flour
Pepper
1/2 grapefruit
1 tablespoon margarine
1/2 teaspoon sugar
Approx. 2 tablespoons cinnamon sugar mixture (1/8-1/4 teaspoon
    cinnamon to 2 tablespoons sugar)

Preheat oven to broil.
Spray small saute pan with a vegetable oil cooking spray, heat and saute
chicken liver that has been dredged in flour and seasoned with pepper.
    Have fruit at room temperature so it will be heated through when top is
browned. To cut grapefruit: Cut in half and section with grapefruit knife.
    Fill center of grapefruit with margarine. Sprinkle sugar and cinnamon
sugar mixture over grapefruit.

Broil grapefruit in shallow baking pan 4 inches from heat about 8-10 minutes or just long enough to brown tops, and heat until bubbling hot. At end of broiling time, place chicken liver in center of grapefruit half and serve.

Nutritional info. per serving

Calories	225	
Protein	5	g
Carbohydrate	35	g
Fat	34	%
Sodium	106	mg
Cholesterol	89	g
Fiber	2	g

Note: Delicious also as a dessert - broil grapefruit without chicken liver and use only 1/2 tablespoon margarine; can be flamed tableside.

The Blueberry Patch
414 East Liberty St., Brookville (904)796-6005

Paula Hopan, General Manager, has 10 years of hands-on experience.
Favorite meal - Roast Beef with Brown Potatoes and Carrots.

♥ Blueberry Cake
Yield: 20 servings

3/4 cup margarine
2 cups sugar
2 teaspoons vanilla
3 eggs, separated
3 cups flour
2 teaspoons baking powder
2/3 cup nonfat milk
2 egg whites
1 pint (2 cups) blueberries
6 teaspoons confectioners sugar (powdered sugar)

Preheat oven to 350 F.
In large bowl, cream margarine, sugar and vanilla. Add egg yolks that
have been beaten; beat until light and fluffy, 2 minutes. In a separate bowl,
mix flour and baking powder. Add milk and flour mixture slowly to sugar
and egg mixture. In a separate bowl, beat egg whites until stiff; gently fold
whites into batter. Mix all.
Spray 9"x13" pan with a vegetable oil cooking spray and dust with flour.
Pour 2/3 batter in pan then sprinkle blueberries over top. Add the rest of
the batter and bake in oven for 45 minutes. Cool and sprinkle confectioners
sugar over top of cake.

Nutritional info. per serving

Calories	230	
Protein	4	g
Carbohydrate	37	g
Fat	30	%
Sodium	146	mg
Cholesterol	32	mg
Fiber	1	g

♥♥ Variation - Blueberry Coffee Cake: 1. Decrease sugar to 1 3/4 cups. 2. Substitute 2/3-1 cup nonfat plain yogurt for the milk. 3. In a small bowl mix 1/4 cup brown sugar and 1/2 teaspoon cinnamon.

Follow above instructions for mixing and baking. Sprinkle 1/2 of brown sugar/cinnamon mixture over blueberries, add the rest of the batter and sprinkle the remainder of mixture over top. You can swirl some of the mixture into the batter with a knife, if desired.

SOUTHWEST

Armani's

Hyatt Regency Westshore 6200 Courtney Campbell Causeway, Tampa (813)874-1234

Hans J. Hickle, Executive Chef, is a culinary school graduate. He has worked in London, Guernsey, France and The Caribbean prior to arriving in the U.S.A, at which time he joined Hyatt Hotels in Pittsburgh, Pa. He opened Hyatt Regency Austin, Columbus and Hyatt Regency Westshore in Tampa, Fla., home of Armani's and Oystercatchers Restaurants.
Hans' mentor - "Carl Duch, principal of the culinary school in Vienna, and author of several books which are used today in teaching the culinary profession."

♥ Eggplant and Tomato Terrine
Yield: 12 servings

2 lbs. eggplant, sliced thinly into rounds
2 tablespoons olive oil
4 teaspoons ground cumin
2 1/2 lbs. very ripe tomatoes, peeled, seeded, diced into 1/4"-1/2" pieces
7 oz. sundried tomatoes, rehydrated and sliced thinly into strips
1 bunch fresh basil, coarsely chopped

Brush eggplant slices with olive oil and sprinkle with cumin. Grill (or use saute pan and saute) eggplant slices on both sides until lightly brown (use a vegetable oil cooking spray, if needed). Line 12"x3"x2 1/2" terrine/pate mold with clear food wrap and arrange layers of grilled eggplant slices on bottom of mold. Cover with layers of chopped tomatoes followed by a sprinkling of chopped basil and sundried tomatoes. Continue the layers alternating eggplant, tomatoes, sliced sundried tomatoes and basil, finishing with eggplant as the top layer.

Fold clear food wrap over top and place a weight such as a dish on top of terrine. Refrigerate overnight.

To serve, unmold terrine opening clear food wrap and turn out onto a plate large enough to accommodate terrine. Garnish with fresh basil sprigs.

Nutritional info. per serving

Calories	73	
Protein	2	g
Carbohydrate	12	g
Fat	33	%
Sodium	15	mg
Cholesterol	-	
Fiber	4	g

Chef's serving suggestion: May be served with a light vinaigrette dressing of your choice.

Donatello

232 N. Dale Mabry, Tampa (813)875-6660

Ricardo, Executive Chef.

♥ Spaghetti Al Tonno
Spaghetti with Tuna Sauce
Yield: 4 servings

1 lb. tomatoes, quartered
1/3 cup olive oil
1/3 cup of celery, chopped
1/3 cup of carrots, chopped
1 garlic clove minced
1 medium onion, finely chopped
10 basil leaves
Pepper to taste
2 - 6 1/2 oz. cans of water-packed tuna, drained
1 lb. spaghetti

Puree tomatoes in blender and set aside. Heat olive oil in pan and saute celery, carrots, garlic and onion. Add tomato puree, pepper and basil. Simmer until liquid is reduced, to produce a thickened sauce (approximately 20 minutes). Add tuna to the thickened sauce.

Cook spaghetti as directed on package, drain and add to sauce.

Nutritional info. per serving

Calories	626	
Protein	34	g
Carbohydrate	74	g
Fat	32	%
Sodium	358	mg
Cholesterol	35	mg
Fiber	7	g

J. Fitzgeralds

Sheraton Grand Hotel 4860 West Kennedy Blvd., Tampa (813)286-4400

Tony Granaghan, Executive Chef, was a steward at 15, then moved into the kitchen for dishes and peeling vegetables before he was offered a scholarship to school. He graduated from Westminster College and apprenticed in London. In the U. S. he has worked in Colorado, New York and Palm Beach.
Most memorable meals - Mixed grill with couscous in Brittany, France; a meal he helped cook for The Queen during his apprenticeship; and helping orchestrate a Presidential luncheon when the Republican Convention was in Miami.
Tony's mentor - his mother!

♥ Grilled Swordfish with Pineapple Mustard Sauce
Yield: 4 servings

4 - 6 oz. swordfish steaks
Pepper to taste
1 tablespoon canola oil
1/2 pineapple (2 cups), diced
1 cup pineapple juice or to taste
2-3 tablespoons Pommery mustard (use more or less to suit taste)

Brush oil on swordfish, season with pepper, and grill or broil 8-10 minutes, turning once.

Cook pineapple and pineapple juice in saucepan 5-10 minutes (if you want a thicker sauce, dissolve up to 1 tablespoon cornstarch in pineapple juice and add to pineapple/pineapple juice mixture).

Remove from heat and blend in mustard. Place on fish and serve.

Nutritional info. per serving

Calories	289	
Protein	30	g
Carbohydrate	18	g
Fat	32	%
Sodium	254	mg
Cholesterol	57	mg
Fiber	1	g

Chef's serving suggestion: Serve with lentil pilaf with cabbage - use Near East Pilaf and shred 1 cup white cabbage into rice while cooking.

Cafe Creole and Oyster Bar

1330 9th Ave.,Ybor City (Tampa's Historic Latin Quarter) (813)247-6283

Anthony D'Avanza, Jr., Owner, was born and raised in New Orleans, and went to Loyola University. He first cooked for fraternity friends, and then on tugs, barges and oil rigs in The Gulf of Mexico, and on The Mississippi River. He cooked in the French Quarter, and on commercial fishing and salvage boats in The Florida Keys, Bahamas and California. Before Cafe Creole, he opened "Selena's," Sicilian and Creole cooking, in Old Hyde Park, Tampa.
Most memorable meals - those "great meals" prepared by his mother (Selena), from whom he learned most of his cooking; by his aunt Claire Giacona, grandmother Giacona and grandmother D'Avanza, who also taught him to cook!

♥ Shrimp Remoulade Salad
A classic New Orleans Creole Dish!
Yield: 8 servings

Sauce:
1/2 cup chopped onion
1/2 cup chopped celery
1/2 cup chopped parsley
Garlic to taste
2 teaspoons lemon juice
1 cup lite mayonnaise
1/4 cup wine vinegar
1 1/2 teaspoons Dijon mustard
2 tablespoons horseradish
4 tablespoons ketchup
2 tablespoons Worcestershire sauce
1 1/2 teaspoons Tabasco sauce
1 1/2 teaspoons black pepper or to taste
2 teaspoons paprika
1 tablespoon Old Bay seasoning (or other seafood seasoning)

Place onion, celery, parsley, garlic and lemon juice in a food processor and blend until vegetables are almost pureed. Add all other ingredients and blend well. Cover and refrigerate. Will keep 2 weeks or more.

To cook shrimp:
1 1/2 gallons water
1 lemon cut in half
4 bay leaves
2 celery stalks, cut in fourths
1 large onion, cut in fourths
6 medium garlic cloves
2 tablespoons black pepper
1 tablespoon cayenne pepper
4 tablespoons of Old Bay seasoning or other powdered seafood seasoning
1 bag of crab or shrimp boil
2 lbs. medium shrimp (31-35 count) in shell

Place all ingredients, except shrimp, in pot of water and bring to a boil. Cook until vegetables are soft, about 20 minutes. At a rolling boil, add shrimp and return to a boil. Turn off heat and let soak for 20 minutes. Chill and peel.

Salad:
Yield: 1 serving
Consists of a blend of 2 or 3 of your favorite greens, including:
romaine lettuce, boston bibb, red leaf lettuce or escarole
1/4 tomato, cut in 2 wedges
1/2 hard boiled egg white, cut in 2 wedges
2 calamata (greek) olives
2 pepperoncini peppers
1 serving shrimp, cooked and chilled
1 thin slice warm french bread or 1/2 pita bread pocket

Prepare salad and top with approx. 1 1/2 oz. (3 tablespoons) of Remoulade sauce.

Nutritional info. per serving

Calories	268	
Protein	20	g
Carbohydrate	25	g
Fat	34	%
Sodium	624	mg
Cholesterol	121	mg
Fiber	5	g

Le Pompano
19325 Gulf Blvd., Indian Shores (813)596-0333

Andrew M. Denis, a graduate of the C.I.A., is the Manager/Chef at Le Pompano, a family business for 17 years. Previously, Andrew worked at The Peabody Hotel in Orlando.
Andrew's mentor - his father Michel Denis. Michel trained in Cannes on the warm coast of the French Riviera, and later gained more experience in Deauville on The Normandy Coast. He has been associated with Prunier and The Bristol Hotel in Paris and later in 1958 came to New York where he was Executive Chef at the Park Lane, The Barclay, Delmonico's on Park Avenue and The Colony Club. Michel and his wife, Clarine, came to Florida in 1973 and opened a small restaurant, which later needed to be expanded to the present one.

♥ Breast of Chicken Andrew
Yield: 4 servings

4 - 6 oz. chicken breasts, skinless

Marinade:
2 oz. red wine vinegar
1 1/2 shallots, finely diced
Pinch of tarragon, basil and parsley or to taste
2 tablespoons canola oil

Sauce:
1/2 oz. (1 tablespoon) margarine
1 tablespoon chopped shallots
1 oz. (1 medium) carrots, julienned
1 oz. leeks (1/2-1, white part only), julienned
1 oz. (1 small stalk) celery, julienned
2-3 oz. (1/4-1/3 cup) evaporated skim milk
Pepper and spices (i.e. nutmeg, lemon) to taste
1/2 teaspoon cornstarch
3 cups cooked brown rice (or grain of your choice)

Poke chicken with fork to allow marinade to penetrate, and pound breasts with the back of a knife to help tenderize. Place vinegar in a bowl with herbs and slowly whip in the oil. Place chicken breasts in marinade and marinate, covered, in refrigerator for at least 4 hours.

Grill chicken breasts.

To make sauce: Melt margarine in pan; add shallots and vegetables, cover and cook until tender. Uncover, add evaporated skim milk, heat and bring to a simmer. Season to taste. If sauce needs thickening, thicken with cornstarch diluted in a small amount of evaporated skim milk and bring sauce to the boiling point, stirring.

Place chicken on plate and top with the sauce and vegetables. Serve with 3/4 cup cooked brown rice (or grain of choice) per serving.

Nutritional info. per serving

Calories	470	
Protein	41	g
Carbohydrate	42	g
Fat	28	%
Sodium	153	mg
Cholesterol	97	mg
Fiber	3	g

♥ You can bake chicken in marinade, in uncovered pan, in 350 F oven for approx. 1/2 hour, or sear in cast iron skillet until bronzed.

Heat leftover marinade to boiling point and reduce, and serve over vegetables!

Saddlebrook Resort
100 Saddlebrook Way, Wesley Chapel (813)973-1111

Vince Shrewsbury, Executive Sous Chef, is responsible for 5 restaurants: The Little Club, Patio, Snack Shack, Gourmet Room and The Cypress Room; and banquet functions of up to 3,500 people!
Most memorable meal - at the Hyatt in Sarasota: tossed greens La Rosa with Italian dressing, baked Manicotti with 3 cheeses and Italian sausage and Strawberry Swirl Cheesecake with Raspberry Truffles.
Vince's mentor - Al Wibbels, the Food and Beverage Director here at the resort, and Lance Stumph, Corporate Executive Chef - Hyatt Regency, Cincinnati.

♥ Fresh Berries and Fruit with Peach Kirsch Sauce
Yield: 5 servings

1 cup raspberries
1 cup sliced strawberries
1 cup diced cantaloupe
1 cup diced honeydew
1 cup diced pineapple

Puree together:
2 cups vanilla nonfat frozen yogurt
1 cup fresh peaches, peeled* and chopped
1 oz. Kirsch liquor

Mix fruit and top with Peach-Kirsch sauce.

Nutritional info. per serving
Calories	180	
Protein	4	g
Carbohydrate	37	g
Fat	6	%
Sodium	7	mg
Cholesterol	-	
Fiber	3	g

* See how to peel a tomato.

♥♥ To make a Raspberry-Chambord sauce, substitute raspberries for the peaches, and Chambord (raspberry liqueur) for the Kirsch.

Use your imagination for other combination sauces to top fruit with, such as, substituting bananas and banana liqueur for the peaches and Kirsch, chocolate nonfat frozen yogurt with Kahlua...!

The Blue Heron

Shoppes at Cloverplace 3285 Tampa Rd., Palm Harbor (813)789-5176

Robert Stea and Larry Lloyd have been creating together for 6 years. Al Bessett joined them at Il Nido Restaurant in Indian Rocks Beach 3 years ago. Since then they have fused their talents and created the Blue Heron Restaurant.
Most memorable meal - "was the first dinner they had in their own restaurant, on December 17, 1989. A real cause to celebrate!"

♥ Marinated Grilled Swordfish with Florida Citrus Sauce
Yield: 4 servings

4 - 6 oz. swordfish steaks
1 tablespoon olive oil
Juice of 1 lime
1 teaspoon white pepper

Marinate steaks in olive oil and lime juice for 3 minutes. Season and grill steaks 3-4 minutes per side. Keep warm until ready to serve.

Florida Citrus sauce:
2 large pink grapefruit
1 large orange
2 key limes or regular limes
1 teaspoon Dijon mustard
1 teaspoon tomato paste
1 tablespoon extra virgin olive oil
6 leaves of fresh basil, finely chopped
1 tablespoon cornstarch diluted in 1/4 cup cold water (if you desire
   thicker sauce)
Scallions, chopped
3 cups cooked brown rice (or grain of your choice)

Squeeze first three ingredients and reserve juice. Place juice, dijon mustard and tomato paste in saucepan and reduce by half, stirring occasionally. When reduced, whisk in olive oil. Simmer and reduce slightly while whisking. Turn off heat, add fresh basil and stir.
Immediately serve over grilled swordfish. Garnish with chopped scallion. Serve with 3/4 cup cooked rice (or grain of choice) per serving.

Nutritional info. per serving

Calories	442	
Protein	33	g
Carbohydrate	44	g
Fat	29	%
Sodium	156	mg
Cholesterol	57	mg
Fiber	3	g

♥ Zucchini Pizza
Yield: 10 servings

1 cup yellow cornmeal
1 cup all purpose flour
1 cup lowfat milk
1/2 cup (4) egg whites
1 tablespoon baking powder
2 medium zucchini washed, ends trimmed and sliced lengthwise
    into thin strips
1/8 cup all purpose flour (for dredging zucchini)
1 tablespoon crushed red pepper, or to taste, or 1 finely chopped jalapeno
1/4 cup parmesan cheese

Preheat oven to 350 F.
Use a small baking sheet with raised edges, and spray liberally with a vegetable oil cooking spray.

Mix the cornmeal, flour, milk, egg whites and baking powder to form a batter. Take the still damp zucchini strips and dredge in reserved flour; then dip zucchini into the batter and lay on the bottom of the sheet pan. Add the crushed red pepper (or chopped jalapeno) to the batter and pour over the strips in the sheet pan.

Bake in oven for 15 minutes. Remove the pan and sprinkle with parmesan cheese; return to oven for 10 minutes or until crust is a nice golden brown. Cut into squares and serve as an accompaniment to a green salad for lunch or as an appetizer before dinner.

Nutritional info. per serving

Calories	139	
Protein	6	g
Carbohydrate	24	g
Fat	11	%
Sodium	182	mg
Cholesterol	4	mg
Fiber	2	g

Black Swan

13707 58th St. North, Clearwater (813)535-SWAN(7926)

Gary A. Brockney - Baker.
Mark Andresick, Executive Chef, apprenticed with a Dutch Chef for 4 years. He has worked in California: San Diego, Santa Barbara and Sonoma for the last 8 years, specializing in French provencial cuisine. In Florida he is adapting to local fresh products.
Most memorable meal - 1986 March of Dimes Charity Dinner in San Diego, California: 5 restaurants and over 15 chefs from around the country participated!
His mentor - Alice Waters, Jeremiah Tower, Larry Forgione, among others who are at the forefront of modern American cuisine. He recommends Madeleine Kamman's books!

♥ Fresh Basil Parmesan Bread
Yield: 2 loaves - 12 servings/loaf

2 cups warm water 110 F.
3 tablespoons dry yeast
1 tablespoon sugar
1/4 cup canola oil
2 teaspoons salt
2 tablespoons fresh basil, chopped
3 tablespoons fresh grated parmesan cheese
5-6 cups flour
1 egg white mixed with 2 tablespoons water
4 tablespoons sesame seeds

Preheat oven to 325 F.
In a large mixing bowl dissolve yeast and sugar in warm water. Let stand about 10 minutes, until frothy. Then add oil, salt, basil and parmesan cheese; gradually add flour.

Knead dough until smooth and easy to touch; let rise double in size.

Roll onto floured surface, divide dough in half. Roll each loaf until bubbles are released. Shape dough into long wide shape. Place each loaf onto cooking sheet liberally sprayed with a vegetable oil cooking spray. With a sharp knife, gently make 5-6 slits into dough. With a pastry brush, brush dough with egg white wash, and sprinkle with sesame seeds. Let dough rise until double in size.

Bake in oven 30-40 minutes.

Nutritional info. per serving

Calories	151	
Protein	4	g
Carbohydrate	25	g
Fat	21	%
Sodium	18	mg
Cholesterol	1	mg
Fiber	1	g

♥ Angel Hair Pasta with Scallop and Pistachio Quenelles in a Wild Mushroom and Fennel Broth
Yield: 2 servings

Quenelles:
1 1/2 oz. pistachio nuts
4 oz. scallops
1/2 tablespoon evaporated skim milk
1 egg white
Pepper
1/2 cup white wine

Combine all ingredients, except wine, in food processor and grind for 30 seconds into a thick paste. Season mixture to taste with pepper.

In large saucepan, simmer 1 quart of water with 1/2 cup of white wine. Roll paste with two spoons into 4 small football shapes and poach lightly in water. Toothpick should come clean when inserted. Set aside.

6 oz. (dry) angel hair pasta; cooked al dente
6 large spinach leaves

Broth:
12 oz. fish fume or bottled clam juice
3 oz. wild mushrooms (shiitake, woodear, oyster), sliced
1 oz. fennel, minced (lightly browned in 1 teaspoon oil and strained)
1/2 tablespoon minced garlic
1/2 tablespoon minced shallot

Add all broth ingredients to saucepan and simmer for 15 minutes. Add quenelles, cooked angel hair and spinach. Heat an additional 7 minutes and serve in soup bowls.

Nutritional info. per serving

Calories	669	
Protein	32	g
Carbohydrate	107	g
Fat	21	%
Sodium	536	mg
Carbohydrate	19	mg
Fiber	3	g

If dried fennel is used, no oil is needed and fat content is less than indicated.

Ile de France

13911 Old Dixie Highway, Hudson (813)863-7994

Gaeton and Michele Gessat, Owners. Gaeton is originally from Corsica, France and sings French songs in the restaurant each night. Michele is from Brussels, Belgium. Most memorable guest - pop artist James Rosenquist.

♥ Coq au Vin
Yield: 4 servings

4 - 6 oz. chicken breasts, skinless, boneless
3 tablespoons flour
1 oz. (2 tablespoons) olive oil
3 cups mushrooms, sliced
1 oz. (2 tablespoons) margarine
3 oz. canadian bacon, julienned
25 pearl onions or other small onions
8 cloves garlic
6 bay leaves
Pinch parsley, thyme
1 oz. (2 tablespoons) cognac
1-2 cups Burgundy wine (If thicker sauce is desired, reserve 1/4
    cup of wine and mix with 1 tablespoon cornstarch)
1/2 cup croutons
Pepper
4 medium white potatoes, steamed

Dredge chicken lightly in flour. Heat 1 1/2 tablespoons olive oil in large pan and saute chicken; add mushrooms. Cook until chicken is just about done.

While chicken is cooking, melt margarine in separate small pan and heat with remaining 1/2 tablespoon olive oil. Saute bacon, onions, garlic, bay leaves, parsley and thyme until onions and bacon are a nice golden color. Add cognac and heat.

Bring the wine to a boil in another saucepan. Add the wine and bacon-onion mixture to the chicken and mushrooms and bring to a second boil, stirring constantly. (Thicken sauce if desired). Add croutons and pepper, and serve with 1 potato per serving.

Nutritional info. per serving

Calories	536	
Protein	45	g
Carbohydrate	30	g
Fat	33	%
Sodium	581	mg
Cholesterol	109	mg
Fiber	2	g

The Don Cesar - A Registry Resort

3400 Gulf Blvd., St. Petersburg Beach (813)360-1881

Michael J. Clark, Executive Chef, is a graduate of the C.I.A. He has worked at the Playboy C.C. Andresort, at Intercontinental and Fairmont Hotels, Adam's Mark Hotel and South Seas Plantation. He came from Chicago to work with Andrew Szilagyi, Corporate Food and Beverage Director of Registry Hotels and Resorts.
Most memorable meal - The night his assistant had his appendix taken out on New Year's Eve. "Holidays in the food service industry are extremely difficult!"
Michael's mentor - his grandmother, who taught him that the true essence of cooking was bringing people together to celebrate life.

♥ Chocolate Dipped Pear with Citrus Sections and Berry Coulis
Yield: 4 servings

4 Seckle pears (or substitute best available)
2 oz. white wine
4 teaspoons sugar substitute
1 stick cinnamon
1 lemon
8 tablespoons (2 tablespoons per person) semi-sweet
    chocolate, melted
2 large oranges
2 grapefruit (pink or ruby)
2 cups strawberries (any other fresh/frozen berries)
1 teaspoon lemon juice
1 oz. Grand Marnier
4 large sprigs mint

Peel and core pears, leave stem on; place in small pot and add wine, sugar substitute, cinnamon stick and lemon. Cover with water, bring to boil, and simmer until tender, about 10 minutes. Cool pears in their liquid.

Melt chocolate over a double boiler, stirring often. Chocolate should be warm but not hot to touch.

Section orange and grapefruit using a grapefruit knife, reserve fruit.

Wash berries lightly in cold water and puree in a blender with lemon juice and Grand Marnier. Strain through a mesh strainer to remove any seeds.

Chill pears until <u>very cold</u> and dry them well with a towel. Dip into chocolate and place on a plate or rack - pear should be coated entirely with chocolate.

Presentation: Sauce each plate with berry puree, place pears on puree (if necessary to avoid sliding, cut bottom side flat) and arrange alternating orange and grapefruit sections in a pinwheel fashion around pear. Garnish with mint sprig. For further decoration, plates can be dusted with powdered sugar or cocoa powder.

Nutritional info. per serving

Calories	324	
Protein	3	g
Carbohydrate	61	g
Fat	22	%
Sodium	16	mg
Cholesterol	-	
Fiber	9	g

♥ Chinese Rice Noodle Roll with Five Spice Beef
Yield: 4 servings

3 large garlic cloves, minced
1/2 teaspoon five spice powder
1- 8 oz. beef tenderloin filet, cut in 4 pieces
1/2 teaspoon sesame seed oil
1/4 cup rice wine vinegar
1 teaspoon olive oil
3 tablespoons lite soy sauce
1/2 teaspoon fresh grated ginger

Rub garlic and five spice powder into filets. Mix sesame seed oil, rice wine vinegar, olive oil, soy sauce and ginger together in bowl. Lightly coat meat and marinate for 1/2 hour. Reserve remainder of marinade.

Heat a non-stick skillet until hot. Add marinated filet and sear well on both sides leaving it quite rare. Set aside.

Sauce:
1 ripe papaya, peeled and seeded (save some seeds for garnish)
Juice from 1 lemon or lime
1/2 cup orange juice

Cut papaya and puree in a blender with lemon or lime juice and orange juice until smooth. Set aside.

4 oz. Chinese rice noodles
1-2 heads romaine lettuce (large leaves)
1 red or green pepper, julienned
1 fresh chili or dash chili paste, to taste
1/2 cucumber, seeds removed, julienned
1 large carrot, julienned
3 green onions, minced
1/2 cup or 3 oz. daikon or turnip, julienned
1 large yellow squash, seeds removed, julienned
1 heeping tablespoon fresh cilantro, mint or basil

Prepare noodle roll: Soak noodles in water 5 minutes; bring pot of water to boil, add noodles and cook al dente. Drain, cool under water and put aside in a bowl. Blanch romaine leaves in boiling water for 10 seconds, cool and reserve. Mix all vegetables with noodles, herbs and reserved marinade.
Lay out romaine lettuce, overlapping leaves to form a 6"x16" rectangle; flatten well and pat dry with towel. Place noodle and vegetable mixture about 1" from top of lettuce and about 2" wide. Shred beef fine with a knife and place in middle of noodles. Roll romaine over noodle and beef mixture like a cigar, tubular shape. Dry and shape with towel.
Cut roll into 8 - 2" pieces (2 per person); sauce plates with papaya coulis and place rolls on top. Garnish with papaya seeds and fresh herb sprigs, and serve at room temperature.

Nutritional info. per serving

Calories	333	
Protein	23	g
Carbohydrate	42	g
Fat	22	%
Sodium	526	mg
Cholesterol	51	mg
Fiber	4	g

♥ If you have problems rolling, try tying roll with scallions, or portion separately: put romaine on top of coulis and spoon noodle mixture on top. Great with chicken too.

♥ Tea Smoked Red Snapper with Cucumber Sauce and Vegetable Fried Rice
Yield: 4 servings

Cucumber sauce:
1/4 cup rice wine vinegar
2 cucumbers, peeled, seeded and diced
1/4 teaspoon sesame seed oil
White pepper
1 teaspoon sugar or 1/2 teaspoon sugar substitute

Preparation for sauce: Place rice wine vinegar in blender, add cucumber in batches; add other ingredients and puree until smooth. Refrigerate until ready to serve.

Rice:
3/4 cup long grain white rice
1 teaspoon olive oil
2 egg whites or 1/4 cup scrambled egg substitute
4 large garlic cloves
1/2 teaspoon fresh grated ginger
1 large carrot, diced
3 green onions, sliced
1 red or yellow pepper, diced
1 cup snow peas or broccoli, cut into small pieces
1/2 cup sliced mushrooms
1 tablespoon lite soy sauce
1 cup bok choy or spinach leaves, chopped
   (almost any combination of vegetables can be added)

Preparation for rice: In pan, add water to white rice and cover 1/4" over rice (check package directions for amount of liquid); bring to a boil, cover and cook over very low heat for about 18 minutes, without stirring, until tender. When cooked remove from pot and allow to cool. Coat a non-stick skillet with 1/2 teaspoon olive oil and a vegetable oil cooking spray.

When hot, scramble egg whites or egg substitute; remove from pan. Add vegetable oil cooking spray and remainder of olive oil to pan; add garlic, ginger, then all vegetables except spinach. Saute a few minutes then add rice and soy sauce; cook a few more minutes then finish with green vegetables. Add egg whites back, remove from heat, keep covered and warm.

Fish:
4 - 6 oz. red snapper, skin on, score skin
1 tablespoon whole seed or whole grain mustard
Juice of 1 lemon
Pinch fresh herbs or to taste such as dill, cilantro, basil or parsley
1 tablespoon lite soy sauce
1/2 teaspoon fresh grated ginger
Course ground black pepper
Paprika
1 tablespoon brown sugar
1/4 cup white wine
1 heeping tablespoon Chinese black tea leaves
Olive oil
Disposable aluminum pie tin

Preparation for fish: Marinate the snapper in all the ingredients listed except tea leaves and olive oil. Prepare a smoker by inverting an aluminum pie tin and punching holes into it, or place snapper on a wire rack which fits into another roasting or saute pan. Place snapper on tin or rack and coat with marinade. Heat pan with olive oil, scatter tea leaves and heat, place tin or rack with fish on top of smoking leaves and cover tightly with aluminum foil. Allow leaves to smoke at medium temperature until fish firms and cooks, being careful not to overcook. Remove fish from rack.

Presentation: Make a mound or portion rice in a cup then unmold. Sauce plate with cucumber sauce, place fish on sauce, exposing part of the sauce. Garnish with fresh herbs or wakame seaweed if available.

Nutritional info. per serving

Calories	404	
Protein	43	g
Carbohydrate	44	g
Fat	10	%
Sodium	525	mg
Cholesterol	62	mg
Fiber	4	g

The Wine Cellar
17307 Gulf Blvd., N. Redington Bch. (813)393-3491

Ted Sonnenschein, Manager/Co-Owner, is originally from West Germany. In the U.S. he has previously worked as Executive Chef at Busch Gardens and for various firms. Ted is very involved with the Pinellas County and the Florida Restaurant Associations.

♥ Lobster Cantonese
Yield: 4 servings

2 tablespoons peanut oil
1 small onion, chopped
1 lb. lobster meat
1/2 cup bamboo shoots
1 teaspoon garlic, finely chopped
1 cup chicken broth
2 tablespoons rice flour
2 oz. rice wine
Cayenne pepper
2 teaspoons lite soy sauce
1/2 teaspoon sugar
1 egg and 1 egg white, beaten
3 scallions, chopped
3 cups cooked rice

In a large pan heat the oil, add onion and saute until light golden. Add lobster meat, bamboo shoots and garlic; saute for 3 minutes, then add the chicken broth and thicken with rice flour. Add the rice wine, cayenne pepper, soy sauce and sugar; bring to a boil. Pull pan off the heat and add the beaten egg and egg white into stew, stirring gently. Top with chopped scallions.

Serve with 3/4 cup cooked white rice per serving.

Nutritional info. per serving

Calories	426	
Protein	27	g
Carbohydrate	54	g
Fat	21	%
Sodium	662	mg
Cholesterol	115	mg
Fiber	3	g

Cafe L'Europe

431 St. Armands Circle, Sarasota (813)388-4415

August Mrozowski, Executive Chef, apprenticed under his father at The St. Nicholas Hotel in Springfield, Illinois for 3 years. He has worked at hotels and restaurants in Illinois and Indiana. Most memorable meal - his father's 70th birthday at Anthony's restaurant in St. Louis. They had Veal Piccata, homemade Canneloni, and a special butter cream pastry and spice cake. His dad blew out the 70 candles with one breath!!!
August's mentor - his father!
The following recipes are from the "Light L'Europe" menu, which meets the dietary standards established by the American Heart Association.

♥ Fillet of Sole Picasso
Yield: 1 serving

6 oz. fillet of lemon sole
1 teaspoon rice (or plain) flour
1 teaspoon white pepper
2 teaspoons canola oil
1 tablespoon white wine
Juice of 1/2 lemon
1/2 orange, sliced
1 kiwi, sliced
1 strawberry, halved
3/4 teaspoon margarine, melted (optional)

Lightly dust the sole with the rice flour and season with pepper. In a hot skillet add oil then saute the sole on both sides to a golden brown (add a vegetable oil cooking spray if needed); just before removing from the skillet add the lemon juice and wine. Put onto a sheet tray or oven proof plate (or leave in skillet if ovenproof), and arrange the sliced fruit on top. Place under broiler to warm fruit. (For added flavor you might want to pour melted margarine over the fruit).

Nutritional info. per serving

Calories	374	
Protein	33	g
Carbohydrate	27	g
Fat	34	%
Sodium	180	mg
Cholesterol	86	mg
Fiber	5	g

Chef's suggestion: Serve with steamed vegetables.

♥ Mahi Mahi Oporto
Yield: 3 servings

1 lb. Mahi Mahi
3 tablespoons fresh lime juice
1/8 teaspoon cayenne pepper
1/2 onion, sliced
1 medium tomato, diced
1/2 sweet pepper - green, red and yellow pepper mixed, diced
1/2 green chile, seeded and chopped
2 tablespoons white wine
1 teaspoon lemon juice

Sprinkle lime juice and cayenne pepper on fish and marinate. Coat skillet with a vegetable oil cooking spray and saute vegetables until almost cooked. Place fish in pan and cover with vegetables; combine lemon juice and wine, and pour over. Simmer on each side until done.

Nutritional info. per serving

Calories	166	
Protein	28	g
Carbohydrate	7	g
Fat	11	%
Sodium	190	mg
Cholesterol	77	mg
Fiber	1	g

Chez Sylvie

1849 South Osprey Ave., Sarasota (813)365-1921

Jean-Francois Mettraux, Chef de Cuisine, trained with Paul Bocuse in Lyon, France. He worked at "Hotel du Parc," Geneva, Switzerland,; "La Guillade," Playa de Aro, Spain; and "La Peryola Hotel," The French Riviera.
His mentor - Escoffier.

♥ Filet of Duck Breast a La Bigarade
Yield: 4 servings

4 - 6 oz. duck breasts, skinless, boneless
Pinch of pepper, parsley and thyme or to taste
1 bay leaf
2 tablespoons shallots, chopped
1 tablespoon lemon juice
3/4 tablespoon (2 1/4 teaspoons) vegetable oil

Preheat oven to 350 F.
Season duck and marinate in above. Bake in uncovered baking pan in oven for approx. 1/2 hour.

Brown sauce:
3/4 tablespoon (2 1/4 teaspoons) margarine
1/2 garlic clove
1 1/2 tablespoons flour
8 1/2 oz. beef bouillon or beef broth

Bigarade Sauce:
4 teaspoons sugar
1 tablespoon red wine vinegar
Juice of 1 orange
Squeeze of lemon juice
2 tablespoons orange peel, julienned, blanched, cooled in cold
    water and drained
1/2 tablespoon Curacao (optional)
3 cups cooked brown rice (or grain of your choice)

For 1 cup of brown sauce: Melt margarine in saucepan over medium-low heat; add garlic; stir in 3/4 tablespoon flour. Dissolve the other 3/4 tablespoon of flour in cold bouillon; heat in separate saucepan. When hot, add to margarine/flour mixture, and boil. Stir constantly.

In a separate pan, cook sugar soaked in wine vinegar to a pale caramel. When the sugar begins to change color, pour in the 1 cup of brown sauce. Blend this mixure with the pan juices. Cook mixture for 5 minutes over a medium-high heat. At the last moment add the orange and lemon juice. Add the orange peel and Curacao, if desired.

Garnish with quarters of peeled and seeded oranges and surround with a border of half slices of oranges.

Serve with 3/4 cup cooked brown rice (or grain of choice) per serving.

Nutritional info. per serving

Calories	474	
Protein	32	g
Carbohydrate	44	g
Fat	35	%
Sodium	304	mg
Cholesterol	102	mg
Fiber	3	g

♥ Sauce is also great with chicken breast.

Michael's on East

1212 East Ave. South, Sarasota, (813)366-0007

Michael Klauber, Owner, grew up in the business at The Colony Beach Resort (owned by his dad) doing every job! He went to the Cornell School of Hotel Administration and completed a cooking apprenticeship at Arnaud's in New Orleans.
Most memorable meal - cooking for President Reagan's inauguration for 10,000 people over 3 days at The Colony!
Michael's mentor - Archie Casbarian, owner of Arnaud's.
Frank Caldwell, the Chef, worked with Michael for 7 years at The Colony. They joined together again 2 years ago.

♥ Marinated Breast of Chicken, Oak Grilled With Glazed Apple and Balsamic Vinaigrette
Yield: 2 servings

2 - 6 oz. chicken breasts, boneless, skinless (free-range if possible)
1/2 oz. (1 tablespoon) red wine
1 teaspoon olive oil
Rosemary
Fresh basil

   Marinate chicken in above for 45-60 minutes. Grill over oak or mesquite wood, 2-3 minutes on each side. Top with warm apple mixture.

Apple Mixture:
2 teaspoons margarine
2 granny smith apples,cook and puree 1/2 of an apple* and thinly
   slice remainder
2 tablespoons good red wine
2 teaspoons balsamic vinegar
1 teaspoon honey
1 teaspoon Grand Marnier

In pan, melt margarine and saute apples. Add cooked pureed apple (applesauce), wine, vinegar and honey. Cover and simmer until apples soften, then take cover off. Reduce; add Grand Marnier at end.

Nutritional info. per serving

Calories	331	
Protein	36	g
Carbohydrate	25	g
Fat	21	%
Sodium	96	mg
Cholesterol	96	mg
Fiber	3	g

* Can substitute 1/4 cup unsweetened applesauce.

♥ Thinly slice 1/4 lb. (4 oz.) red onions; follow recipe adding onions along with apples.

Euphemia Haye
5540 Gulf of Mexico Dr., Longboat Key (813)383-3633

Raymond Arpke, Chef/Owner, bought Euphemia Haye in 1980 and has expanded the restaurant several times! He went to a Milwaukee area technical school, and has a degree in Hotel and Restaurant Cookery. Raymond has worked at The Colony Resort and Cafe L'Europe.

♥ Black Bean Hummus
Yield: 1 Quart - 16 1/4 cup servings

1/2 pound dry black beans - rinsed well and soaked overnight
1/4 red pepper, diced
1/4 green pepper, diced
1/2 onion, diced
1 tablespoon fish base
1 1/2 garlic cloves, crushed
1/2 gallon water

In large pot cook all ingredients until mush, approx. 5 hours. Cool.
Note: You can use 3 cups canned black beans (drained) - omit fish base and water, and cook for approx. 1/2 hour. Cool.

3 1/2 oz. Tahini (sesame seed paste)
1 1/2 oz. (3 tablespoons) lemon juice
5 garlic cloves
2/3 oz. (4 teaspoons) olive oil
1 1/3 oz water/cornstarch mixture (see preparation tips) (If using canned beans, use chicken broth/cornstarch mixture)
1 dash cayenne pepper
1 dash hot sauce

8 pita bread pockets (or grain of your choice)

Puree cold beans with the rest of ingredients (except pita) in processor. Serve with 1/2 pita (or grain of choice) per serving.

Nutritional info. per serving

Calories	149	
Protein	6	g
Carbohydrate	20	g
Fat	30	%
Sodium	230	mg
Cholesterol	-	
Fiber	2	g

Harry's Continental Kitchens

525 St. Judes Dr., Longboat Key (813)383-0777

Harold R. Christensen, Chef/Owner, has an Associate of Science Degree in Hotel and Restaurant Cookery from Milwaukee, Wisconsin. He has 20 years working experience in resorts, country clubs, hotels, private clubs and restaurants.
Most memorable meals - cooking for Green Bay Packers training camp and cooking at The Waldorf Astoria. He also remembers a disaster: at his first catering job, his car broke down and he had to call a cab to get the food to the party. When they arrived, the guests were eating peanut butter on saltines and their drinks were straight up with no ice!
Harry's mentor - his Mom!

♥ Hot Flounder Salad over Fresh Spinach
Yield: 6 servings

2 lbs. flounder fillets, cut in one inch pieces
1/4 cup flour
Pepper to taste
1/3 cup olive oil
1 1/2 lbs. fresh spinach
2 tablespoons shallots, chopped fine
2 cups tomatoes, peeled, seeded and diced
1/2 cup fresh lemon juice
2 tablespoons of sugar
1/2 tablespoon chopped fresh basil
3 scallions, chopped
3 pita bread pockets (or grain of your choice)

Lightly flour and season flounder; heat oil in large pan and saute flounder until lightly browned. Turn and cook completely. Remove and place over spinach. Put shallots, tomatoes, lemon juice, sugar and basil in pan and heat. Pour over flounder and spinach.

Garnish with scallions and serve with 1/2 pita (or grain of choice) per serving.

Nutritional info. per serving

Calories	372	
Protein	34	g
Carbohydrate	28	g
Fat	34	%
Sodium	323	mg
Cholesterol	77	mg
Fiber	5	g

The Colony Beach & Tennis Resort
1620 Gulf of Mexico Dr., Longboat Key (813)383-6464

Tom Klauber, a graduate of the C.I.A., also received The Grand Diploma from Ecole de Cuisine La Varenne, Paris, France. He has worked at Patrissrie Chatton in Paris; Ristorante La Loggie in Florence, Italy; for Baron Rothchild in Normandy and Holland; and at the Royal Sonesta in New Orleans, before joining The Colony in 1981. Tom is the recipient of many culinary awards, is one of the founders of the American Institute of Wine and Food and a Maitre Rotisseur - Confrerie de la Chaine des Rotisseurs!
His best experience was hosting The Colony's Annual Stone Crab and Seafood Festival! "Bringing together chefs and winemakers from all over the country to celebrate the outstanding local seafoods -it gives all of us a forum to share, create and learn from each other."

♥ Warm Salad of Shellfish and White Beans
Yield: 4 servings

For the white beans:
1/2 cup dry white beans
2 cups chicken stock
1 bouquet of fresh herbs

For the shellfish:
3 tablespoons olive oil
36 small clams
2 - 5 oz. lobster tails, meat (poached and shells removed)
1 cup white wine
1/2 cup plum tomato concasse
1 tablespoon lemon juice

For the salad:
2 1/2 tablespoons olive oil
2 teaspoons lemon juice
1 teaspoon sherry vinegar
1 cup mixed salad greens (use more if desired)
Pepper to taste
1/4 cup chopped fresh parsley
4 pita bread pockets (or grain of your choice)

Soak the beans overnight. Drain and cook them in a large pot for 1 to 1 1/2 hours in stock with the bouquet of herbs until they are tender but firm. Reserve on the side.

Heat 1 1/2 tablespoons of the olive oil in a large skillet and saute the clams and lobster; deglaze with wine and cook just to where the clams open. Remove the seafood and reduce the remaining liquid by 1/2; add the remaining olive oil, lemon juice, tomato concasse and white beans. As this simmers, deshell the clams, saving 12 for garnish, and slice the lobster tails into 4 medallions each; return all the seafood to the pan.

To serve: Make a dressing of the olive oil, lemon juice, and vinegar; season with pepper. Lightly toss with the greens and divide onto the center of each dish. Arrange the shellfish and beans over the salad with the warm broth and garnish with the whole clams and chopped parsley. Serve with 1 pita (or grain of choice) per serving.

Nutritional info. per serving

Calories	561	
Protein	37	g
Carbohydrate	44	g
Fat	35	%
Sodium	692	mg
Cholesterol	97	mg
Fiber	4	g

Ophelia's On The Bay

9105 Midnight Pass Rd., Siesta Key (813)349-2212

Stanley Ferro, Chef/Owner, got hands on experience when he "fell into the restaurant business in Cape Cod." He and his wife had "The Playhouse Restaurant," which was associated with The Summer Stock Theater. They served the theater patrons, locals and stars! Stanley likes to read cookbooks.

Most memorable meal - the first banquet for The Playhouse. A buffet was planned for 125-150 people as a celebration for the end of the season and instead, 350 people showed up and they ran out of food. Twenty cases of champagne saved the evening!

♥ Swordfish Chandelier
Yield: 1 serving

1 tablespoon olive oil
4 oz. swordfish, sliced thin
1 tablespoon flour
3 oz. scallops
1 oz. shiitake mushrooms
Touch of garlic
Pinch fresh oregano
Pepper
Juice of lemon wedge
1 oz. white wine
1/2 cup cooked brown rice (or grain of your choice)

Heat olive oil in pan; saute swordfish, dredged in flour. Turn when swordfish is brown. Add scallops,mushrooms, garlic, oregano, pepper, squeeze of lemon and wine. Reduce (thicken with up to 1/2 tablespoon cornstarch diluted in 1/8 cup cold water, if desired).

Serve with 1/2 cup cooked brown rice (or grain of choice).

Nutritional info. per serving

Calories	562	
Protein	41	g
Carbohydrate	54	g
Fat	31	%
Sodium	275	mg
Cholesterol	73	mg
Fiber	2	g

Summer House

6101 Midnight Pass Rd., Siesta Key (813)349-1100

Michael A. Medico, Sous Chef, has worked at The Summer House on and off since he was 17. He has also worked at Tossattis Restaurant and The Hyatt in Sarasota.
Most memorable meal - since his mother is "one of the best cooks he knows," the best meals he has ever had were those at home on holidays with the whole family. Michael feels that "coming from an all Italian background, cooking must be in their blood."
Michael's mentors - Chef Jean Pierre and Chef Joe Tossatti.

♥ Chicken (or Fish) Veracruz
Yield: 4 servings

4 - 6 oz. chicken breasts, skinless, boneless
Fresh garlic
2 teaspoons oil
Cilantro

Preheat oven to 350 F.
Marinate chicken in above, and bake in covered baking pan for 1/2 hour until cooked. Top with sauce.

Sauce:
2 teaspoons oil
4 garlic cloves
2 cups mushrooms, sliced
2 cups diced tomatoes
2 cups artichoke hearts, quartered
1 cup chicken stock
1 tablespoon margarine
Pepper to taste
1 teaspoon fresh chopped cilantro

In a large pan heat oil and saute garlic; reduce heat. Add mushrooms, tomatoes and artichoke hearts and cook vegetables. Add chicken stock and heat; add margarine, pepper to taste and cilantro.

Nutritional info. per serving

Calories	316	
Protein	40	g
Carbohydrate	14	g
Fat	32	%
Sodium	363	mg
Cholesterol	97	mg
Fiber	1	g

Prawnbroker

13451-16 McGregor Blvd., Fort Myers (813)489-2226

Steve Wolfe, Chef, has 19 years "hands-on experience" in the restaurant business. His mentor - Michael Schilling, Owner of The Prawnbroker.

♥ Tuna Monte Bella
Yield: 6 servings

Sauce:
3 tablespoons olive oil (2 tablespoons for sauce and 1 for fish)
1 3/4 cups water/cornstarch mixture (optional, see preparation tips)
1/2 cup red wine vinegar
1/2 cup capers
2 green olives, sliced
2 tablespoons anchovy paste
2 teaspoons rosemary
2 teaspoons thyme
4 scallions, tops only, chopped

6 - 6 oz. tuna steaks, 1/2 inch thick, cut into medallions
4 1/2 cups cooked brown rice (or grain of your choice)

Prepare above sauce one day in advance: Mix all sauce ingredients together (if you don't wish to dilute sauce with water/cornstarch mixture, you can omit this and serve mix as a relish on fish).

In large saute pan, heat 1 tablespoon olive oil and a vegetable oil cooking spray; place tuna medallions in pan and saute fish approximately 3-4 minutes on each side.

Stir sauce and ladle over fish just before removing from heat.
Serve with 3/4 cup cooked brown rice (or grain of choice) per serving.

Nutritional info. per serving

Calories	465	
Protein	39	g
Carbohydrate	35	g
Fat	35	%
Sodium	1016	mg
Cholesterol	56	mg
Fiber	3	g

Sonesta Sanibel Harbour Resort and Spa
17260 Harbour Pointe Dr., Ft. Myers (813)466-4000

Gerard M. Pinault, Executive Chef, went to The Hotel School of Thonon les Baines, France. He has owned two restaurants, one in the city of La Rochelle, France and the other on Balboa Island, Newport Beach, CA. Gerard has worked at "L.A.X. Marriott," "Anaheim Marriott;" opened "Hotel Meridien," Newport Beach, CA; worked at "Grand Hotel," Point Clear, AL.; "Royal Sonesta," Cambridge, MA; and finally opened Sonesta Sanibel Harbour Resort and Spa.
Most memorable meal- 1969 Dinner Auction at the "Hospices de Beaune," France. The greatest Burgundy Wines are auctioned that night after dinner which included:

Foul "consomme"
Hare "Pate"
Trout Almondine
Wild Boar "civet" Stew
Roast Pheasant in Cabbage

Gerard's mentor - his father.

♥ Baked Grouper Florentine
Yield: 4 servings

1 1/4 lbs. grouper fillet, sliced very thin
1 tablespoon water
10 oz. spinach leaves, washed, stems off
1 tablespoon sherry wine
1 medium onion, diced
1/2 cup chicken broth
1 cup skim milk
1 tablespoon cornstarch
2 tablespoons grated swiss cheese

Preheat oven to 375 F.
In skillet, put 1 tablespoon water, spinach leaves, cover with lid and bring to a boil for 3 minutes. Drain, set spinach leaves in individual baker dish and lay 2 - 2 1/2 oz. slices of grouper on spinach.

Pour sherry wine in skillet and flambe to burn and evaporate the alcohol; add the diced onion and cook 2 minutes. Add chicken broth, 3/4 cup of milk and bring to a boil.

Dilute the cornstarch in 1/4 cup of milk; add to boiling stock and cook at low heat for 5 minutes. Pour over fish in baking pan and sprinkle grated swiss cheese over sauce. Bake 20 minutes and serve.

Nutritional info. per serving

Calories	215	
Protein	34	g
Carbohydrate	11	g
Fat	13	%
Sodium	255	mg
Cholesterol	58	mg
Fiber	3	g

Note: If lowfat swiss cheese is used, the fat content will decrease.

The Chef's Garden/Truffles
1300 Third Street South, Naples (813)262-5500

Michael McMahan, Executive Chef, learned his culinary skills the traditional way - through hands - on experience.
Beirne Brown, a partner in the Cuisine Management group, is the 1991 President of the Florida Restaurant Association.

♥ Truffles' Warm Oriental Chicken Salad
Yield: 4 servings

Dressing:
1 cup chicken stock
1/8 cup lite soy sauce
1/8 cup dry sherry
1/4 tablespoon Oriental chili-garlic paste (if unavailable, use Tabasco
     sauce to taste)
1/2 tablespoon Oriental oyster sauce
1/8 cup brown sugar
1 garlic clove, grated or crushed fine
1/4 tablespoon fresh grated ginger root
1/2 teaspoon coriander
1/2 teaspoon cornstarch mixed with 1/8 cup water

Combine above ingredients in large saucepan. After thoroughly combining all ingredients, bring to a boil and cook until all ingredients are blended. After the sauce has been prepared, assemble the following ingredients and proceed with the rest of the recipe.

4 - 6 oz. chicken breasts, skinless, boneless

Marinate the chicken breasts in a small amount of the dressing for 1 hour. Grill the chicken, cool, then slice.

1 tablespoon oil
1/2 head bok choy, chopped
2 oz. bamboo shoots, canned
2 oz. water chestnuts, canned
1 red bell pepper, sliced
1/2 lb. snow peas

2 oz. (1/2 cup) cashew nuts
4 cups cooked angel hair pasta

Heat oil in saute pan; add sliced chicken, vegetables and nuts and heat. Toss with Oriental dressing, finally adding angel hair.

Nutritional info. per serving

Calories	618	
Protein	51	g
Carbohydrate	68	g
Fat	23	%
Sodium	776	mg
Cholesterol	97	mg
Fiber	5	g

Michael's Cafe
2950 Ninth St. North, Naples (813)434-2550

Scott Daning, Executive Chef, has "had training from some of the best chefs in various parts of the country." He has experience from both hotels and restaurants. While in Boston, James Burke, the owner and chef of two restaurants, taught him "the wonders of life beyond French cooking." He then perfected his own "style" of cooking, combining a little of Northern Italian with French cuisine.
Most memorable meal - Four Seasons in Boston: Soft Shell Crab, mixed bittergreen salad, Veal, Beef and Lamb Combo, and Tiramisu.
Scott's mentor - David Beier, Owner/Chef of Walloon Lake Inn, N. Michigan.

♥ Roselline
"Pasta Roses"
Yield: 1 serving

1/4 lb. fresh pasta sheets (any flavor will do, but Scott prefers
    sheets flavored with cracked black pepper)
2 1/2 oz. Fontina cheese from Italy, cut into 1" slices
1 bunch of fresh basil leaves
1/2 cup sundried tomatoes, rehydrated
1/4 teaspoon fresh ground pepper
1 tablespoon freshly grated parmesan cheese
2 tomatoes

Preheat oven to 400 F.
    Cut fresh pasta sheets in 1 inch wide strips; you should have about 6 strips.
    Lay out pasta strips and arrange cheese on pasta lengthwise. Then lay out basil leaves on top of cheese. Slice tomatoes into thirds and place every inch or so on top of basil, so you now have layers. Roll up completed strips firmly and set on their sides, keeping rolls tight together. Don't let them unravel.
    Spray casserole dish with a vegetable oil cooking spray and place completed roses on bottom. Bake covered with aluminum foil for 10-15 minutes. Carefully remove foil and garnish with parmesan cheese.

Puree and strain tomatoes. Dress pasta roses with this coulis, and serve immediately.

Nutritional info. per serving

Calories	737	
Protein	35	g
Carbohydrate	91	g
Fat	32	%
Sodium	161	mg
Cholesterol	110	mg
Fiber	8	g

You can substitute 4 oz. skim mozzarrella cheese for the Fontina! Pasta roses would make a great appetizer too!

The Dining Room

The Ritz Carlton Naples 280 Vanderbilt Beach Rd., C.S., Naples (813)598-3300

James Mario Iacovino, Executive Sous Chef, graduated with a Professional Chef's Degree from the State University of New York at Cobleskill. He has worked in various restaurants in New York and Florida, and with the Sheraton and Marriott Hotels in Ft. Lauderdale. James loves the West Coast of Florida!
Most memorable meal - "serving President Jimmy Carter, and Donald Trump was a thrill!"
James' mentor - Executive Chef, Pierre Dousson, formally of Maxim's of Paris, and Chicago and Fairmont Hotels.

♥ Poppyseed Cake
Yield: 2 cakes - 16 servings/cake

3 cups plain nonfat yogurt
3/4 cup poppyseeds
7 oz. (14 tablespoons) soft margarine
2 cups sugar
3 eggs
6 egg whites
2 tablespoons lemon juice
6 cups cake flour
1 tablespoon baking powder
1 tablespoon baking soda

Preheat oven to 350 F.
Mix together yogurt and poppyseeds in small bowl.
In large bowl, cream margarine and sugar until fluffy. Beat in eggs and egg whites slowly; add lemon juice. In separate bowl combine dry ingredients. Beat dry mixture into margarine mixture alternately with yogurt and poppy seed mix.

Pour into Kugelhofpan - bundt pans that have been sprayed with a vegetable oil cooking spray.
Bake for 1 hour in oven.

Nutritional info. per serving

Calories	207	
Protein	5	g
Carbohydrate	31	g
Fat	33	%
Sodium	210	mg
Cholesterol	20	mg
Fiber	-	

Sprinkle confectioners sugar over cooled cake, if desired.

South Seas Plantation
Resort and Yacht Harbour, Captiva Island (813)472-5111

Poul Grav, Executive Chef, is originally from the Chesapeake Bay area of Maryland. His career started at the age of 13 under the direction of his father, Danish Master Chef Gudmon Lee Grav. Poul apprenticed under the Olympic winning chef, Sture Olaf Andersson. During this time period, he was also attending select courses given at the C.I.A. Prior to South Seas Plantation, Poul was a chef with the Pinehurst resorts.

♥ Pineapple Muffins
Yield: 12 <u>large</u>

2 cups all purpose flour
2 1/2 teaspoons baking powder
1 teaspoon ground cinnamon (optional)
1/3 cup margarine
1 cup sugar (reserve 1 tablespoon)
1 egg
2 egg whites
1 1/2 cups mashed ripe pineapple (or canned crushed pineapple packed in juice)
1/4 cup skim milk

Preheat oven to 375 F.
In a bowl, sift together flour, baking powder and cinnamon; place to one side. In separate bowl, cream margarine and sugar until light and fluffy. Add egg and egg whites and mix for 1 minute; add (drained) pineapple and milk at low speed. Add dry ingredients, and mix until just combined. Spoon into large muffin cups that have been sprayed with a vegetable oil cooking spray; sprinkle the tops with reserved sugar. Bake in oven for 25 minutes, until a toothpick inserted in the center of one muffin comes out clean.

Nutritional info. per serving

Calories	189	
Protein	4	g
Carbohydrate	35	g
Fat	20	%
Sodium	131	mg
Cholesterol	18	mg
Fiber	1	g

♥♥ Mix cinnamon with your reserved sugar and sprinkle tops of muffins with cinnamon sugar mix before baking.

♥ Island Fajitas
Yield: 4 servings

1/2 teaspoon crushed red pepper, or to taste
1 1/2 teaspoons sugar
1 lb. medium size shrimp
1 oz. (2 tablespoons) olive oil
1 bell pepper, sliced into long strips
1 large onion, sliced into long strips
2 carrots, sliced into long strips
1/2 lb. mushrooms, sliced
2 green onions, diced
8 oz. picante sauce
8 pieces soft fajita bread (tortillas)

Mix sugar and crushed red pepper together and dust the shrimp with the mixture. In a large saute pan heat oil until hot, almost smoking. Saute vegetables for 30 seconds, then add shrimp, and saute for 30 seconds more. Add picante sauce and simmer 30 seconds, or until shrimp is cooked.

Spoon on fajita bread (tortillas) and serve.

Nutritional info. per serving

Calories	411	
Protein	26	g
Carbohydrate	51	g
Fat	28	%
Sodium	642	mg
Cholesterol	166	mg*
Fiber	3	g

* To lower cholesterol to 111 mg per serving, use only 3/4 lb. shrimp in recipe.

♥ Chicken Kew
Yield: 4 servings

4 - 6 oz. chicken breasts, boneless, skinless, cut into large strips
4 teaspoons teriyaki sauce (1)
2 oz. (4 tablespoons) olive oil or sesame seed oil

1/2 lb. snow peas
1/2 red bell pepper, large dice
1/2 green pepper, large dice
1/4 cup teriyaki sauce (2)
1 teaspoon ground ginger
1 tablespoon cornstarch diluted in 1/4 cup cold water
3 cups cooked white rice

Marinate chicken in teriyaki sauce (1). Heat 1 oz. oil in large pan,or wok, and saute chicken; when chicken is cooked, drain any remaining oil and remove from pan. Heat remaining 1 oz. of oil and saute vegetables for 60 seconds; add teriyaki sauce (2) and ginger, and thicken with cornstarch mix. Add the chicken back to the pan and stir while cooking 40-60 seconds. Serve on 3/4 cup cooked rice per serving.

Nutritional info. per serving

Calories	577	
Protein	42	g
Carbohydrate	59	g
Fat	29	%
Sodium	1000	mg
Cholesterol	96	mg
Fiber	3	g

♥♥ Try experimenting with other vegetables, i.e. broccoli, carrots, onions... Add garlic, sesame seeds .

♥ Caribbean Fruit Stuffed Pork Loin
Yield: 6 servings

Fruit Stuffing:
1 papaya, skinned, 1/4 inch dice
1 mango, skinned, 1/4 inch dice
1 passion fruit, halved, pulp removed
1/4 cup raisins
1/8 cup pecans
1/2 cup orange marmalade
Cinnamon to taste
Nutmeg to taste
1/2 teaspoon brown sugar

2 1/4 lbs. pork loin
2 tablespoons rosemary
2 tablespoons black pepper
2 tablespoons shallots in 1/4 teaspoon oil
Butcher twine
3 cups cooked brown rice (or grain of your choice)

Preheat oven to 350 F.
In a bowl, mix all the fruit with the rest of stuffing ingredients well.
Cut pork loin down the center 3/4 the way through and pound out with a meat mallet. Place stuffing on one end of the pork loin and roll. Tie with butcher twine. Season with herbs.
Roast in pan for 1 hour or until internal temperature is 170 F.
Serve with 1/2 cup cooked brown rice (or grain of choice) per serving.

Nutritional info. per serving

Calories	548	
Protein	37	g
Carbohydrate	59	g
Fat	30	%
Sodium	94	mg
Cholesterol	107	mg
Fiber	4	g

The Greenhouse

Captiva Village Square, Captiva Island (813)472-6006

Kevin Barr, Chef, attended a 2 year restaurant management course at Bucks County College in Pennsylvania. For the past 14 years he has been working in restaurants throughout the country. Kevin has worked under many great chefs with various styles of cooking, who in turn helped him create his own style!

♥ Oriental Buckwheat Pasta Salad
Yield: 6 servings

1 1/2 tablespoons peanut butter
1/4 cup vinegar
3/8 cup water/cornstarch mixture (optional, see
    preparation tips)
1/8 cup (2 tablespoons) sesame oil
.2 cups (3 tablespoons) Tahini (sesame seed paste)
1 teaspoon tamari or lite soy sauce
2 teaspoons fresh chopped garlic
1/4 teaspoon lemon juice
1/2 teaspoon fresh chopped cilantro
2 tablespoons white wine
1/4 cup firm tofu, chopped small
3 scallions, chopped
1 teaspoon fresh grated ginger
1-2 kirbies or small cucumbers, seeded, chopped small

6 oz. soba, Japanese buckwheat, noodles
6 - 4 oz. grilled chicken breasts, skinless

Vinaigrette: In a small bowl mix the peanut butter and vinegar. Add the water/cornstarch mixture and sesame oil in a steady stream whipping the entire time until the dressing thickens. Add the remaining ingredients.

Bring a large pot of water to a rapid boil; add noodles and bring back to boil and cook, stirring occasionally until they just begin to soften (about 3 minutes). Drain noodles in colander and rinse well under cold running water; drain well. Chill all ingredients, toss with vinaigrette and serve immediately. Note: It may not be necessary to use all the dressing; noodles should be well coated but not soggy.

Serve with a 4 oz. grilled chicken breast per serving.

Nutritional info. per serving

Calories	432	
Protein	44	g
Carbohydrate	28	g
Fat	34	%
Sodium	392	mg
Cholesterol	96	mg
Fiber	2	g

The Nutmeg House
2761 Gulf Dr., Sanibel Island (813)472-1141

David McCreary, Chef/Kitchen Manager, a native Floridian, is a C.I.A. graduate. He has previously worked at Casa Ybel Resort, Thistle Lodge Restaurant; Joey's; and Landlubber Restaurant. He prefers "varied styles and regions of cooking."
Many memorable meals - those serving celebrities, wealthy patrons and "walk-ins of all nationalities and classes."

♥ Grilled Salmon with Angel Hair
Yield: 1 serving

6 oz. salmon steak
2 teaspoons margarine
Pinch parsley, basil, mint and dill or to taste
Juice of 1 lemon or more to taste
1 tablespoon water
4 oz. angel hair pasta; cooked according to package directions
Parsley
Scallions

Grill salmon steak.
Sauce: In saucepan, melt margarine and add fresh herbs. Add lemon juice and water, heat.
Place pasta as bed on plate for salmon steak; top with sauce.
Garnish with parsley and scallions.

Nutritional info. per serving

Calories	679	
Protein	47	g
Carbohydrate	87	g
Fat	21	%
Sodium	138	mg
Cholesterol	56	mg
Fiber	-	

Truffles at Casa Ybel

2255 West Gulf Dr., Sanibel Island (813)472-9200

Mike Jacob, Executive Chef, originally from Milwaukee, Wisconsin has 18 years of on the job training.
Most memorable meals - serving The Wisconsin Chefs Club Annual Fall Anniversary Dinner: a dinner for 300 peers!
This past August, he dined at the Lafayette restaurant in The Drake Hotel (with 6 other cuisine management executive chefs, and C.M.I. partner Tony Ridgeway). The meal at The Lafayette consisted of 12 courses, and Mike said he literally had to be "force fed" because he was so full. Of course that is somewhat understandable since he had just come from an 8 course meal at the San Dominico restaurant!

♥ Grilled Swordfish with Onion Relish
Yield: 4 servings

2 shallots, minced
1/2 cup cider vinegar
1/4 cup water
4 tablespoons sugar
1/2 teaspoon white pepper
1/2 teaspoon cumin
Pinch chili powder
1/2 tablespoon jalapeno pepper, minced
1 tablespoon cornstarch diluted in 1/4 cup cold water
1/2 spring onion, grilled and chopped fine
1/2 red onion, grilled and chopped fine
2 scallions, grilled and chopped fine
1 leek - whites only, grilled and chopped fine
4 - 6 oz. swordfish steaks; grilled

Spray medium pan with a vegetable oil cooking spray, heat and saute shallots until transparent. Add cider vinegar, water, sugar, pepper, cumin, chili powder and jalapeno. Bring to a boil, add cornstarch mix and cook until smooth and thick. Mix in onions and cook 5 minutes. Use water if the mix gets too thick.

Serve over grilled swordfish.

Nutritional info. per serving

Calories	316	
Protein	37	g
Carbohydrate	26	g
Fat	21	%
Sodium	173	mg
Cholesterol	72	mg
Fiber	2	g

Chef's serving suggestion: Accompany with steamed okra and corn-bread.

O'Sheas
1081 Bald Eagle Dr., Marco Island (813)394-7531

Dolores Shea, Owner/Operator.
Most memorable meal - at the Americana Hotel in New York.
Dolores' mentor - her husband and her mother.
Mike Sleater, the Chef, has 20 years on-the-job training. He has previously worked at The Stable Inn chain, and Adams Rib Restaurant in Indianapolis.

♥ Polynesian Scallops
Yield: 1 serving

1/4 cup diced green pepper
1/2 bunch green onions, chopped
1/4 cup water chestnuts, sliced
1/4 cup pineapple cubes
2 teaspoons Worcestershire sauce
1 tablespoon wine vinegar
1/4 cup pineapple juice
1 teaspoon lime juice
1 pimento, diced
6 oz. bean sprouts

6 oz. scallops
1/2 tablespoon margarine

Spray medium pan with a vegetable oil cooking spray, heat and saute green pepper and onions partially. Add remaining ingredients and cook for 5 minutes, covered, over medium heat. (Mixture may be thickened slightly with 1 tablespoon cornstarch dissolved in 1/4 cup cold pineapple juice, if a heavier consistency is desired).

Heat margarine in another pan over medium heat and saute scallops for 2 minutes. Add polynesian mix, from other pan, and continue cooking 2 minutes.

Nutritional info. per serving

Calories	319	
Protein	27	g
Carbohydrate	44	g
Fat	17	%
Sodium	345	mg
Cholesterol	37	mg
Fiber	4	g

Chef's serving suggestion: Serve with rice and garnish with lemon, wedge or crown, and kale.

♥ Would be great with chicken too!

The Black Pearl
1409 A1A, Vero Beach (407)234-4426

Bruce Turner, Head Chef, has 16 years kitchen experience from restaurants in England. He went to the "City and Guilds of London Institute in conjunction with the Hotel Catering and Institutional Management Association." Bruce came to the U.S.A. to work at the Black Pearl with Ian Greenwood, another fellow Englishman, and he's still with him.
Most memorable meal - when Bruce ate raw fish for the first time, in the form of sushi, at a Japanese restaurant. Now he loves it, and is excited about trying new things - except "sea urchin with quail egg....no thanks!"
Bruce admires the chefs and restaurant owners who successfully run their operations over the years, and dedicate their time and energy to pleasing the public! He specifically mentions Ian Greenwood, Owner-Black Pearl, who after much success is still going strong.

♥ Curried Scallops and Shrimp
Yield: 4 servings

Curry Sauce:
1/2 oz. (1 tablespoon) olive oil
2 oz. onion, chopped
1 garlic clove
1/2 oz. (1/8 cup) flour
1/2 oz. (1 tablespoon) curry powder (approximately)
1/2 oz. (1 tablespoon) tomato paste
3/4 pint clam/fish stock
1 small Granny Smith apple (peeled and cored), diced
1 tablespoon mango chutney
1/2 oz. (4 teaspoons) raisins, optional

In saucepan, heat oil; add the onion and garlic and cook without coloring. Mix in the flour and curry powder, and cook to a sandy texture. Add tomato paste and stock to smooth sauce. Add diced apple, mango chutney and raisins; simmer approximately 30 minutes. Skim sauce and adjust seasoning.

Braised Rice:
1/2 oz. (1 tablespoon) margarine
1 small onion, chopped
1 garlic clove
1/2 teaspoon fennel seed
1/4 teaspoon thyme leaf

1/4 teaspoon rosemary
6 oz. long grain rice
14 oz. chicken stock
Pepper

Preheat oven to 250 F.

In saucepan, melt margarine; cook the onion and garlic then add herbs and rice, stirring until well mixed. Add the stock (adjust quantity of liquid according to package directions) and pepper, cover with parchment paper sprayed with a vegetable oil cooking spray, and bring to a boil. Place in oven for 15-20 minutes (can be cooked on stove in covered pan). Remove from pan, check seasoning.

1 oz. (2 tablespoons) oil
8-10 oz. large shrimp
8-10 oz. large sea scallops
2 oz. green onions, sliced fine, chopped
2 oz. tomato, seeded, diced
2 oz. (1/4 cup) white wine
1 teaspoon chopped parsley
4 teaspoons toasted almonds

In large saute pan, heat oil and saute the scallops and shrimp, season, and add tomatoes and onions. Add white wine and reduce. Add the curry sauce and chopped parsley.

Serve with rice topped with toasted almonds.

Nutritional info. per serving

Calories	505	
Protein	28	g
Carbohydrate	56	g
Fat	33	%
Sodium	806	mg
Cholesterol	106	mg
Fiber	4	g

Backstage

Reynolds Plaza 1061 East Indiantown Rd. Jupiter (407)747-9533

David Glenn Duncan, Chef de Cuisine/Assistant Manager, has previously worked at The Breakers, Le Virage in California, Vinton's, The Hasta and The Yorkshire Inn. David has been in the food business since age 11!

Most memorable meal - At Le Virage in 1982: he and Lolek Jacinski were doing tableside flambe service for Tom Jones and his party of 11. Lolek splattered some flaming brandy on the curtains and it burst into flames. Lolek said "Dave, take care of that, won't you" and kept on with the show. His nonchalance "cracked Dave up" and he, along with Tom Jones and party, laughed while he put the fire out; then dessert was served.

His mentors - Chris Markanti who taught him the basics; Hans Eichmen showed him real gourmet cuisine; and Lolek Jacinski taught him that if you really love what you are doing, the recognition will come!

♥ Breast of Chicken Paillard on Fresh Mixed Greens with Warmed Vinaigrette
Yield: 4 servings

4 - 6 oz. chicken breasts, skinless, boneless
Pepper
1 oz. (2 tablespoons) sesame oil
1 1/2 cups pineapple juice
2 fresh lemons (juiced)
1/3 cup pickled ginger, julienned
1/3 cup balsamic vinegar
2 tablespoons lite soy sauce
1 level tablespoon light brown sugar
1 cello bag (10 oz.) of fresh spinach
1 head of Bibb lettuce
1/2 cup mandarin orange sections
1/2 cup fresh scallions

Very lightly season both sides of each chicken breast with pepper. In a large wide skillet mix together the sesame oil, pineapple and lemon juice, ginger, balsamic vinegar, soy sauce and brown sugar; marinate chicken breasts for approx. 10-15 minutes.

Thoroughly wash and trim spinach and bibb lettuce. Drain well, then place in a large salad bowl for tossing. Add the mandarin orange sections and scallions.

Remove chicken from marinade and charbroil on medium heat. Place the skillet with the marinade on high heat. Cook the chicken breasts until they are done and place on a side plate. Reduce the marinade by half.

Place a small amount of the marinade in the mixed greens and toss. Divide onto four plates. Top with the chicken breast and a little more dressing.

Nutritional info. per serving

Calories	362	
Protein	39	g
Carbohydrate	27	g
Fat	28	%
Sodium	647	mg
Cholesterol	96	mg
Fiber	3	g

Harpoon Louie's
1065 N. Highway A1A, Jupiter (407)744-1300

Ken Wade, Executive Chef, has had experience in all facets of the industry: luxury and banquet hotels, clubs and restaurants- multi-unit, high volume, gourmet and country club. He graduated from College in Ireland and spent years working there in different places, one of them being Ashford Castle. Ken also has a lot of teaching experience and is very involved with The American Culinary Federation.
Most memorable meal - at Palmer Le Notre's Restaurant in Paris, France.

♥ Tuna Steaks with Papaya Salsa
Yield: 4 servings

1 large papaya, seeded, peeled and cut into 1/4" cubes
2 jalapeno chiles, seeded and finely chopped
1/2 medium red onion, coarsely chopped
1/2 cup fresh cilantro, finely chopped
2 tablespoons olive oil
1 tablespoon fresh lime juice
Ground pepper
3 cups cooked brown rice (or grain of your choice)
4 - 6 oz. 3/4" thick tuna steaks (or other firm flesh fish,
    i.e. mahi mahi or yellowtail)

Combine papaya, chiles, onion, cilantro, oil and lime juice in medium bowl. Season with pepper. Cover salsa and let flavors blend at least one hour. (Can be prepared 2 days ahead, refrigerate; bring to room temperature before using).

Spray fish with a vegetable oil cooking spray and grill; serve salsa, on top or side, along with 3/4 cup cooked brown rice (or grain of choice) per serving.

Nutritional info. per serving

Calories	514	
Protein	47	g
Carbohydrate	41	g
Fat	30	%
Sodium	84	mg
Cholesterol	70	mg
Fiber	4	g

Sinclairs

Jupiter Beach Hilton Five North A1A, Jupiter (407)744-5700

Billy Poirier, Executive Chef, previously worked at Seasons Restaurant in Boston, and came to know Sinclairs through its visiting Chefs program! He is a graduate of Johnson and Wales Culinary School in Providence, R.I.; and has experience from The Charles Hotel in Cambridge, The Biltmore in Providence, The Fourways Restaurant in Washington, D.C. and The 800 room Playboy ski resort at Great Gorge, New Jersey.
Billy has long been balancing various traditions and styles in his cooking, since he is the product of a French father and an Italian mother!

♥ Caribbean Poached Snapper
"Blaff"
Yield: 4 servings

1 sweet potato, peeled and sliced 1/4 inch thick
1 white potato, peeled and sliced 1/4 inch thick

Broth:
1 teaspoon canola oil
1 medium onion, thinly sliced
1 stalk celery, thinly sliced
3 garlic cloves, minced
2 lbs. of washed fish frames (bones)
2 limes, juiced
1/4 cup white wine
1 sprig thyme
1 bay leaf
4 allspice berries
1/2 scotch bonnet pepper (or jalapeno)

4 - 6 oz. snapper fillets, skinned
3 scallions, finely sliced
1/2 tomato, peeled, seeded and diced
8 lime slices

In saucepan, blanch potatoes separately in boiling water until done. Remove and cool on ice.
Preparation of broth: Heat canola oil in stock pot and saute onion, celery and garlic over medium heat until translucent. Add chopped fish

frames and saute 5 minutes more. Add wine, lime juice, water to cover and bring to a simmer. Remove any foam on surface. Add thyme, bay leaf, allspice and pepper. Simmer on low for 1 hour, strain and adjust seasoning.

Final assembly: Bring broth to a simmer and add seasoned fish fillets. Simmer 5 minutes or until done. Carefully remove the fish and divide among 4 warm soup plates. Re-heat broth again and add potatoes, scallions and tomatoes. Divide potatoes and broth among the plates and garnish with lime slices. Serve at once.

Nutritional info. per serving

Calories	285	
Protein	37	g
Carbohydrate	22	g
Fat	12	%
Sodium	134	mg
Cholesterol	62	mg
Fiber	3	g

Cafe Chardonnay

Garden Square Shoppes 4533 PGA Blvd., Palm Beach Gardens (407)627-2662

Frank Eucalitto, Chef/Owner, graduated from Johnson and Wales Culinary Arts program. He and his wife Gigi opened the restaurant 4 years ago, and serve "Regional American Specialties." Frank loves to read different cookbooks and magazines!
His most memorable meal was dinner at "The Belvedere" in Italy, where he was served Northern Italian specialties.

♥ Fresh Basil Angel Hair with Scallops and Wild Mushrooms
Yield: 4 servings

1 lb. angel hair pasta; cooked according to package directions
2 oz. (1/4 cup) extra virgin olive oil
1 1/2 lbs. sea scallops
Pepper
1 cup fresh wild mushrooms, sliced (shiitake, oyster,
    button or chanterelle)
3 cloves garlic, minced
1 cup fish or chicken stock
1 fresh tomato, peeled, seeded and diced
2 tablespoons chopped fresh basil
2 tablespoons Italian parsley
2 tablespoons mint
4 tablespoons parmesan cheese

Coat medium size teflon saute pan with oil over medium heat. Season scallops with pepper and saute until lightly browned on 1 side. Turn scallops, add mushrooms and cook 1 minute. Add garlic; cook for 30 seconds. Add stock, tomato and herbs; simmer 1-2 minutes until scallops are cooked. Season to taste with pepper. Toss with pasta, add parmesan cheese and serve.

Nutritional info. per serving

Calories	741	
Protein	49	g
Carbohydrate	93	g
Fat	23	%
Sodium	594	mg
Cholesterol	61	mg
Fiber	1	g

Explorers Restaurant
PGA National Resort 400 Avenue of the Champions, Palm Beach Gardens (407)627-2000

Jeff Summerour, Executive Chef, is responsible for three restaurants including The Explorers, Signature Restaurant and Members Clubhouse; special event catering and banquet facilities at the resort. Previously he worked as the Executive Chef at several establishments in South Carolina and Tennessee.
Jeff has won many employee, as well as Culinary Food Honors!

♥ Roast Loin of Axis Venison with Lingonberry Sauce
Yield: 6 servings

1 oz. margarine
6 - 6 oz. Venison loin medallions
Pepper
Approx. 1 oz. lingonberry sauce/serving (recipe below)

Heat margarine in saute pan and sear seasoned meat; finish cooking in oven until desired doneness. Fan out on top of sauce.

Lingonberry Sauce:
1 tablespoon lingonberries
1 teaspoon green peppercorns
1 teaspoon garlic
1 teaspoon shallots
1 sprig thyme
1/2 cup raspberry vinegar
1 1/2 cups Demi-glace (recipe below)
4 tablespoons lingonberry preserves
2 tablespoons margarine

Demi-glace:
3/4 tablespoon margarine
1/2 garlic clove
2 1/4 tablespoons flour
1 1/2 cups beef broth

For demi-glace: Melt margarine in saucepan over medium low heat and saute garlic; stir in 1/2 of flour. Mix remaining flour with cold broth; heat in separate saucepan. When hot, add to margarine/flour mixture, and boil, stir constantly.

For sauce: In saucepan, combine lingonberries, green peppercorns, garlic, shallots, thyme and raspberry vinegar. Reduce to 1/3 of original quantity; add demi-glace and lingonberry preserves, finish with margarine.

Nutritional info. per serving

Calories	279	
Protein	35	g
Carbohydrate	14	g
Fat	30	%
Sodium	364	mg
Cholesterol	-	
Fiber	-	

Chef's serving suggestion: Serve with Corn Cakes (see recipe below), vegetables of your choice and additional lingonberries, if desired.

♥ The sauce is delicious on chicken too!

♥ Corn Cakes
Yield: 6 servings

3/4 cup flour
1/2 cup corn meal
1/2 teaspoon baking powder
Pepper
1 egg
3/4 cup evaporated skim milk
1/4 cup onion, chopped
1 baking potato, peeled and shredded
1/2 cup corn kernels
2 tablespoons sugar

In a large bowl, mix flour, corn meal, baking powder and pepper. Then mix in egg and evaporated skim milk; whip until smooth. Mix in remaining ingredients.

Preheat griddle.

Drop batter by large spoonfuls and grill (or use a non-stick pan sprayed with a vegetable oil cooking spray).

Nutritional info. per serving

Calories	108	
Protein	4	g
Carbohydrate	21	g
Fat	7	%
Sodium	49	mg
Cholesterol	22	mg
Fiber	1	g

Cafe L'Europe

150 Worth Ave., Palm Beach (407)655-4020

Norbert M. and Lidia Goldner, Owners. They have opened a new restaurant - Bistro L'Europe in Mizner Park in Boca Raton.

♥ Florida Yellow Tail Snapper Wrapped In Phyllo With Roasted Red Pepper, Basil-Yogurt Sauce
Yield: 2 servings

2 - 6 oz. snapper fillets, boneless
Pepper
1 bunch basil
1 red bell pepper, roasted and julienned
2 oz. (4 tablespoons) margarine
8 phyllo sheets
2 shallots, minced
1 garlic clove
1/2 cup (4 oz) dry white wine (optional)
1/2 cup lowfat yogurt
10 pencil thin asparagus

Preheat oven to 375 F.
Season snapper with pepper; place 2 leaves of basil on top of snapper then place roasted pepper on top.
In saucepan, melt 1 oz. of margarine. Lay out sheets of phyllo and brush with melted margarine - lay 4 sheets on top of each other, 4 for each portion. Place snapper in the middle a third-way down. Start at the top, pull phyllo over top of snapper, then fold in left side and then right side so that they meet (or as close as possible); then turn over until all phyllo is wrapped around snapper. Repeat process with other fillet. Bake in oven on flat sheet pan for 15 minutes (use a vegetable oil cooking spray for phyllo, if needed).
Sauce: Melt 1 oz. of margarine in sauce pan; add shallots and garlic, and saute. Add wine and reduce to 1/2. Add yogurt and simmer; add basil to sauce. Blend in blender until emulsified. Steam asparagus, season with pepper.

To serve: Fan asparagus on plate and add snapper sliced in three with sauce surrounding it.

Nutritional info. per serving

Calories	730	
Protein	45	g
Carbohydrate	68	g
Fat	34	%
Sodium	752	mg
Cholesterol	57	mg
Fiber	2	g

♥ Grilled Chicken Breasts With Pasta Shells, Roasted Red, Green And Yellow Peppers, Tomato, Black Olives, Scallions, Tarragon and Chicken Bouillon
Yield: 2 servings

1- 2 1/2-3 lb. natural feed chicken, roaster or broiler
1 carrot
1 onion
1 stalk of celery
1 leek
Bay leaf, thyme, peppercorn, bouillon herbs, parsley stalks
1 teaspoon vegetable oil
1 red, green and yellow pepper, roasted, diced 1/4" cubes
1 vine ripe tomato, blanched, seeded and diced 1/4" cubes
6 pitted small black olives, quartered
1 bunch scallions, sliced thin
1 bunch tarragon, finely chopped
1 oz. grated parmesan cheese
2 oz. dried pasta shells; cooked according to package directions

Remove breasts and legs from chicken. Roughly chop carrot, onion, leek and celery; place in stock pot with chicken bones, 2 quarts of water, spices and bouillon herbs. Simmer covered on stove for 4 hours, skimming grease off top.

Brush oil on chicken with skin, season, and grill over charcoal flame. When cooked, remove skin and cut into 1/2" dice. Strain chicken stock and reduce to 1/3 of original quantity; add chicken, peppers, tomato, olives, scallions, tarragon and cheese. Toss with pasta and season to taste. Serve on plate or shallow soup bowl with tarragon flower.

Nutritional info. per serving

Calories	527	
Protein	51	g
Carbohydrate	49	g
Fat	25	%
Sodium	846	mg
Cholesterol	108	mg
Fiber	8	g

Renatos
87 Via Mizner, Palm Beach (407)655-9745

John Jones, Sous Chef, was an apprentice at Petite Marmite, and worked there for 11 years. John's mentor - Wolfgang Puck.

♥ Bordeaux Capellini
Yield: 1 serving

1 tablespoon oil
1 teaspoon garlic
4 escargot
10 asparagus tips
1/2 cup sliced shiitake mushrooms
1/2 cup carrots, julienned
3 cups red wine, Burgundy
1/4 lb. capellini (angel hair pasta)
1/2 cup tomato concasse (1 tomato, peeled,seeded and diced)
1 teaspoon parmesan cheese, if desired

   Heat oil in medium-large saute pan and saute garlic; add escargot, asparagus, mushrooms and carrot, and saute until cooked. In saucepan, heat wine to boiling point and reduce slightly. While escargot and vegetables are cooking, put capellini into red wine and cook al dente.
   Add tomato to escargot and vegetables, heat.
   When capellini is cooked, strain and reserve wine. Add capellini to rest of ingredients in saute pan, toss, and add parmesan. Add reserved wine as desired.

Nutritional info.per serving
(using all wine after reducing)

Calories	1040	
Protein	44	g
Carbohydrate	127	g
Fat	14	%
Sodium	484	mg
Cholesterol	57	mg
Fiber	4	g

The Breakers
Palm Beach (407)655-6611

Matthias Radits, Executive Chef, completed an eight year apprenticeship in Austria, then spent five years in Germany, Spain and the Bahamas before moving to the United States in 1983. He has been at The Breakers since 1989.
His most memorable meal - one he cooked in Miami with Paul Bocuse, who is, also his mentor.

♥ Chicken Dijon
Yield: 4 servings

4 - 6 oz. chicken breasts, skinless, boneless
8 bibb lettuce leaves
32 each (about 1 lb.) pencil thin asparagus spears
1 medium head radicchio (about 4-6 oz.), julienned
1 large vine-ripened tomato, cut into 1/8ths

Dressing:
1 tablespoon Pumpkinseed oil (other flavored nut oil can be
    substituted)
2 tablespoons extra virgin olive oil
1/2 teaspoon Dijon mustard
1/2 teaspoon lite soy sauce
1 1/2 tablespoons sherry vinegar
Pepper to taste
20 slices melba wheat toast (or grain of your choice)

Poach or grill chicken breast portions. Slice thinly on the diagonal.
Arrange two lettuce leaves at the top of each plate.
Place about 8 asparagus spears around each plate. Place the julienned radiccio down the center of each plate and top with chicken slices.
Arrange tomato slices between the asparagus spears.
Blend all dressing ingredients together well and drizzle over salads.

Note: Serve the chicken hot and the salad ingredients cold along with 5 slices melba toast (or grain of choice) per serving.

Nutritional info. per serving:

Calories	401	
Protein	44	g
Carbohydrate	23	g
Fat	33	%
Sodium	279	mg
Cholesterol	98	mg
Fiber	4	g

♥ Key Lime and Papaya Vinaigrette (for Lobster)
Yield: 4 servings

1 ripe papaya
1/2 red pepper, diced fine
1/2 purple pepper, diced fine
1/2 green pepper, diced fine
2 tablespoons rice vinegar
3 tablespoons key lime juice
1 teaspoon ginger juice
2 tablespoons extra virgin olive oil

16 oz. (1 lb.) steamed lobster meat, cut into medallions

Dice 1/2 of the papaya very fine and mix with the diced peppers in a small mixing bowl. Put the other 1/2 of the papaya in a blender with the rice vinegar, key lime juice and the ginger juice. Blend until smooth then blend in the olive oil. Mix with papaya and peppers.
Serve over 4 oz. cooked (steamed and chilled) lobster meat medallions per serving.

Nutritional info. per serving:

Calories	209	
Protein	24	g
Carbohydrate	11	g
Fat	33	%
Sodium	434	mg
Cholesterol	81	mg
Fiber	1	g

The Mark

222 Lakeview Ave., West Palm Beach (407)835-8686

Gregory Williamson, Executive Chef, graduated from Johnson and Wales Culinary Arts Program. He previously worked in Boston at The Dover Sea Grille, which won several awards! He came to Florida "for a chance to work with Norman Van Aken, to utilize local seafoods and lie on the beach."
Gregory's mentor - his mother.

♥ Chicken Breast Stuffed with Feta Cheese and served on Spinach with Canellini Beans, Oregano, Roasted Garlic and Tomato

Yield: 4 servings

1 head roasted garlic
1 teaspoon olive oil
1 medium onion, diced
1/2 lb. (1 cup) dry Canellini beans (can substitute
    large navy beans)
2 cups chicken stock
1 tablespoon chopped fresh oregano
1 large or 2 small tomatoes, chopped
Pepper
4 - 5 oz. chicken breasts, skinless, boneless*
1/4 lb. feta cheese
1/4 cup parsley
1 lb. clean spinach

To roast garlic: In a small pan roast garlic cloves in oven at 300 F for 1 hour.

Soak beans in water for 6 hours or overnight. Rinse and simmer in water to cover until almost soft, then drain.

Preheat oven to 350 F.

Heat olive oil in large pan and saute onions until soft. Add beans and chicken stock, and cook until tender. Add oregano, garlic, tomatoes and pepper.

Mix the parsley and feta cheese together; place on top of each chicken breast and bake covered in baking pan in oven for 30 minutes or until cooked. Remove cover last 10 minutes. Steam spinach. To serve: Place beans on a plate, place 1 small pile of spinach in the center of the plate and serve the chicken on the spinach.

Nutritional info. per serving

Calories	466	
Protein	49	g
Carbohydrate	42	g
Fat	24	%
Sodium	875	mg
Cholesterol	98	mg
Fiber	11	g

* Chicken portion is smaller due to the fact that feta cheese, another protein source, is portioned on top.

The Ocean Grand Hotel
2800 South Ocean Blvd., Palm Beach (407)582-2800

Hubert A. Des Marais IV, Executive Chef, is a graduate of the C.I.A. He has used his culinary skills in The Carolinas, New York and Texas, as well as here in Florida.
Most memorable meal - Deportanova and Placido Domingo.
Hubert's mentor - his grandmother!

Adam N. Votaw, a graduate of the C.I.A., has had much experience in London, England as well as in the States.
His most memorable meal - when he "cooked dinner for his grandmother, uncle, aunt and wife in his miniature London flat."
Adam's mentor- Albert Roux of Le Gavroche, London, England.

♥ Seared Yellowtail Snapper with A Smoked Citrus and Ginger Sauce
Yield: 6 servings

6 - 6 oz. snapper fillets
2 tablespoons peanut oil
1 teaspoon pepper

Relish:
2 honey murcetts (or other sweet orange)
2 tangelos
2 sunburst tangerines
Juice of 4 key limes
2 ruby red grapefruit
2 blood oranges
1 bunch orange mint, chopped
3 oz. dark rum

Sauce:
1/4 cup grated ginger root
1 small bermuda onion, diced
2 cups dark rum
3 cups citrus juice
1 tablespoon margarine
6 tablespoons smoked citrus (or 2 tablespoons dry lemon and orange zest)
Pepper

Heat peanut oil in a skillet and saute snapper fillets. Season with pepper and finish cooking in oven, if necessary, in skillet if ovenproof or baking pan.

For relish: Zest, peel and section fruit. Save zest for the sauce. Toss sections with rum and mint. Refrigerate until ready to use.

For sauce: Smoke zest with orange, guava or tamarind wood chips in a smoker just long enough to impart flavor. If you don't have a smoker use an outdoor grill with a cover. Light one charcoal briquette and when its red hot, cover with wood chips. After the chips start to smolder, place zest on a metal screen then place the screen on top of the grill rack. Cover and smoke for 15 minutes. This may be done well in advance or you can use dry zest if desired.

Place ginger and onion in a sauce pan along with the rum and citrus juice. Reduce to a syrup over a medium high flame. Whip in margarine. Strain sauce and add smoked citrus, season with pepper. Keep warm until ready to use.

To serve: Arrange relish in center of plates and place snapper fillets on top; warm in oven, if plate is ovenproof. When serving, place sauce on the outer edge of the plates.

Nutritional info. per serving

Calories	585	
Protein	33	g
Carbohydrate	38	g
Fat	13	%
Sodium	87	mg
Cholesterol	53	mg
Fiber	5	g

♥ Fresh Tropical Fruit Compote for Angel Food Cake
Yield: 10 servings

1/2 cup papaya, diced
1/2 cup mango, pureed
1/2 cup pineapple, diced
1/2 cup melon (watermelon, honeydew, cantaloupe), diced
*1/2 cup carambola (starfruit), diced
*1/2 cup kiwi, diced

Toss fruit together in mango puree. * If tropical fruit is not available any fresh fruits can be substituted, such as: strawberries, raspberries, blackberries, blueberries or any other favorites.

Optional: add 1/2 teaspoon of cinnamon and 1 oz. rum and lightly toss with fruit mix.

Serve over your favorite angel food cake.

Note: The fresh tropical fruit compote and angel food cake will fit into heart healthy recipe guidelines, as the fat content of fruit and angel food cake is negligible.

Auberge Le Grillon
6900 N. Federal Highway, Boca Raton (407)997-6888

Brian Shaw, Executive Chef, started restaurant work at 14 and worked as an apprentice in New Orleans. He came to South Florida "primarily for the weather and the amount of fine dining establishments."
Brian's most memorable meal - Christmas morning, 1982, when he was working as a breakfast cook in a Florida Resort: by 8:15 a.m. he realized he was the only one who showed up to work. "He spent an hour and a half running to take orders, back to cook and then to serve. The guests must have been pleased because he made excellent tips!"

♥ Supreme de Poulet et Homard Garci Naturel
(Lobster Stuffed Breast of Chicken with Natural Sauce)
Yield: 2 servings

1- 2 oz. lobster tail
1 1/2 cups chicken stock or broth
1/2 cup sweet white wine
2 - 5-6 oz. chicken breasts, skinless, boneless
1 teaspoon green peppercorns, smashed
3-4 leaves of fresh spinach (washed)
2 teaspoons arrowroot (dissolved in 1/4 cup wine)
Pepper
1 sheet of wax paper, damp cloth napkin (or aluminum foil)

Preheat oven to 350 F.
In medium saucepan poach lobster tail in stock and wine approximately 5-8 minutes; remove and reserve stock. Remove tail from shell and divide in two; chop shell slightly and save.

Gently pound chicken breasts; spread peppercorns on inside of chicken breast and cover with spinach. Place lobster meat on chicken breast and roll up. Put stuffed chicken breast seam side down in large casserole and cover breast by 3/4 with remaining stock. Cover with damp napkin or aluminum foil and bake in oven for 15-20 minutes.

Pour stock into saucepan with lobster shell and reduce by half. Thicken sauce with arrowroot mixture, just enough to coat back of spoon, and strain. Season with pepper to taste.

To serve, slice breast on a bias and spoon sauce over top.

Nutritional info. per serving

Calories	336	
Protein	42	g
Carbohydrate	11	g
Fat	15	%
Sodium	736	mg
Cholesterol	107	mg
Fiber	-	

The Boca Raton Resort and Club
501 East Camino Real, Boca Raton (407)395-3000

Located in the heart of Florida's Gold Coast, The Boca Raton Resort and Club is one of the country's most prestigious resorts. The recipient of the Mobil Travel Guide's Five-Star Award and Triple A's Five-Diamond Award, the resort boasts lavish amenities, and a number of fine restaurant options, all with superb food and ambiance.

♥ Vitello Milano
Yield: 2 servings

2 tablespoons olive oil
1/2 cup porcini mushrooms, sliced
1/4 cup minced shallots
1/2 cup sundried tomatoes, rehydrated and julienned
8 oz. scallopini veal
1 cup dry white wine
1/2 cup artichoke hearts, diced
1/2 cup chopped parsley
6 oz. Polenta (Italian style cornmeal); cooked according to
   package directions
Garnish:
1 oz. red pepper, roasted, peeled and julienned.

Heat oil in medium saute pan over medium heat. Saute mushrooms, shallots and sundried tomatoes. Add veal and lightly saute. Add the white wine, artichokes and parsley; cook a few more minutes.

Place the polenta in the center of a serving plate and surround it with the veal and vegetables. Garnish with julienned pepper.

Nutritional info. per serving:

Calories	729	
Protein	35	g
Carbohydrate	87	g
Fat	24	%
Sodium	838	mg
Cholesterol	91	mg
Fiber	15	g

Coppola's

Crocker Center 5250 Town Center Circle, Boca Raton, (407)368-7400

Louis Coppola, who has been cooking for 20 years, is the 7th generation in the family business! Most memorable meal - although he recalls cooking for many celebrities, Mayors, Presidents....Louis really enjoyed cooking for Jerry Lewis; he came into the kitchen and they had fun cooking together!
His mentors - his father, Vincent and grandfather, Louis. He has a son, Vincent who is the "legacy to go on...."

♥ Risotto Pescatore
Yield: 4 servings

1 teaspoon olive oil
2 cloves garlic, chopped
2 cups Chardonnay Wine
5-6 oz. shrimp
5-6 oz. lobster meat
17 mussels
17 Littleneck clams
4 tablespoons margarine
Pepper
8 sprigs parsley, chopped
4 cups steamed white rice
1 large tomato, diced
1/2 cup green peas

In large pan heat oil and a vegetable oil cooking spray and saute garlic. Add 1 cup Chardonnay and seafood; cook over medium heat until clams and mussels open. Add 2 tablespoons margarine, pepper and parsley; simmer covered 15 minutes.

In a separate pan combine rice, tomato, peas, 1 cup Chardonnay and 2 tablespoons margarine; simmer 5 minutes.

To serve, place rice on a large platter, arrange mussels and clams around the edges, and top with seafood and sauce.

Nutritional info. per serving
Calories	574	
Protein	29	g
Carbohydrate	66	g
Fat	19	%
Sodium	485	mg
Cholesterol	101	mg
Fiber	3	g

Glades Cafe

Bloomingdales, Boca Raton (407)394-2219

Chester W. Barthmaier, Executive Chef.

♥ Pasta and Shrimp Marseilles
Yield: 3 servings

12 snow peas, cut diagonal
1 large carrot, julienned
1 small zucchini, julienned
1 small yellow squash, julienned
1 small red pepper, julienned
1 stalk broccoli, small florets
1 head leaf lettuce
8 oz. peeled and deveined medium shrimp
1 qt. water
5 cloves
2 small bay leaves
3/4 cup lite mayonnaise
1 1/2 tablespoons Dijon mustard
1 1/2 tablespoons horseradish
3 tablespoons balsamic vinegar
4 cups cooked rotini (tricolor)
Lettuce leaves
Lemon wedges

In large saucepan with water, blanch all vegetables; cool in refrigerator.
Bring water to boil with cloves and bay leaves. Reduce heat to simmer and add shrimp, cook 3-4 minutes or until a nice red color and firm. Remove from water and cool in refrigerator.
Mix mayonnaise, mustard, horseradish and vinegar until smooth consistency.
Mix all vegetables and pasta together. Add sauce and let cool in refrigerator 1 hour before serving.

On a large round plate, place 4 lettuce leaves in center, facing out. Place pasta salad in center of plate and place the shrimp around the pasta. Garnish with lemon wedges.

Nutritional info. per serving

Calories	541	
Protein	23	g
Carbohydrate	66	g
Fat	34	%
Sodium	393	mg
Cholesterol	131	mg
Fiber	7	g

Sante Fe Grill

2300 Executive Center Dr., Boca Raton (407)994-1255

Steven K. Mettle, Executive Chef, has worked with many fine chefs coast to coast including stints at the American Restaurant in Kansas City, and the River Cafe in New York City; as well as being Executive Chef at Gordons High Altitude Cuisine in Aspen, Colorado.
Most memorable meal - "The dinner served for Hollywood movie mogul Marvin Davis last winter in Aspen. The party dined on free-range chicken with white truffles, and rabbit with linquisa sausage and okra: price per person $1,000.00. Guests included Gregory Peck, Sidney Portier..., and an army of security people for each attendee."

♥ Five Grain Compote
Yield: 12 - 1/2 cup servings

2 oz. hard winter wheat berries
   1 1/8 cups broth or stock
2 oz. quinoa grain
   3/4 cup broth or stock
2 oz. rye berries
   1 1/8 cups broth or stock
2 oz. brown Texmati rice
   3/4 cup broth or stock
2 oz. teff grain
   3/4 cup broth or stock
1 tablespoon canola oil
1/2 medium red onion, diced
1/4 yellow pepper, diced
1/4 poblano pepper, diced
1/4 carrot, diced
1/2 garlic clove, minced
1/4 bunch cilantro, chopped
3/4 cup chicken stock
Pepper

   In saucepans, cook all grains individually in chicken stock (check package directions for quantity of liquid for each grain) until al dente; rinse grains until water rinses clear.

Heat canola oil in large pan and saute all vegetables until crunchy. Add chicken stock, cilantro, pepper and the grains; mix. Heat until stock is absorbed and serve.

Nutritional info. per serving

Calories	113	
Protein	5	g
Carbohydrate	20	g
Fat	17	%
Sodium	344	mg
Cholesterol	-	
Fiber	2	g

Note: purchase grains in health food store.

♥ Try adding a touch of balsamic vinegar and eat cold as a salad.

The Gazebo Cafe
4199 N. Federal Highway, Boca Raton (407)395-6033

Bob Walsh, Executive Chef, was previously the Garde Manger at Pier 66, The Mayflower Hotel in Washington, D.C. and on the S.S. Rotterdam (Holland America Line).
His most memorable meal - "every meal on The Ship: 4,000 a day."
Bob's mentor - Hiroshi Noguchi, Executive Chef at The Seaworld Resort in Orlando.

♥ Chicken Tomato Herb
Yield: 2 servings

2 tablespoons margarine
2 - 6 oz. chicken breasts, skinless, boneless
1/8 cup flour
4 baby carrots
3 broccoli florets
8 zucchini slices
8 yellow squash slices
4 mushrooms, sliced
Nutmeg, pepper and parsley to taste
1 oz. (2 tablespoons) lemon juice
1/2 fresh tomato, peeled, seeded and diced
2 oz. (1/4 cup) chicken stock
Parsley

Preheat oven to 350 F.
Heat 1 tablespoon margarine in saute pan, and saute chicken that has been lightly dredged in flour; finish cooking in oven in saute pan, if ovenproof, or baking pan.
Heat 1 tablespoon margarine in a separate pan and saute vegetables, adding pinch of nutmeg, pepper and parsley. Deglaze with lemon juice, and add diced tomato. Add chicken stock to vegetables, heat, and pour over top of chicken breast. Garnish with fresh parsley.

Nutritional info. per serving
Calories	335	
Protein	39	g
Carbohydrate	16	g
Fat	34	%
Sodium	295	mg
Cholesterol	96	mg
Fiber	3	g

Brooks

500 South Federal Highway, Deerfield Beach (305)427-9302

Jon Howe graduated from Palm Beach Junior College and then worked 6 years at Bernard's in Boynton Beach (now Ben Venuto) He has been at Brooks for the past 9 years. Jon's mentor - his father-in-law: Bernard Perron!

♥ Duck Breast a la Brooks
Yield: 4 servings

4 - 6 oz. duck breasts, skinless, boneless
Pepper
1/3 cup sugar
1/3 cup water
1/2 cup red wine vinegar
1 1/2 cups veal stock
1 1/2 cups cranberries
1/3 cup Cranberry Liqueur
1/2 cup Cabernet Sauvignon
2 3/4 tablespoons margarine
4 medium potatoes, cooked and mashed
Parsley

Preheat oven to 350 F.
Season duck breasts and bake in covered baking pan for approx. 30 minutes, until cooked.

In a heavy saucepan over low heat dissolve sugar in water and cook until caramelized. Remove from heat and add the wine vinegar. Add veal stock, cranberries, cranberry liqueur and red wine; cook for approx. 15 minutes. Add margarine to sauce.

To serve: Slice the duck breasts and fan on plate, then cover with sauce. Serve with 1 medium mashed potato per serving and decorate with parsley or watercress.

Nutritional info. per serving

Calories	566	
Protein	30	g
Carbohydrate	57	g
Fat	29	%
Sodium	462	mg
Cholesterol	102	mg
Fiber	2	g

 Try sauce on leftover turkey or with chicken breasts!

Cafe Arugula

3150 N. Federal Highway, Lighthouse Point (305)785-7732

Dick Cingolani, the Executive Chef and owner of Cafe Argula, Cafe Grazia and Border Cafe, has a "Passion for Cooking." He was trained in Italy, and combines European influence and flavorings with American products.
His most memorable meal - Tom Cruise was in the restaurant and Dick didn't realize it until he saw Tom's credit card!
His mentor - Mark Militello.

♥ Cannelloni
Yield: 6 servings

Bechamel Sauce:
3 tablespoons margarine
3 tablespoons flour
4 cups skim milk
2 tablespoons fresh grated parmesan cheese
Pinch of fresh grated nutmeg

In large saucepan melt margarine; add flour and whisk until smooth. Add milk, simmer until thick, stirring frequently. Add cheese and seasoning and remove from heat (if sauce needs thickening, use up to 1 tablespoon cornstarch dissolved in 1/4 cup cold water). Cover with waxed paper until ready to assemble and serve.

Marinara Sauce:
3/4 tablespoon olive oil
1 tablespoon finely chopped garlic
2 cans Imported Plum Tomatoes (crushed by hand)
1 tablespoon fresh or 1 teaspoon dried basil
1 tablespoon fresh chopped parsley
Pepper

Heat oil in large saucepan and saute garlic until light brown. Quickly add tomatoes and bring to a boil. Lower to simmer, add the rest of ingredients and cook 20 minutes.

3/4 tablespoon olive oil
1/2 cup chopped onion
1 lb. ground skinless, boneless chicken breast

1 lb. ground lean stewing veal
1 pkg. (8 oz). frozen chopped spinach, cooked (or 1 lb. fresh steamed)
1/3 cup fresh grated parmesan cheese
Pepper to taste
12 fresh or dried 6" Pasta Squares (Cannelloni)*

Heat olive oil in large saute pan and cook onions until transparent. Add chicken and veal, cook through, do not brown. Remove to bowl and drain off any fat or liquid. Add cooked spinach, cheese and seasoning. Stir in 1 cup of Bechamel sauce to bind.

Preheat oven to 350 F.
Cook pasta until al dente and rinse in ice water, drain and dry.
Divide filling into 12 portions - put filling at one end of the pasta square and roll up.
Put a thin layer of marinara sauce in a baking pan large enough to put all cannelloni in a single layer. Put filled cannelloni in pan then drizzle Bechamel sauce down middle of all cannelloni, using all the sauce. Pour Marinara over both ends of pasta making sure all of the pasta is covered. Cover with foil, shiny side in, and bake 30-40 minutes until bubbling hot. Serve 2 per person with more Marinara sauce if desired.

Nutritional info. per serving

Calories	586	
Protein	49	g
Carbohydrate	50	g
Fat	33	%
Sodium	835	mg
Cholesterol	120	mg
Fiber	3	g

*Can use dry manicotti.

♥ Three Berry Crisp
Yield: 10 servings

Use seasonal fresh berries; we prefer a combination of raspberries, blueberries and blackberries or strawberries. This also can be done with one or two berries by adjusting quantities (for sweetness).

Preheat oven to 350 F.
1 pint each raspberries, blueberries, blackberries
1/2 cup flour
3/4 cup sugar

Clean berries; mix together in a large bowl with the flour and sugar. Distribute in heatproof baking cups and top with the crumb mixture (recipes below).

Crumb mixture - A:
1 cup flour
1 cup sugar
1/4 lb. margarine

Cut margarine in to flour and sugar to crumbly stage - mixture should be crumbly and come together when pressed firmly. Crumble in lumps over top of berries. Bake until brown and bubbly, 35-40 minutes.

Nutritional info. per serving

Calories	319	
Protein	3	g
Carbohydrate	59	g
Fat	26	%
Sodium	109	mg
Cholesterol	-	
Fiber	4	g

Serve warm with a dollop of yogurt mixed with 1 teaspoon of cinnamon if desired.

Alternate crumb mixture - B:
1 1/2 cups quick cooking oats
3/4 cup lite brown sugar
1 1/8 cups all-purpose flour
1 1/2 tablespoons cinnamon
15 tablespoons margarine

Mix all ingredients, and cut in chilled margarine to coarse meal stage. Sprinkle over berries (mixed with flour and sugar, and distributed in heat-proof baking cups, as above) and bake 35-40 minutes, until crisp and bubbly.

Nutritional info. per serving

Calories	478	
Protein	7	g
Carbohydrate	73	g
Fat	35	%
Sodium	206	mg
Cholesterol	-	
Fiber	4	g

♥ Chocolate Sauce
Yield: 1 1/2 cups - 24 tablespoons

8 tablespoons of Hershey's cocoa
1 cup water
3/4 cup sugar
2 tablespoons Kahlua

Mix cocoa with 1/4 cup of water. Mix remainder of the water with sugar in a saucepan, bring to boil until dissolved. Add cocoa mixture and simmer until thick. (Cook over low heat - be careful not to burn. You may want to use the top of a double boiler). Add Kahlua and heat.

Nutritional info. per tablespoon

Calories	53	
Protein	-	
Carbohydrate	12	g
Fat	2	%
Sodium	17	mg
Cholesterol	-	
Fiber	-	

Use over iced milk, nonfat frozen yogurt, or fresh fruit - berries, bananas... for dessert.

Cafe Grazia
3850 North Federal Highway, Lighthouse Point (305)942-7206

♥ Grazia's Cavatelli
Yield: 6 servings

1 lb. durum flour
4 oz. semolina flour
1 tablespoon baking powder
2 teaspoons olive oil
10 oz. water

In food processor, mix all dry ingredients 2 seconds; add oil and enough water to make a thick dough. Let rest 3 minutes wrapped in plastic. Roll out into 1/2" cylinders and cut into 1" pieces (or use a cavatelli machine, available at Italian markets).

Cook in boiling (salted) water 8-10 minutes until tender. Drain and serve with your favorite tomato sauce.

Nutritional info. per serving

Calories	369	
Protein	33	g
Carbohydrate	51	g
Fat	8	%
Sodium	167	mg
Cholesterol	-	
Fiber	1	g

Border Cafe

♥ Santa Fe Sushi
Yield: 10 servings

1 can black beans (or 8 oz. fresh- soak overnight and cook
   until tender. Use only 2 cups cooked black beans)
2 tablespoons cilantro
1 fresh jalapeno
Pepper
8 oz. skinless, boneless chicken breast, cut into 1/2" strips
1 package frozen spinach (or fresh steamed)
10 flour tortillas
6 oz. low fat jalapeno jack cheese cut into 1/4"
   julienne (if unavailable, use lowfat monterey jack)
6 oz. low fat colby cheese cut into 1/4" julienne
1 red pepper, blanched, julienned
2 carrots, blanched, julienned

Puree cooked beans with cilantro, jalapeno and red pepper in processor, to make a thick paste; add cooking liquid, or broth, if necessary.
   Grill, broil or saute (with vegetable oil cooking spray) chicken breast and
season with pepper.
   Lightly blanch spinach and season with pepper.
   Warm tortilla over grill or stove to make it more flexible. Spread black
bean paste on bottom half. Top with slices of grilled chicken, cheese,
spinach and vegetables. Going from one edge to the other carefully roll,
starting at the filled end. Wrap in plastic wrap and refrigerate 1 hour to
firm.
   To serve, slice into 1" pieces.

Nutritional info. per serving

Calories	298	
Protein	23	g
Carbohydrate	33	g
Fat	26	%
Sodium	194	mg
Cholesterol	32	mg
Fiber	3	g

Serve with spicy tomato sauce on the plate. Arrange "Sushi" and garnish with "Border Salsa."

♥ Serve tortilla warm, if desired.

♥ James' Spicy Tomato Sauce
Yield: 12 - 1/2 cup servings

10 lbs. ripe tomatoes (canned can also be used)
2 tablespoons ground cumin
1 medium fresh poblano pepper (canned green chili can be used)
1-2 chilpotle in Adobo*
3 whole garlic cloves
1 serrano or jalapeno pepper
Pepper

In saucepan over medium heat, cook ingredients 10-15 minutes. Remove from heat and puree in blender; add pepper to taste.
*Available in Mexican or Spanish markets. Will keep for weeks in the refrigerator.

Nutritional info. per serving
Calories	26	
Protein	1	g
Carbohydrate	5	g
Fat	14	%
Sodium	21	mg
Cholesterol	-	
Fiber	1	g

Note - analyzed without data for chilpotle in adobo.

♥ Santa Fe Salsa
Yield: 10 - 3 generous tablespoon servings

1/2 cup cooked fresh or frozen corn kernels
1 tomato chopped
1/2 cup diced red pepper

1/2 cup diced yellow pepper
1/4 cup diced poblano pepper
1 small jalapeno, diced
3 tablespoons minced cilantro
1 clove garlic, minced
1/2 cup diced red onion
2/3 tablespoon olive oil
Juice of 1/2 lime (or to taste)
Pepper

Mix all ingredients together in bowl, and refrigerate.

Nutritional info. per serving

Calories	29	
Protein	1	g
Carbohydrate	5	g
Fat	34	%
Sodium	18	mg
Cholesterol	-	
Fiber	1	g

Cafe Max

2601 East Atlantic Blvd., Pompano Beach (305)782-0606

Oliver Saucy, Executive Chef and Co-Owner, is a graduate of the C.I.A. Born in Germany, his father was a chef in a German Castle which had been converted into a resort. He and his Dad "talked cooking all the time." Oliver does a "lot of reading, studying and traveling," besides using his imagination and past experience!
His most memorable meals - at "Citrus" and "Masas" in San Francisco and Los Angeles.
Oliver's mentor - his Dad, who besides being a chef, became an instructor at the C.I.A.

Tom Rittenhouse, the Pastry Chef, Purchasing Agent and Kitchen Manager at Cafe Max, is a graduate of the University of Florida and New England Tech.
He has had many memorable meals throughout the world, as well as in his mom's own kitchen. One of his standout meals was a "Kidney Pizza," which both he and his brother mistakenly ordered at a restaurant in Bonn, during their first week in Germany!

♥ Chef Oliver's Sweet Onion-Crusted Snapper with Madeira Sauce
Yield: 4 servings

Onion-crusted fish:
2 tablespoons olive oil
1 pound red onions, peeled and sliced
2 1/2 teaspoons balsamic vinegar
4 teaspoons light brown sugar
Ground black pepper, to taste
4 - 6 oz. yellowtail snapper fillets, rinsed and pat dry

In a large shallow pan, heat olive oil over high heat. Add onions and cook until browned, but not crisp. Add vinegar, brown sugar and pepper. Continue to cook, stirring, until mixture is brown or caramelized and all the liquid has evaporated from the pan. (Mixture should be a dark brown color; watch carefully to prevent burning). Remove from heat and cool to room temperature. This mixture can be prepared a day ahead and refrigerated.

Preheat oven to broil, and preheat oven-proof casserole (or large oven-proof plate).

Arrange fillets on baking sheet and lightly season with pepper.
Divide onion mixture among fillets, spreading evenly over top of each and pack down. Set aside.

Madeira sauce:
1 cup aged Madeira wine
1 clove garlic, chopped
1 shallot, chopped
1 teaspoon tomato paste
Juice of 1/2 lemon
1/4 cup evaporated skim milk
1 tablespoon cornstarch
1 tablespoon margarine
Ground black pepper, to taste

In a heavy saucepan over medium heat, cook wine, garlic, shallot, tomato paste and lemon. Simmer for 10 minutes. Mix cornstarch with evaporated skim milk; add to Madeira mixture and bring to boiling point, stirring constantly, to thicken. When thickened, whisk in margarine. Strain, if desired, and season with pepper. Set sauce aside and keep warm.

Take oven-proof casserole (plate) out of oven, being careful not to burn your fingers; spray with a vegetable oil cooking spray, and place fillets and onions, onion side down. Broil approx. 10 minutes, until fish is opaque throughout.

To serve, ladle a pool of sauce onto each individual serving plate and top with a snapper fillet.

Nutritional info. per serving

Calories	392	
Protein	38	g
Carbohydrate	19	g
Fat	26	%
Sodium	160	mg
Cholesterol	63	mg
Fiber	2	g

♥ Banana Devils Food Loaf Cake
Yield: 10 servings

5 fl. oz. (1/2 cup + 2 tablespoons) honey
1 cup all purpose flour
3/8 cup cocoa
1 teaspoon baking soda
1/2 teaspoon baking powder

1/8 teaspoon cinnamon
1/2 cup skim milk
1 tablespoon white vinegar
1 tablespoon instant coffee, dissolved in 1 tablespoon water
1/4 cup vegetable oil
1 large egg
2 medium bananas (very ripe), mashed with fork

Preheat oven to 350 F.
Combine all ingredients in a large mixing bowl. Mix until thoroughly combined.
Bake in 9″ x 5″ loaf pan, sprayed with a vegetable oil cooking spray, 30-40 minutes, until toothpick inserted in middle comes out clean.

Nutritional info. per serving
Calories	238	
Protein	3	g
Carbohydrate	43	g
Fat	24	%
Sodium	143	mg
Cholesterol	22	mg
Fiber	1	g

Serve over softened nonfat frozen yogurt and surround with sliced bananas.

♥ Champagne and Flower Petal Sorbet
Yield: 12 servings

1/4 cup water
1/4 cup sugar
1 bottle champagne (your favorite)
2 tablespoons edible flower petals, chiffonade (finely sliced)
6 lemons crowned into 12 crowns (halves)
Edible flowers, mint

In saucepan, dissolve sugar in water over medium heat. Pour straight champagne and simple syrup (sugar and water mixture) into ice cream freezer/maker and freeze according to manufacturer's instructions. Remove frozen sorbet from machine and fold in flower petals. Freeze until firm and serve in lemon crown. Garnish with a fresh whole edible flower and a sprig of mint.

Nutritional info. per serving

Calories	59	
Protein	-	
Carbohydrate	6	g
Fat	-	
Sodium	-	
Cholesterol	-	
Fiber	-	

Note: Remaining calories are alcohol calories.

Palm-Aire Spa Resort

2501 Palm-Aire Dr. North, Pompano Beach (305)968-2700

Karen Manno-Webb is the Department Head and Staff Nutritionist/Dietitian at Palm Aire; she is co-author of Spa Recipes From The Spa At Palm-Aire. Karen's interest in cooking started when she was forced into preparing food for herself when she went to college, and really enjoyed every minute of it!

Her most memorable meal - Buddy Hackett hired her to train him on Spa Cuisine; one evening he cooked a meal, took his first bite and told her "how come when I make a meal it doesn't taste as good as when you make one?"

♥ Pumpkin Muffins
Yield: 24 "mini" muffins

4 tablespoons raisins
2/3 cup dry skim milk powder
6 tablespoons flour
1 teaspoon baking soda
1 tablespoon pumpkin pie spice
1 teaspoon cinnamon
1/4 cup "Sugar Twin" or 8 packets "Sweet'n Low"
1 cup pumpkin (preferably fresh, canned can be substituted)
1 teaspoon vanilla extract
4 egg whites

Preheat oven to 350 F.
Mix dry ingredients in a bowl; mix wet ingredients in a separate bowl. Combine both and mix well. Pour batter into muffin tins and bake in oven for 20-25 minutes.

Nutritional info. per serving

Calories	28	
Protein	2	g
Carbohydrate	5	g
Fat	3	%
Sodium	56	mg
Cholesterol	-	
Fiber	-	

♥ Chocolate Chip Banana Bran Muffins
Yield: 12

1 cup shredded bran cereal (such as Kelloggs All Bran/Fiber One)
3/4 cup skim milk, at room temperature
1 1/2 cups sifted all purpose flour
1/4 cup miniature semi-sweet chocolate chips
1 tablespoon baking powder
1 cup mashed ripe bananas (approx. 2 large bananas)
2 large egg whites at room temperature
1/4 cup molasses
Vegetable oil cooking spray

Position rack in center of oven and preheat to 400 F. Lightly spray vegetable oil cooking spray on 12, 2 3/4" x 1 1/4" (3 oz.) muffin cups.
In a medium bowl combine the bran and milk. Let stand 3-4 minutes until soft. In a large bowl stir together the flour, chocolate chips and baking powder. In another bowl stir the banana, egg whites, molasses and softened bran mixture until blended. Make a well in the center of the dry ingredients. Add the liquid ingredients and stir with a wooden spoon just to combine. Spoon the batter into the prepared muffin cups making each cup 3/4 full. Bake 20-25 minutes or until the muffins are golden brown and a cake tester or toothpick inserted into the center of one muffin comes out clean. Cool the muffins in the pan on a wire rack for 5 minutes. Remove the muffins from the cups and finish cooling on the rack. Serve warm or cool completely. You may store muffins in an airtight container at room temperature for up to 12 days.

Nutritional info. per serving

Calories	130	
Protein	4	g
Carbohydrate	27	g
Fat	11	%
Sodium	186	mg
Cholesterol	-	
Fiber	3	g

♥ Oven Baked Fried Chicken
Yield: 1 serving

5-6 oz. skinless chicken breast
2 tablespoons no-oil Italian Dressing (dip for the chicken) or
    low calorie Italian
1/8 cup Nutri-Grain cereal, crushed as coating for chicken
1/8 cup Grape Nuts, for extra crispy chicken

Preheat oven to 350 F.
Dip chicken breast into the dressing, then roll in the crushed cereal to coat the chicken; add Grape Nuts for crispy chicken. Place in baking pan in oven for 20-30 minutes.

Nutritional info. per serving

Calories	289	
Protein	37	g
Carbohydrate	18	g
Fat	23	%
Sodium	455	mg
Cholesterol	98	mg
Fiber	1	g

Karen suggests this for fish too!

♥ Chicken and Broccoli Quesadillas
Yield: 1 serving

2 oz. skinless chicken breast, diced
1/2 garlic clove, minced
1/4 cup chopped onion
1/4 cup sliced mushrooms
1/4 cup chopped broccoli
1 whole wheat pita bread pocket, cut in half and opened
1/2 oz. lowfat cheese, shredded
Vegetable oil cooking spray

Preheat oven to 375 F.

Spray saute pan with a vegetable oil cooking spray and saute chicken for 2 minutes. Add garlic and vegetables, cook for approx. 4 minutes.

Place half (2 quarters) of the pita on a non-stick baking sheet. Place the chicken-vegetable mixture on top of each pita, top with the shredded cheese and cover with the remaining pita. Bake for 10 minutes.

Nutritional info. per serving

Calories	261	
Protein	27	g
Carbohydrate	26	g
Fat	18	%
Sodium	331	mg
Cholesterol	56	mg
Fiber	2	g

Serve hot with Mexican salsa!

Sea Watch

6002 N. Ocean Blvd., Ft. Lauderdale (305)781-2200

Chef Darryl Shuford.

♥ Beef with Orange-Soy Teriyaki
Yield: 4 servings

Teriyaki Sauce:
1/4 cup orange marmalade
1/4 cup lite soy sauce
1 tablespoon fresh lemon juice (1 large lemon)
1 tablespoon white horseradish
1 tablespoon sesame oil
1 teaspoon minced fresh garlic
1/2 teaspoon ground ginger
1/8 teaspoon or to taste cayenne pepper
1/2 teaspoon minced cilantro
1/8 red pepper, minced

1 lb. lean top round or eye round beef, sliced
Bamboo skewers
1 cup dry couscous (or grain of your choice); cooked according
    to package directions

Combine all marinade ingredients together and marinate beef slices 2 to 4 hours. Skewer beef onto skewers and broil or grill until done. Serve with 3/4 cup couscous (or grain of choice) per serving.

Nutritional info. per serving:

Calories	452	
Protein	39	g
Carbohydrate	46	g
Fat	24	%
Sodium	687	mg
Cholesterol	92	mg
Fiber	4	g

♥ Paella Sea Watch
Yield: 8 servings

Paella Stock:
2 tablespoons olive oil
1 garlic clove, minced
1/2 red pepper, chopped
1/2 medium onion, chopped
1 large tomato, diced
3 cups fresh fish or chicken stock (or mixture of bottled clam
    broth and low-salt canned chicken broth)
Pinch saffron
1 tablespoon paprika
2 teaspoons cumin

   In large pot, heat oil over medium heat and saute garlic and vegetables. Add stock and seasonings and simmer 1/2 hour.

Paella Rice:
3 tablespoons olive oil
1/4 red pepper, chopped
1/4 onion, chopped
1/2 garlic clove, minced
1/2 fresh tomato, diced
2 cups raw rice
2 cups each fish stock and chicken stock
Pinch saffron
Black pepper to taste

Paella:
32 oz. (2 lb.) raw/skinless chicken breast, cut into bite-size pieces
12 oz. Cod or other lean fish fillet, cut into chunks
1/2 lb. peeled and deveined shrimp
1/4 lb. clam meat or 16 each clams, scrubbed clean
1/4 lb. mussel meat or 32 each mussels, scrubbed clean
1/2 cup green peas

Garnish:
1 lemon, sliced thin
2 tablespoons pimento strips
2 tablespoons chopped parsley

Preheat oven to 400 F.

Heat oil in large pot (preferably one that can go from stovetop to oven) over medium heat. Saute pepper, onion and garlic until onion is translucent. Add tomatoes and rice and saute until rice is well coated. Add stocks and seasonings and remove from heat.

Add chicken pieces and saute one minute; stir in cod pieces. Cover and bake in hot oven approx. 20 minutes or until liquid is absorbed, turning rice once or twice during cooking. After 10 minutes add shrimp.

In a separate pot, steam clams and mussels until shells open.

Before serving, stir in green peas to paella rice.

To assemble: Place paella rice in serving dishes and top with clams and mussels. Pour paella stock over each portion. Garnish with lemon wheels, pimento strips and chopped parsley, if desired.

Nutritional info. per serving:

Calories	506	
Protein	51	g
Carbohydrate	43	g
Fat	28	%
Sodium	1012	mg
Cholesterol	142	mg*
Fiber	2	g

* If you are watching your cholesterol, decrease the amount of shellfish used in the recipe.

The Cypress Room

The Westin Hotel Cypress Creek, 400 Corporate Dr., Ft. Lauderdale (305)772-1331

Executive Chef Geoff Davies was born in England and has worked at a number of U.S. hotels, including the Fairmont Hotel in Dallas, before joining Westin in 1985.
He is inspired by his wife, who has endured years of his leaving for work before dawn and return-ing from work late at night.

Paul Riso, Chef de Cuisine, has worked with Westin Hotels and Resorts for the past five years. He began his chef career with a small French restaurant in New York, then opened the Westin La Paloma Resort in Tucson, Arizona before moving to Florida.

♥ Potato Leek Soup with Apple
Yield: 4 servings

3 3/4 cups chicken broth
2 average baking potatoes, peeled and large diced
1 large leek, chopped
1 teaspoon thyme
1/2 teaspoon marjoram
2 average apples (Red Delicious or Cortland, preferred), peeled and diced
Black pepper to taste

In a 1 1/2 qt. saucepan, bring broth to a boil with potatoes. Add leeks and simmer until potatoes are tender. Add herbs, remove from heat, and puree soup in a blender. Season to taste, and stir in apple.

Nutritional info. per serving

Calories	153	
Protein	4	g
Carbohydrate	34	g
Fat	8	%
Sodium	597	mg
Cholesterol	-	
Fiber	3	g

♥ Chicken and Spinach Salad with Hot-'n'-Sour Dressing
Yield: 1 serving

2 cups fresh cleaned spinach
6 mandarin orange segments
4 oz. grilled or poached skinless chicken breast, cut into strips
2 tablespoons walnut pieces *
1/2 teaspoon finely grated orange zest

Dressing:
4 tablespoons (1/4 cup) orange marmalade
2 tablespoons rice wine vinegar
1/2 tablespoon horseradish

Arrange spinach and orange segments on plate.
In small saucepan, heat all dressing ingredients together. Toss chicken pieces in dressing. Arrange chicken pieces on spinach and pour remaining dressing over chicken. Top with walnuts and a bit of fresh orange zest.

Nutritional info. per serving

Calories	476	
Protein	33	g
Carbohydrate	69	g
Fat	9	%
Sodium	186	mg
Cholesterol	65	mg
Fiber	6	g

* Chef Davies recommends caramelizing walnut pieces first by cooking them in Simple Syrup: a simmering mixture of 1/4 cup water and 6 table-spoons sugar.

♥ Lamb Medallions with Gin and Mango
Yield: 1 serving

1/2 teaspoon peanut oil
6 oz. lamb loin, cleaned and cut into 3 - 2 oz. medallions
1/2 shallot, minced
1 oz. (2 tablespoons) Gin
4 oz. (1/2 cup) lamb stock (or chicken or beef stock)

1/2 average mango, diced
4 oz. fresh spinach, cleaned and trimmed
1 teaspoon minced garlic
4 each juniper berries
Pepper to taste

Heat peanut oil in medium skillet and saute lamb medallions to desired doneness. Remove lamb from pan; drain off accumulated fat. Add shallots, and deglaze pan with Gin; bring to boil. Add all but 2 tablespoons of the stock to the pan and 1/2 of the mango; simmer and reduce by 1/3. Strain, if desired, and season to taste.

Steam spinach and garlic with remaining stock.

To serve: Ladle sauce onto plate, place spinach in the middle and arrange lamb on spinach. Garnish the rest of the plate with the remaining mango.

Nutritional info. per serving

Calories	498	
Protein	47	g
Carbohydrate	22	g
Fat	30	%
Sodium	536	mg
Cholesterol	133	mg
Fiber	7	g

♥ Try with chicken medallions!

Aruba Beach Cafe
1 Commercial Blvd., Lauderdale-by-the Sea (305)776-0001

Chef Matt Collins graduated from the California Culinary Academy in 1979, and has worked in San Francisco, the Bahamas and Washington, D.C.
His most memorable cooking experience was trying to prepare an 800 lb. Manna Ray in the Bahamas.
His mentor is Chef Wendy Little of Mustard's Grill in Napa Valley, California.

♥ Chicken Satay
Yield: 4 servings

4 - 6 oz. chicken breasts, skinless, boneless and sliced into 1" wide strips

Satay marinade:
2 tablespoons lite soy sauce
2 tablespoons coconut cream
6 oz. pineapple juice (3/4 cup)
1 oz. ginger root, peeled and sliced
6 tablespoons honey
2 tablespoons fresh lemon juice

Peanut Satay Sauce:
1/2 cup creamy peanut butter
1/3 cup coconut cream
1/2 cup pineapple Juice
1 teaspoon sesame oil
1 teaspoon ginger root, peeled and sliced
3 tablespoons lite soy sauce
Pinch cayenne pepper or to taste

1 cup raw white rice, cooked according to package directions
4 green onions (scallions), chopped
Bamboo skewers

Mix all marinade ingredients together and marinate chicken pieces 30 minutes to 1 hour. Meanwhile, prepare Peanut Satay Sauce:

Mix all sauce ingredients together in medium saucepan and heat, stirring to simmer. Cover and let simmer until ready to serve.

Skewer chicken pieces on bamboo skewers and grill on both sides.

Serve chicken on 3/4 cup hot rice per serving with sauce. Sprinkle chopped scallions over top of each portion.

Nutritional info. per serving:

Calories	779	
Protein	55	g
Carbohydrate	78	g
Fat	33	%
Sodium	1000	mg
Cholesterol	98	mg
Fiber	3	g

Note: Most of the fat in this recipe comes from the coconut cream which is high in saturated fat. Therefore enjoy the Chicken Satay only occasionally.

Cafe Phoenix

4403 W. Tradewinds Ave., Lauderdale-by-the-Sea (305)351-0221

Executive Chef William Ludwig, who trained in such four star restaurants as Cafe Max and the Morada Cafe, is now creating his style of "New American Southwestern" cuisine at Cafe Phoenix. His mentor is Mennan Tekeli, formerly executive chef at Regines in the Grand Bay Hotel in Miami.

♥ Mushroom and Sweet Pepper Quesadilla with Black Bean Chili, Tomato Salsa and Lime Sour Cream
Yield: 4 generous portions

Black Bean Chili:
1 cup dried or 3 cups cooked (canned) black beans
1 tablespoon vegetable oil
1/4 large (about 2-3 oz.) Bermuda onion, finely diced
1 stalk celery, finely diced
1/2 carrot, finely diced
1/2 red pepper, finely diced
1/2 yellow pepper, finely diced
2 tablespoons minced cilantro
1/2 teaspoon chopped shallots
1/2 teaspoon minced garlic
1 1/2 teaspoons cumin
1/2 cup chicken stock
1/4 cup honey
2 tablespoons barbeque sauce (any brand)
1/2 teaspoon chili powder
Pepper to taste

Rinse dried black beans and soak overnight. Cook in large stockpot with 6 cups water until tender. Reserve.

In a separate saute pan, heat oil over medium heat and saute onions, celery and carrots until onions are translucent; add to black beans. Add diced peppers to black beans; add remaining ingredients and heat through, stirring. Adjust seasoning and hold until ready to assemble quesadilla.

Mushroom and Sweet Pepper Mix:
1 tablespoon vegetable oil
1/2 teaspoon minced garlic

1/2 teaspoon minced shallot
1 red pepper, julienned
1 yellow pepper, julienned
1/4 Bermuda onion, julienned
1/4 Spanish onion, julienned
1/2 jalapeno pepper, finely minced
1 1/2 teaspoons cumin or to taste
1 tablespoon minced cilantro
5 oz. common mushrooms or a mixture of different exotic mushrooms
1/4 cup chicken stock
Pepper to taste

Heat oil in large saute pan and saute garlic and shallots. Add peppers, onions and jalapeno pepper and cook until onions are translucent. Stir in spices, mushrooms and chicken stock. Season to taste.

Tomato Salsa:
2 tomatoes, peeled and diced
1/3 Bermuda onion, finely diced
1/2 jalapeno pepper, finely minced
1/4 bunch cilantro, minced
2 tablespoons vegetable oil
1/4 cup balsamic vinegar
1 1/2 oz. lime juice
1 tablespoon cumin
1 teaspoon minced garlic
1 teaspoon minced shallot
Pepper to taste

Combine all ingredients in a mixing bowl and mix. Adjust seasoning to taste.

Lime Sour Cream:
4 tablespoons light sour cream or plain lowfat yogurt
2 tablespoons lime juice (1-2 limes)

Blend ingredients together well.

Assembly:
4 - 12 inch diameter flour tortilla shells

4 oz. mixture of shredded cheddar and monterey jack cheese

Sprinkle tortilla shells with cheese mixture. Top with a portion of hot Mushroom and Sweet Pepper Mix and fold tortilla shell in a half moon shape. Cut into three triangles and place each triangle with the points facing center on large serving plates. Fill the spaces between each triangle with Black Bean Chili. Place a portion of Tomato Salsa in the middle of the plate where the points of the triangles meet. Serve with a dollop of the Lime Sour Cream.

Nutritional info. per serving:

Calories	756	
Protein	29	g
Carbohydrate	106	g
Fat	33	%
Sodium	659	mg
Cholesterol	26	mg
Fiber	20	g

Note: With lowfat cheddar and monterey jack cheese the fat and calorie content will decrease.

Cafe Seville
2768 East Oakland Park Blvd., Ft. Lauderdale (305)565-1148

A restaurant with a touch of Spain. Antonio (Chef) and Jose Servan (Owner/Manager) learned from a master...their father in Spain!

♥ Caracoles Riojana
Escargots sauteed with Garlic, Tomato, Mushrooms and Sherry Wine
Yield: 1 serving

1 tablespoon olive oil
3 1/2 oz. escargots
4 mushrooms, sliced
1 clove garlic, minced
1/2 cup whole, peeled and crushed tomatoes
1/2 teaspoon chopped basil
1/4 cup Sherry
Pinch red pepper
Pinch pepper

Heat olive oil in medium pan and saute escargots; add mushrooms and garlic, and saute. Add remaining ingredients and cook for 1 minute. Serve in clay casserole (if available).

Nutritional info. per serving

Calories	380	
Protein	26	g
Carbohydrate	21	g
Fat	33	%
Sodium	220	mg
Cholesterol	65	mg
Fiber	2	g

15th Street Fisheries

1900 E. 15th Street, Ft. Lauderdale (305)763-2777

Michael Hurst, owner of 15th Street Fisheries, is also a Professor with the F.I.U.'s School of Hospitality Management in Miami and past President of the National Restaurant Association. A Magna Cum Laude graduate of the Restaurant Management Program at Michigan State University, he is a captivating speaker who speaks at more than 40 meetings a year both nationally and internationally, and is a consultant with such clients as Walt Disney World and Lion Breweries of New Zealand.
His most memorable experience - was his first visit to New York, during which time he visited 42 restaurants between the hours of 6 p.m. to 1 a.m.; yet never got to eat dinner!
Michael's mentor - Win Schuler.

♥ Sunflower Wheat Bread
Yield: 2 - 1 1/4 lb. loaves. 12 servings/loaf

1 1/2 cups water
2 - 1/4 oz. pkgs. dry active yeast
1 tablespoon sugar
1/2 tablespoon honey
1 tablespoon molasses
2 tablespoons sunflower oil
2 tablespoons onion, finely minced and softened in 1/4 cup hot water
1 1/2 teaspoons salt
1 1/2 cups whole wheat flour
2 1/2 cups bread flour
1 egg
1/3 cup skim milk
2 1/2 oz. sunflower seeds

Heat water in small saucepan to approx. 110 F., until warm but not hot to touch. Pour water into large mixing bowl or into bowl of electric mixer that has a dough hook attachment. Add yeast, sugar, honey, molasses, oil and onion, and stir. Add salt and whole wheat flour, and stir.

Stir in bread flour until dough starts to form a ball. Continue to add flour, while mixing at low speed with dough hook attachment for electric mixer or while kneading bread on a floured surface, if kneading by hand. Knead by machine approx. 6-7 minutes or by hand 8-10 minutes. Add more bread flour, if necessary, until dough pulls away from the bowl and is no longer sticky.

Turn dough into lightly oiled bowl, turning once and cover with damp towel or plastic wrap. Let dough proof 1 hr. or until doubled in bulk.

Punch dough down and let rest 5 minutes. Scale and shape dough into 2 even round loaves.

Mix egg together with milk and brush loaves well with mixture. Coat tops of loaves with sunflower seeds.

Place loaves on baking sheets that have been sprayed with a vegetable oil cooking spray and proof until doubled, approx. 35-45 minutes.

Preheat oven to 350 F and bake loaves approx. 35-45 minutes or until golden brown and they sound "hollow" to the touch. Cool at least 20 minutes before slicing.

Nutritional info. per serving:

Calories	118	
Protein	8	g
Carbohydrate	14	g
Fat	24	%
Sodium	140	mg
Cholesterol	9	mg
Fiber	2	g

♥ Rum Raisin Bread
Yield: 1 - 8" X 8" pan. 16 servings

1/2 cup margarine (1 stick)
3/4 cup sugar
1 egg
1/2 teaspoon each Almond, Coconut, Rum and Banana extracts (Banana Liqueur may be substituted)
1/4 teaspoon lemon juice
2 cups skim milk
1/4 teaspoon salt
2 3/4 cups flour
1 1/2 teaspoons baking powder
1 large biscuit Shredded Wheat, crumbled
3/4 cup granola cereal
1/2 cup raisins
1 tablespoon Rum
Appleton Rum

Preheat oven to 350 F.

In large mixing bowl, cream together margarine and sugar. Add egg and beat until well incorporated. Add extracts, lemon juice, 1/2 of the milk and salt. Stir in 1/2 of the flour, then the remaining milk, shredded wheat, granola, raisins, rum and baking powder that has been sifted with the remaining flour.

Pour batter into an 8" X 8" pan that has been sprayed with a vegetable oil cooking spray and bake 1 - 1 1/2 hours or until toothpick inserted in center is almost dry.

To serve, brush cut squares with Appleton Rum (it MUST be Appleton Rum!) and lightly toast first.

Nutritional info. per serving:

Calories	237	
Protein	5	g
Carbohydrate	38	g
Fat	28	%
Sodium	163	mg
Cholesterol	14	mg
Fiber	2	g

Gibby's
2900 N.E. 12th Terrace, Ft. Lauderdale (305)565-2929

Art Goodman, Pastry Chef/Head Baker, went to the University of Nevada College of Hotel/Restaurant Management. Art received his training the "old fashioned way," working in small shops throughout New Jersey.
Two memorable occasions stand out in his mind:
Baking a 8 by 12 foot cake for 3,000 people for Miami Beach's 75th Birthday Party!
Helping bake 2 dozen bagels each day which were delivered to Elizabeth Taylor and Richard Burton's suite at Caesars Palace, where they were working on a picture.
At different times his mentor has been different people, but he specifically cites Albert Kumin, a Swiss Pastry Chef at The World Trade Center.

♥ Apple Pillows
Yield: 4 servings

1/4 cup golden (yellow) raisins
1/4 cup dried apricots, chopped to raisin size
1/2 oz. (1 tablespoon) Brandy
2 large baking apples (1/2/portion)
4 sheets Phyllo dough
3 tablespoons melted margarine

Mix:
1 1/2 teaspoons cinnamon
1/3 cup sugar
Pinch of nutmeg (if you like cloves, add a pinch)

Preheat oven to 350-375 F.
Mix raisins and apricots, sprinkle with brandy and soak for 1 hour or more.

Peel apples, cut into halves, remove stems and core (use melon baller). Score apples on opposite side of core, by making cuts 1/2 way through to make baking easier and faster.

Take 1 phyllo sheet, brush margarine on 1/2 and fold in half. Brush scored side of apple with margarine, sprinkle cinnamon-sugar mix on top, and turn and place on phyllo.

Put 1/4 raisin and apricot mixture on inside (cored) part of apple. Fold 4 corners of phyllo into center. Turn over and place on baking sheet that has been sprayed with a vegetable oil cooking spray. Brush with margarine and sprinkle more cinnamon-sugar on top.

Bake for 25-30 minutes, or until golden brown.

Nutritional info. per serving

Calories	292	
Protein	3	g
Carbohydrate	52	g
Fat	26	%
Sodium	162	mg
Cholesterol	-	
Fiber	2	g

♥ To lower fat and calories, spray a vegetable oil cooking spray, instead of margarine, on phyllo sheets. Can serve on softened vanilla ice milk or nonfat frozen yogurt.

Il Giardino

609 East Las Olas Blvd., Ft. Lauderdale (305)763-3733

Chef Larry Lombardo spent 10 years training in French Kitchens before returning to his native Italian cuisine. He has been with Il Giardino for 10 years; the last four as a partner in the restaurant..

♥ Pasta e Fagioli Soup
Yield: 4 servings

2 tablespoons olive oil
1 large onion, finely chopped
7 oz. can plum tomatoes, drained and coarsely chopped
1- 22 oz. can northern (white) beans
1 quart (4 cups) chicken stock
1 tablespoon minced garlic
2 bay leaves
Pinch each dried basil and oregano
2 oz. dried pasta, such as small shells
4 tablespoons grated parmesan cheese

Heat olive oil in large stockpot and saute onions over moderate heat until translucent. Add all other ingredients and bring to a simmer. Simmer 30 minutes or longer before serving, stirring occasionally.

Serve each portion topped with 1 tablespoon parmesan cheese.

Nutritional info. per serving:

Calories	431	
Protein	25	g
Carbohydrate	58	g
Fat	24	%
Sodium	933	mg
Cholesterol	8	mg
Fiber	14	g

La Ferme

1601 East Sunrise Blvd., Ft. Lauderdale (305)764-0987

Chef Henri and Marie Paule Terrier have been the proprietors for 16 years. A delightful man from France, Henri started apprenticing at the age of 14 and has experience from many different restaurants!

♥ Flounder aux Epinards et Champignons (Flounder with Spinach and Mushrooms)
Yield: 4 servings

1 1/2 tablespoons oil
1 shallot, chopped
1 small garlic clove, chopped
1 tablespoon chopped parsley
1/2 lb. fresh mushrooms, sliced
1/2 lb. fresh spinach leaves
4 - 5-6 oz. flounder fillets
Pepper

Heat oil in a large saute pan and lightly saute the shallots, garlic and parsley. Add mushrooms and spinach, saute quickly to mix. Place the flounder flat in the pan so that it is surrounded by the mushroom and spinach mixture. Add pepper and cover tightly with foil; boil approx. 4- 6 minutes.

Nutritional info. per serving

Calories	222	
Protein	33	g
Carbohydrate	6	g
Fat	30	%
Sodium	111	mg
Cholesterol	53	mg
Fiber	2	g

Henri suggests the dish with snapper as well.

La Reserve

3115 N.E. 32nd Ave., Ft. Lauderdale (305)563-6644

Guy and Richard Teboul, Proprietors. On the intracoastal waterway, La Reserve has won many awards including the Wine Spectator Award and the Holiday Award.

♥ Citrus Chicken Breast
Yield: 4 servings

2 lemons
2 oranges
1 large pink grapefruit
4 - 6 oz. chicken breastas, skinless, boneless
4 oz. (8 tablespoons) honey
1 tablespoon margarine
4 oz. (1/2 cup) dry white wine
4 oz. (1/2 cup) chicken broth

Take a 1/2 lemon, a 1/2 orange, and 1/4 of grapefruit and peel, skin and cut in small wedges to use to garnish plates. Squeeze juices out of the rest of the fruit into a bowl; add chicken and marinate for 20 minutes.

Take chicken out of marinade and reserve.

Brush both sides of chicken with honey. Heat margarine in a large pan and cook chicken at a high temperature to give a nice color, then reduce heat (add chicken broth if needed). When cooked, remove chicken from pan also removing excess fat. Heat pan, pour in wine, wait 1 minute, then pour the reserved juices in; heat thoroughly and reduce for a few minutes.

To serve: Pour 1 teaspoon of the reduced juices on each serving of chicken and garnish with a wedge of lemon, orange and grapefruit.

Nutritional info. per serving

Calories	273	
Protein	36	g
Carbohydrate	16	g
Fat	18	%
Sodium	202	mg
Cholesterol	96	mg
Fiber	1	g

Chef's serving suggestion: Guy and Richard suggest that steamed rice, snow peas and spinach be served with the chicken. Serve with a Fume Blanc from California or the Loire Valley.

Paesano Restaurant
1301 East Las Olas Blvd., Ft. Lauderdale (305)467-3266

Mario and Maria Spinaci, Proprietors. Mario, the Chef, was given an award for professional culinary leadership from Chefs in America foundation.

♥ Linguini e Broccoli
Yield: 4 servings

1 lb. bunch broccoli, trimmed and chopped
8 oz. dry linguini
2 tablespoons olive oil
8 garlic cloves, minced
1/2 cup chicken broth
Pinch or to taste cayenne pepper
4 tablespoons grated parmesan cheese

Steam broccoli for five to eight minutes or until tender crisp in large pot. Remove broccoli and hold. Add enough water to the pot to cook pasta in. Cook pasta according to package directions and drain.

In a large skillet, heat olive oil over medium heat and saute garlic until soft. Add chicken broth and pepper and heat through. Add the cooked broccoli and pasta and toss together.

Serve each portion topped with 1 tablespoon grated parmesan cheese.

Nutritional info. per serving:

Calories	293	
Protein	12	g
Carbohydrate	42	g
Fat	28	%
Sodium	224	mg
Cholesterol	4	mg
Fiber	6	g

Pier 66 Resort & Marina
2301 SE 17th Street Causeway, Ft. Lauderdale (305)525-6666

Executive Chef John Turner was born and raised in England, where he completed his apprenticeship training and culinary education. His work experience includes chef positions with luxury cruise ships, the Marriott Corporation and properties in Bermuda. He is an active member of the Chaine des Rotisseurs and the International Foodservice Executives Association, and teaches foodservice classes at the hotel to students in the Nova University Hospitality Education Program. He was named one of the top 500 master chefs of America by "Chefs of America."
His most memorable experience was hosting the 25th anniversary of Preferred Hotels at Pier 66 in 1988.

♥ Amaretto Souffle
Yield: 6 servings

3 tablespoons honey
1/4 cup fresh orange juice
1 teaspoon lemon juice
1 teaspoon grated orange rind
1/2 teaspoon grated lemon rind
1/4 cup Amaretto or other almond liqueur
1 tablespoon arrowroot mixed with 1 tablespoon orange juice
2 whole eggs, separated + 2 egg whites

Combine honey, orange and lemon juice, grated rinds and liqueur in a saucepan and bring to a boil. Remove pan from heat and whisk in arrowroot/juice mixture and return pan to heat. Bring to the boiling point, stirring. When thickened, remove from heat and allow to cool 15 minutes.

Preheat oven to 400 F.
Spray 1 quart souffle dish with a vegetable oil cooking spray.
Whisk egg yolks quickly into cooled mixture.
In a separate bowl with clean beaters whip egg whites until stiff but not dry. Fold beaten egg whites into cooled egg yolk mixture. Pour into prepare souffle dish. Bake in oven 15-20 minutes, or until puffed and golden.
Serve immediately.

Nutritional info. per serving:

Calories	114	
Protein	3	g
Carbohydrate	17	g
Fat	14	%
Sodium	38	mg
Cholesterol	71	mg
Fiber	-	

Primavera Restaurant
830 East Oakland Park Blvd., Ft. Lauderdale (305)564-6363

Chef Aldo Rabottini graduated from hotel school in Italy, with apprenticeships at such properties as the Hotel Danieli in Venice and the Excelsier in Florence.
His most memorable experience was in 1989 when he took care of Frank Sinatra and a party of 20 guests, with only 20 minutes warning to get ready!

♥ Risotto con Vodka e Limone
(Risotto with Vodka and Lemon)
Yield: 4 servings

1 tablespoon olive oil
1/3 small onion, chopped
1 cup raw Arborio rice
2 tablespoons Vodka
3 cups chicken broth
Juice of 1/2 lemon, plus zest of lemon
3 tablespoons cream cheese*

In a medium saucepan, heat olive oil over medium heat and saute onions until translucent. Stir in Vodka and rice and stir until rice is well coated.

In a separate pot, heat chicken broth to boiling. Add hot broth, slowly, to rice mixture and reduce heat to simmer. Cover and simmer 15 minutes or until "al dente." Rice should still be a bit wet.

Remove pot from heat and stir in lemon juice, zest and cream cheese.
Serve immediately with a garnish of a bit more lemon zest, if desired.

Nutritional info. per serving:

Calories	282	
Protein	8	g
Carbohydrate	39	g
Fat	27	%
Sodium	617	mg
Cholesterol	13	mg
Fiber	5	g

* To decrease fat and calorie content, substitute light cream cheese (Neufchatel).

♥ Bavarese alle Fragole
(Strawberry Bavarian Cream)
Yield: 4 servings

1 pint fresh strawberries, washed and trimmed
1 envelope unflavored gelatin
1/2 cup canned evaporated whole milk
1/3 cup sugar
Juice of 1/2 lemon
3/4 cup plain lowfat yogurt

Puree approx. 1 1/4 cups strawberries, reserving the rest for garnish. Press the strawberry puree through a strainer and reserve 1/3 of the puree. Put the rest of the puree in a bowl.

In a small saucepan, dissolve gelatin in milk and heat, stirring, over low heat until gelatin is dissolved and milk is warm to the touch. Add the sugar, lemon juice and the softened gelatin/milk mixture to the bowl of strawberry puree. Place bowl in refrigerator and cool just until the mixture begins to set. Fold in plain yogurt, then turn mixture into 4 - 6 oz. souffle cups or other molds that have been sprayed with a vegetable oil cooking spray. Let bavarian set at least two hours.

To serve: Pour some of the reserved strawberry puree on the bottom of each serving plate. Unmold the bavarians onto puree. Garnish with reserved strawberries.

Nutritional info. per serving:

Calories	183	
Protein	7	g
Carbohydrate	33	g
Fat	15	%
Sodium	67	g
Cholesterol	12	mg
Fiber	3	g

Shirttail Charlie's

400 S.W. 3rd Ave., Ft. Lauderdale (305)463-FISH

Shirttail Charlie's features fresh Florida fish, conch, shrimp, alligator, steaks and chicken, with casual dining poolside, downstairs, or elegant dining, upstairs.
Chef Leslie Finley, originally from Cape Cod, Ma. became interested in becoming a chef from his aunt, who owned the Wequasset Inn in Cape Cod.
His most memorable cooking experience - winning a "Conch Off" at Pier 66 in Ft. Lauderdale, at which he could barely keep up with the demand for tastes of his dish!

♥ Grouper "in the Bag"
Yield: 1 serving

1 oz. each (1 small stalk) celery, (1/10 large) red onion, (1/4 large)
    zucchini and (1 medium) carrot, julienned
1 oz. (2 tablespoons) margarine, melted
1 tablespoon grated parmesan cheese
2 tablespoons seasoned bread crumbs
2 tablespoons lemon juice
2 tablespoons white wine
Pepper and paprika to taste
6 oz. grouper fillet

Preheat oven to 400 F.
    Combine vegetables and all remaining ingredients together and spread on top of grouper. Carefully place grouper in a brown paper (lunch) bag. Roll ends of bag up tightly. Brush the entire outside of the bag with vegetable oil (or spray with vegetable oil cooking spray), especially the ends to help "seal" the bag closed.
    Place bag on baking sheet and bake in hot oven 15 minutes or until bag is puffed (from steam created during cooking).
    Slit bag open carefully on serving plates immediately before serving - watch the heat of the steam!

Nutritional info. per serving:

Calories	428	
Protein	42	g
Carbohydrate	30	g
Fat	29	%
Sodium	539	mg
Cholesterol	68	mg
Fiber	3	g

Chef's serving suggestion: Serve with rice or red skinned potatoes.

Stan's Restaurant and Lounge
3300 East Commercial Blvd., Ft. Lauderdale (305)772-3777

Chef Jacques Hodent was born in Paris, where he also attended cooking school and began his cooking career. His international cooking experience includes chef positions in Montreal, Washington D.C., St. Martin and New York.
His most disasterous affair was a wedding in the Time Life Building in New York when the wedding table WITH the wedding cake fell down!
Chef Jacques admires and longs to dine with Paul Prudomme of New Orleans.

♥ Halibut Fillets in Lettuce Leaves
Yield: 4 servings

4 - 6 oz. halibut fillets
1 cup dry white wine
14-16 leaf lettuce leaves
2 small leeks, white parts only, cut into crosswise slices
2 small carrots, sliced
1 cup fish stock (or bottled clam broth)
2 tablespoons cooked mushrooms, pureed
2 tablespoons lowfat cottage cheese
Pepper to taste

Marinate fish in wine for 15 minutes. Remove fish and reserve the wine. Spread lettuce leaves on work surface and arrange fish on top. Sprinkle fish with pepper and scatter leek and carrot slices over.

Wrap lettuce around fish and vegetables, making four "packages." Place packages in medium-sized saucepan that has been sprayed with a vegetable oil cooking spray and that has 1" sides and a tight-fitting lid.

Pour reserved wine over fish and add enough of the fish stock to cover fish. Simmer fish, covered, over low heat for 15 minutes. Remove packages from pan and keep them warm in the oven.

Reduce cooking liquid in pan to about 1/2 cup. Blend in mushroom puree and cottage cheese and keep sauce warm - do not boil.

Arrange fish packages on serving plates and serve sauce on the side.

Nutritional info. per serving:

Calories	268	
Protein	38	g
Carbohydrate	8	g
Fat	14	%
Sodium	140	mg
Cholesterol	55	mg
Fiber	2	g

The Down Under
3000 East Oakland Park Blvd., Ft. Lauderdale (305)563-4123

The Down Under, as well as Casa Vecchia in Ft. Lauderdale and La Vieille Maison in Boca Raton, is owned by Al Kocab and Leonce Picot. The Down Under features American and European favorites in a beautiful setting on the Intracoastal Waterway. The Down Under has been awarded the Wine Spectator Grand Award from 1981-1990.

♥ Snapper Down Under
Yield: 4 servings

4 - 6 oz. snapper fillet
1/4 cup skim milk
1 egg or 1/4 cup egg substitute
1/3 cup flour
2 tablespoons peanut oil
1/4 teaspoon white pepper
8 oz. (4 cups) white mushrooms, diced
1 cup white wine
1 tablespoon margarine
1/2 cup cleaned and sliced leeks
2 teaspoons lemon juice

Preheat oven to 400 F.
Mix milk and egg together in a small bowl. Dip snapper fillets in mixture, then dust with flour.

In a large skillet, heat oil over medium high heat. Carefully put snapper in pan, season and brown each side, approx. 2-3 minutes per side. Add mushrooms and wine, and bake 10-12 minutes in oven - in skillet, if ovenproof, or baking pan.

Remove pan from oven and place back on medium high heat. Remove fish to serving plates. Add margarine, leeks and lemon juice to pan and bring to a boil, stirring constantly. Spoon sauce over fish and serve.

Nutritional info. per serving:

Calories	383	
Protein	40	g
Carbohydrate	14	g
Fat	33	%
Sodium	191	mg
Cholesterol	116	mg*
Fiber	2	g

* Analyzed with whole egg.

♥ Gazpacho
Yield: 4 servings (1 quart total)

1 tablespoon extra virgin olive oil
2 chives, chopped
1 clove garlic, peeled and crushed
2 whole peeled tomatoes
1/2 green bell pepper, seeds removed
1 medium cucumber, peeled and seeded
1 small red onion
2 leaves fresh basil
1 sprig fresh thyme
1 sprig fresh tarragon
1 cup tomato juice
1 teaspoon sugar
2 tablespoons Worcestershire sauce
1 teaspoon pepper
4 tablespoons unseasoned croutons

Combine all ingredients together in blender or food processor and process until relatively smooth, but with some chunky pieces. More tomato juice can be added to thin, if desired. Garnish with croutons.

Nutritional info. per serving:

Calories	101	
Protein	2	g
Carbohydrate	15	g
Fat	33	%
Sodium	417	mg
Cholesterol	-	
Fiber	3	g

The Flambe Room

Times Square Plaza 3042 N. Federal Highway, Ft. Lauderdale (305)563-7455

Dennis Burke, one of the Chefs at The Flambe Room, came to Fort Lauderdale seeking warm weather and light cooking. He has worked at Le Dome, Pier 66 and The Plum Room at Yesterdays.
Most memorable meal - "A Spinach Stuffed Veal Loin that knocked Robert (Wild West) Conrad out of his chair one night."
His mentor - Chef Jean Claude Galan of The Mansion on Turtle Creek in Dallas.

♥ Veal Scallopini Stella
created and named after Maria Talerico (one of the owners).
Yield: 4 servings

Marinara Sauce:
2 teaspoons olive oil
6 cloves garlic, chopped
1- 15 oz. can imported whole plum tomatoes, crushed
2 tablespoons dried sweet basil (or 1/3 cup fresh basil)

Heat olive oil in heavy saucepan; add garlic, cook until lightly browned. Add tomatoes with juice and cook 15 minutes. Add basil, cook for 5 additional minutes. Set aside.

1/2 oz. (1 tablespoon) olive oil
1/2 cup chicken or beef (broth) stock
16 - 1 oz. slices veal loin
Approx. 1 tablespoon flour
2 tablespoons chopped fresh garlic
5- 20 small pepperoncini peppers (depending on your taste for spice)
1 cup sliced mushrooms (domestic or wild)
1/3 cup dry red wine
1/4 teaspoon oregano leaves
1/4 teaspoon chopped fresh basil
2 teaspoons chopped fresh parsley
1/4 teaspoon freshly ground pepper

Heat a large heavy skillet on a hot flame. Add olive oil (broth or vegetable oil cooking spray when needed), and saute lightly floured veal one minute on each side. Remove veal from pan and set aside. Lower heat to medium and add the garlic, peppers and mushrooms to the pan. When mushrooms have begun to brown, add the red wine and then the marinara sauce with the herbs and seasonings. Cook until sauce is bubbly; return the veal to the sauce, heat and serve.

Note: Although pieces of veal loin are tender enough to eat without tedious pounding, we recommend flattening them a bit to ensure uniformity in cooking.

Nutritional info. per serving

Calories	296	
Protein	34	g
Carbohydrate	11	g
Fat	35	%
Sodium	342	mg
Cholesterol	114	mg
Fiber	1	g

♥ Try using Turkey medallions too.

The Left Bank
214 S.E. Sixth Ave., Ft. Lauderdale (305)462-5376

Jean-Pierre Brehier, the Chef/Owner, graduated from the Culinary Cooking School of Nice. He came to us from France after getting experience with Roge Verge (his mentor, whose philosophy is to use only the best and freshest ingredients. He also felt, as does Jean-Pierre, that cooking "must be FUN and feel good")! While working as a Sous Chef on the Renaissance Cruise Ship, they stopped over for a few days in Port Everglades. Jean-Pierre liked it so much he moved here. After working in several restaurants, he opened The Left Bank at 24 years of age.
His most memorable meal was when he cooked Bouillabaisse for Jackie Gleason without knowing who he was. After dinner Jackie Gleason came to the kitchen and gave him a $200 tip!

♥ Breast of Chicken with a Champagne Mustard Sauce
Yield: 4 servings

4 - 6 oz. chicken breasts, skinless, boneless
1/4 cup flour
6 teaspoons margarine
1/2 cup chicken broth
2 shallots, finely minced
1/2 teaspoon fresh ginger, finely chopped
1/4 cup chopped tomatoes
1/4 cup sliced mushrooms
1 oz. (2 tablespoons) Brandy
1/4 cup champagne
1/4 cup evaporated skim milk
1 teaspoon cornstarch dissolved in 1/4 cup evaporated skim milk
2 tablespoons Dijon mustard
Pepper to taste

Lightly dredge chicken breasts in flour. In a skillet large enough to hold the chicken without crowding, heat 4 teaspoons of margarine (set aside the remaining 2 teaspoons to soften); when it turns golden brown, add the breasts of chicken and cook 2-3 minutes on each side (add chicken broth when needed). While moving the pan back and forth to avoid sticking, add the shallots, ginger, tomatoes and mushrooms, and cook for 1 minute.

Deglaze with brandy and flambe (if possible). After the flame goes out, add the champagne and evaporated skim milk and let reduce for 3-4 minutes. Add cornstarch mixture, bring to a boil stirring constantly, and thicken. Transfer the chicken breasts to a warm platter.

In the same skillet add the mustard and the remaining softened margarine, 1 teaspoon at a time, to sauce. Heat a few seconds until all the margarine is melted, season and pour over the chicken.

Nutritional info. per serving

Calories	300	
Protein	38	g
Carbohydrate	8	g
Fat	27	%
Sodium	346	mg
Cholesterol	97	mg
Fiber	-	

♥ Try with Tuna Steaks.

♥ Orange and Honey Sauce
Yield: 6 oz.

1 teaspoon margarine
2 shallots, chopped finely
1/4 cup red wine vinegar
1/4 cup red wine
1 tablespoon honey
2 tablespoons frozen orange juice concentrate
1/4 cup evaporated skim milk
Pepper to taste

Heat margarine in saucepan and cook shallots for 1 minute. Add vinegar, red wine and reduce by one third. Add honey, orange juice concentrate and evaporated skim milk, stirring constantly and bring mixture to boil. Adjust seasoning and serve.

Nutritional info. per 1 Tablespoon

Calories	22	
Protein	1	g
Carbohydrate	4	g
Fat	10	%
Sodium	12	mg
Cholesterol	-	
Fiber	-	

♥ Use with pork, beef, chicken...

Yesterday's on the Intracoastal

2881 East Oakland Park Blvd., Ft. Lauderdale (305)561-4400

Executive Chef Fred Gilbert trained under a chef who was the personal chef to Charles de Gaulle and who had trained under the great culinary master, Auguste Escoffier.
His most disasterous experience was on Mothers Day when Fred was just a young apprentice. He did not take the initiative to put 60 Prime Ribs of beef in to roast, after having been told by his most intimidating chef to season them. Hours later, when the chef ordered Fred to pull the roasts from the oven, he had to tell the chef he had not cooked them yet! Fred received a reprimanding like none he has seen since, but certainly learned a lesson from the experience!

♥ Key Lime Pasta Vinaigrette
Yield: 4 servings

Dressing:
1/4 cup orange juice
1 tablespoon lime juice
1/4 cup honey
1/4 cup safflower oil
1 1/2 oz. raspberry vinegar

4 cups cooked macaroni or small shell pasta
6 oz. bay scallops, steamed or poached
6 oz. peeled and deveined shrimp, cooked
4 oz. crabmeat
1 grapefruit, sectioned
2 cups chopped romaine lettuce
2 large oranges, sectioned

Whisk all dressing ingredients together in a medium bowl. Chill until ready to use.

To serve: Toss pasta in dressing. Line serving plates with 1/2 cup each romaine lettuce; top with pasta portions. Arrange seafood over the top of pasta and garnish with fresh fruit sections.

Nutritional info. per serving:

Calories	470	
Protein	27	g
Carbohydrate	57	g
Fat	30	%
Sodium	215	mg
Cholesterol	107	mg
Fiber	4	g

Old Florida Seafood House
1414 NE 26th Street, Wilton Manors (305)566-1044 4535 Pine Island Road, Sunrise (305)572-0444

♥ Chicken or Shrimp Diane
Yield: 1 serving

1/4 cup raw rice; cooked according to package directions
1 tablespoon margarine
1 1/2 oz. (3/4 cup) mushrooms, sliced
1 1/2 oz. (1/4 medium) onions, chopped
1 oz. (about 4-5) scallions, chopped
2 garlic cloves, chopped
1 teaspoon or to taste blackened or "Cajun" seasoning*
6 oz. chicken breast, skinless, boneless or 4 oz. raw shrimp
2 teaspoons chopped parsley
2 oz. (1/4 cup) white wine

Heat margarine over medium heat in medium skillet. Saute mushrooms, onions, scallions and garlic for five minutes or until onions are soft.

Add seasoning, chicken or shrimp, parsley and wine and stir until chicken or shrimp is done. Serve over rice.

* Use South Seas Plantation Blackening Mix or try K-Pauls Seafood Magic with shrimp or Poultry Magic with chicken.

Nutritional info. per serving:

	Shrimp		Chicken	
Calories	444		510	
Protein	28	g	44	g
Carbohydrate	41	g	40	g
Fat	29	%	25	%
Sodium	322	mg	264	mg
Cholesterol	172	mg**	98	mg
Fiber	4	g	4	g

** If you are watching your cholesterol, decrease the amount of shrimp called for in the recipe.

La Tavernetta

8455 West McNab Rd., Tamarac (305)722-1831

Carol and G.G. Romano, Owners. G.G., the Chef, grew up learning the business from his family. He does his own shopping and baking as well as cooking!
Their most memorable meals include entertaining celebrities such as: Liza Minneli, Don Johnson (who arrived and left by helicopter) and Tip O'Neill. Carol also recalls a night when a man came in by taxi who was in-between flights. He had heard about the restaurant from someone in Colombia!

♥ Minestrone di Savoia
Yield: 10 servings

1 medium onion, finely chopped
2 tablespoons margarine
2 celery stalks, diced
2 carrots, diced
2 zucchini, diced
2 medium boiling potatoes, peeled and diced
Pepper to taste
4 large ripe tomatoes, peeled and chopped
1 cup cooked red beans
1 tablespoon tomato paste
8 cups meat stock (or canned beef broth)
1/2 cup Arborio rice (or small pasta shapes)
2 tablespoons chopped parsley
6 tablespoons grated Parmesan cheese

Combine onion and margarine in a large stock pot and cook stirring frequently. Add celery, carrots, zucchini and potatoes. Season with pepper; cook stirring for 5 minutes. Add tomatoes, beans, tomato paste and broth, bring to boil; lower and simmer for 2 hours. Add rice, cook uncovered over high heat for 20 minutes or longer, until rice is cooked. At this point, the longer you cook, the thicker the soup becomes. Pour soup into bowls and stir grated cheese into each portion.

(**Note** - if soup becomes too thick, add water and thin to desired consistency).

Nutritional info. per serving

Calories	139	
Protein	7	g
Carbohydrate	20	g
Fat	22	%
Sodium	814	mg
Cholesterol	3	mg
Fiber	3	g

♥ Minestra Papazoi
(Sweetcorn, Barley and Bean soup)
Yield: 8 servings

2 slices Canadian bacon, finely chopped
2 garlic cloves, crushed
2 tablespoons olive oil
1 cup pearl barley
1- 16 oz. can navy beans
1 cup fresh or frozen corn kernels
9 cups light (chicken or veal) stock (or broth)
1 cup diced raw potato
1 tablespoon chopped parsley
Fresh ground pepper

Heat oil in large stock pot, add the bacon and garlic; cook until golden brown. Remove from pot; add barley to pot and saute for 1-2 minutes (use a vegetable oil cooking spray if needed).

Add beans, corn, bacon, garlic and stock, bring to a boil. Lower heat and simmer for 45 minutes. Add potato and cook 1 1/2 hours until the vegetables and potato are tender. Stir in parsley, add pepper to taste.

Nutritional info. per serving

Calories	215	
Protein	11	g
Carbohydrate	33	g
Fat	21	%
Sodium	1116	mg
Cholesterol	4	mg
Fiber	3	

Brasserie Max

The Fashion Mall 321 North University Dr., Plantation (305)424-8000

William "Charlie" Brown, past Executive Chef, got his formal training at Johnson and Wales University. He has previously worked at Mustard's Grill in The Napa Valley. Charlie likes straight-forward food - simple in freshness and quality - that makes a statement!
Most memorable meal - The funniest was at Mustards, where Julia Child was to have lunch. Charlie worked for hours on innovative ideas for entrees, sauces, etc. and when Julia came in, she ordered a sandwich!
His mentor- Cindy Pawlcyn (Executive Chef at Mustard's Grill)- Real Restaurants in California.

Andy Williams, Executive Chef, received his B.S. in Hotel & Restaurant Management from F.I.U. He feels that chefs "in the 90's will be preparing more and more heart healthy cuisine!" His most memorable meal was at The Coyote Cafe in Santa Fe, New Mexico.

♥ Grilled Chicken Breast with Peach and Mint Marinade Served with Peach and Plum Salsa
Yield: 4 servings

6 tablespoons peach nectar
3 tablespoons olive oil
1 1/2 tablespoons finely chopped fresh mint
1/4 teaspoon finely chopped fresh garlic
1 teaspoon finely chopped shallots
1/2 teaspoon black pepper
4 - 6 oz. chicken breasts, skinless, boneless

2 cups cooked Wild or Brown Rice

Mix all ingredients in large bowl, except rice, together and add chicken breasts. Let marinate for at least 2 hours, turning occasionally.

Peach and Plum Salsa:
2 large ripe peaches, finely diced
3 ripe plums, finely diced
2 green onions cut on bias, very thin
1/4 cup small diced roasted red pepper
1 teaspoon finely chopped fresh basil
2 1/4 teaspoons finely chopped fresh mint
2 1/4 teaspoons balsamic vinegar
2 1/4 teaspoons olive oil

Pinch black pepper

Toss all ingredients together, taste and adjust seasoning.
To assemble: Grill chicken breasts over a low fire; watch the chicken breasts because the natural sugars in the peach juice may cause the breasts to char.
Top each chicken breast with 1/4 of salsa. Serve with 1/2 cup cooked wild or brown rice per serving.

Nutritional info. per serving

Calories	467	
Protein	38	g
Carbohydrate	39	g
Fat	34	%
Sodium	85	mg
Cholesterol	96	mg
Fiber	3	g

Chef's serving suggestion: Serve with fresh steamed baby vegetables.

♥ Roasted Eggplant and Tomato Sauce
Yield: 6 servings- 1 cup/serving

* 1- 16 oz. eggplant, small diced
* 8 oz. red onion, small diced
8 oz. (8 small stalks) celery, small diced
6 oz. (3 cups) quartered button mushrooms
3 oz. (6 tablespoons) olive oil
1 tablespoon chopped garlic
* 4 cups chopped tomatoes
1 cup red wine
3/4 tablespoon black pepper
1/4 tablespoon crushed red pepper
12 cups cooked pasta

Mix together eggplant, red onion, celery and mushrooms in a large bowl. Place large saute pan (or stock pot) on stove on high heat; heat olive oil and saute garlic for one minute. Add eggplant mix, saute two minutes, stirring constantly. Add tomatoes, red wine, black pepper and crushed red pepper, stir constantly. Cover and reduce to low heat; cook for 10 minutes.

Remove from heat, uncover and stir. Add mixture to your favorite pasta.

* For added flavor, grill your vegetables first using different wood chips or charcoal.

Nutritional info. per serving

Calories	637	
Protein	19	g
Carbohydrate	102	g
Fat	22	%
Sodium	77	mg
Cholesterol	-	
Fiber	5	g

Top with 1 teaspoon of grated cheese per serving if desired.

Armadillo Cafe
4630 S.W. 64th Ave., Davie (305)791-4866

Eve Montella and Kevin McCarthy are the Chef/Owners.
Eve Montella graduated from the school of Hospitality Management at F.I.U.. An interest in culinary arts started in her mother's kitchen and has never stopped. Besides cooking in restaurants, she has directed a cooking school and a catering business.

Kevin McCarthy, a graduate of the C.I.A., has cooked in many restaurants around the country. Working in Dallas introduced him to the foods of the Southwest, and made a lasting impression. His most memorable meal was a party for Burt Reynolds: Kevin was helping cater tons of food, while they showed excerpts from the movie.

♥ Dolphin Baked in Paper with Southwest Vegetables
Yield: 2 servings

Parchment paper
1- 10-12 oz. skinned and boned dolphin fillet
Olive oil cooking spray
1/4 red pepper, cut in thin strips
1/4 yellow pepper, cut in thin strips
1 1/2 oz. jicama, cut in thin strips
1 ea. sundried tomatoes, rehydrated, cut in thin strips
1/2 oz. (1/6 cup) leek, blanched, cut in thin strips
1/4 of ancho chile stemmed, seeded and cut in thin strips
1/4 oz. (1/8 cup) mushrooms, sliced thin
2 teaspoons olive oil
Pinch ground pepper, cumin, chili powder
1 tablespoon washed and chopped cilantro
1 oz. good quality Chardonnay

Preheat oven to 350 F.

Cut parchment paper into the shape of a large heart. Spray inside with olive oil cooking spray. Place the dolphin fillet in the center of one side of the heart. Cover with the peppers, jicama, tomato, ancho chile, leek and the mushrooms. Sprinkle with olive oil, black pepper, cumin, chili powder, cilantro and a splash of chardonnay. Starting from the top seam fold to seal the edges down to the bottom. Spray with olive oil cooking spray top and bottom; place on sheet pan in oven for 15 to 20 minutes or until paper is brown and puffed up. Serve on plate or platter while still puffed up, cutting open just as you are about to eat.

Note: the following fish can be substituted - grouper, yellowtail snapper, pompano and lobster medallions.

Nutritional info. per serving

Calories	217	
Protein	30	g
Carbohydrate	8	g
Fat	27	%
Sodium	109	mg
Cholesterol	52	mg
Fiber	1	g

♥ Raspberry Sauce for Meringues
Yield: sauce for approx. 12 large meringues

Use your favorite meringue recipe; you can make them large and fill (before baking, take a wet tablespoon and press into meringue to make indentation or use a piping bag to create a "shell"), or into small cookies.

To make flavored meringues - experiment with adding 2 tablespoons cocoa, semi-sweet chocolate chips or raisins to your recipe.

1 pint fresh raspberries
1/2 to 1 cup granulated sugar

Crush berries through a sieve or strainer to remove seeds. Sweeten with the sugar and stir until sugar dissolves.

To serve: Pour the raspberry sauce on dessert plate or cup. Place a meringue on top of sauce and fill or top the meringues with a combination of fresh berries or sliced peaches.

Put blueberries in baked meringue shells for a great red, white and blue dessert!

Classic variation: Place a small scoop of frozen nonfat yogurt, sorbet or ice milk in the meringue shell and freeze. Garnish with berries and mint leaf.

Note: Fat content of meringues with raspberry sauce will be well within heart healty recipe guidelines, as the fat content of meringues and fruit is negligible.

♥ Flan
Yield: 2 servings

1 whole large egg plus 1 egg white
2 tablespoons granulated sugar
1 cup skim milk
1 teaspoon vanilla extract

Preheat oven to 350 F.
Place the egg white and whole egg in a small mixing bowl with the sugar. With an electric mixer whip this mixture until light and fluffy. Add the skim milk and vanilla and stir until well mixed.

Divide mixture between two oven-proof custard cups. Bake flans in a waterbath: set the flans in a deep baking pan and place this pan on the lower shelf of the oven. Carefully pour water in the baking pan to surround the flans. Bake the flans in this waterbath for approximately 45 minutes or until firm.

Variations: for Mocha flans add a teaspoon of instant coffee dissolved in the vanilla extract to the flan mixture.

For Caramelized flans dissolve 1/4 cup sugar in 1/4 cup water in a small skillet. Boil this mixture over high heat until the sugar caramelizes (thickens and changes to an amber color). At this point pour the caramel into the bottom of the custard cups and allow to harden. Pour the flan mixture over the caramel and bake as directed. The caramelized sugar will form a sauce under the flan.

For Apple flans slice a small baked apple and place a few slices in the bottom of each custard cup with a pinch of cinnamon. Pour the flan mixture on top and bake as directed.

Nutritional info. per serving

	Plain/Mocha		**Caramelized**		**Apple**	
Calories	141		231		183	
Protein	9	g	9	g	9	g
Carbohydrate	19	g	43	g	30	g
Fat	18	%	11	%	15	%
Sodium	122	mg	123	mg	123	mg
Cholesterol	109	mg	109	mg	109	mg
Fiber	-		-		2	g

This recipe is from Larry Berfond (formerly of Cafe D'Estournel), the owner of the New Silverado Cafe, and his Chef de Cuisine Joseph Naughton, who has been at the restaurant for the past 2 years. Joseph has worked at many restaurants including Filippo's, Gus's Clam House and The Sea Grill.

Veal (Swordfish) Farniente
Yield: 2 servings

Veal:
1 teaspoon oil
8-9 oz. veal
1 tablespoon flour

Heat olive oil in large saute pan and lightly saute veal that has been dredged in flour. Turn over.

For Swordfish:
10-12 oz. swordfish
1 teaspoon oil

Brush swordfish with oil then grill until almost cooked. Place in pan.

Veal or Swordfish:
1-2 tablespoons anisette
2 oz. chicken stock
1 cup cooked fresh spinach, well drained
1/4 oz. (4) sun dried tomatoes, rehydrated, sliced
4 oz. (1/2 cup) marinara sauce (your choice, preferably homemade)
1 oz. (1/4 cup) skim mozzarella cheese

Preheat oven to 400 F.

Add anisette and chicken stock to pan with veal or swordfish; heat. In baking pan, or saute pan if ovenproof, layer the veal or swordfish, then spinach, sun dried tomatoes and marinara sauce. Top with cheese and bake in oven for 10 minutes.

Nutritional info. per serving

	Veal		Swordfish	
Calories	351		297	
Protein	42	g	36	g
Carbohydrate	13	g	10	g
Fat	33	%	33	%
Sodium	696	mg	729	mg
Cholesterol	152	mg	66	mg
Fiber	3	g	3	g

Sheraton Bonaventure Resort and Spa

250 Racquet Club Road, Ft. Lauderdale (305)389-3300

Spa Chef Keith Stuart is a 1987 graduate of the C.I.A.
His most memorable meal was one he prepared for his company's corporate executives without any prior warning that they were coming!

Chicken Scallopini Palermo
Yield: 4 servings

4 - 6 oz. chicken breasts skinless, pounded thin
2 to 3 egg whites, mixed with 2 tablespoons water
3/4 cup whole wheat bread crumbs
1 teaspoon minced garlic
2 tablespoons raspberry vinegar
1/2 cup no sugar added raspberry fruit spread
1 cup fresh raspberries

Preheat oven to 350 F.
Dip chicken pieces in egg white mixture. Mix bread crumbs with garlic. Dip chicken pieces into bread crumb mixture, coating on both sides.

Spray a baking sheet with a vegetable oil cooking spray and place chicken pieces on baking sheet. Bake 25-30 minutes or until golden brown.

Heat raspberry vinegar in a small saucepan over medium heat. Stir in raspberry spread and heat through. Stir in about 3/4 of a cup of the fresh raspberries and remove from heat. Serve over chicken portions. Garnish with the remainder of raspberries.

Nutritional info. per serving:

Calories	396	
Protein	45	g
Carbohydrate	46	g
Fat	7	%
Sodium	289	mg
Cholesterol	99	mg
Fiber	3	g

Blueberry Crepes
Yield: 6 servings

6 prepared crepes *
3 tablespoons farmers cheese
1 tablespoon lowfat milk
1/2 cup unsweetened blueberry conserves
1 1/2 teaspoons cornstarch
1/2 cup apple juice

Garnish:
6 sprigs fresh mint
6 strawberries, stem on, cut in a fanned fashion

In a small bowl mix together farmers cheese and milk, using a fork to combine. Spread mixture very thinly over each crepe.

Heat conserves in a small non-stick saucepan. Dissolve cornstarch in the apple juice and add to the conserves; bring to a boil over medium heat, stirring frequently until mixture boils and thickens. Spread about one tablespoon of the blueberry mixture over each crepe then roll up.

Place one crepe on each of six serving plates. Spoon an additional one tablespoon of the blueberry mixture over each crepe. Garnish each with mint leaves and a strawberry fan.

Nutritional info. per serving:

Calories	143	
Protein	3	g
Carbohydrate	29	g
Fat	12	%
Sodium	129	mg
Cholesterol	43	g
Fiber	.5	g

* See Crepes with Apples and Armagnac, Arthur's 27, Lake Buena Vista Palace.

Tutti's at Weston

1342 S.W. 160 Ave., Sunrise (305)389-5200

Daphne Anderson, Past Chef, is a C.I.A. graduate. She has worked in Vermont, Palm Beach and in Miami at the Doral Saturnia Spa.
Most memorable meals - at the Armadillo Cafe. In addition, she has cooked for Dan Marino and several other Miami Dolphins at Tuttis.
Daphne's mentor - Emeril Lagasse of New Orleans.

Basic Red Sauce
Yield: 3- 5 oz. servings

1 teaspoon olive oil
Few sprigs basil, chopped
Few sprigs parsley, chopped
1 small onion, minced
1 medium carrot
1 rib celery
4 garlic cloves
Few sprigs rosemary
Pinch crushed red pepper
1 bay leaf
Few sprigs thyme, chopped
Few sprigs oregano, chopped
1/4 cup white wine
1- 28 oz. can whole plum tomatoes in juice, crush tomatoes with hands

Heat oil in large pot; add basil, parsley and onion, and saute. In food processor, process carrots, celery, garlic and rosemary until fine, or chop by hand; add and saute. Add red pepper, bay leaf, thyme and oregano, and saute. Add wine, bring to a boil, reduce. Add tomatoes and juice. Bring sauce to a simmer; turn down to low heat, cover and cook for 2-4 hours, until acidity is cooked out and flavors blend.

Nutritional info. per serving

Calories	103	
Protein	4	g
Carbohydrate	19	g
Fat	18	%
Sodium	459	mg
Cholesterol	-	
Fiber	4	g

Rolatina De Spinach
Rainbow Lasagna, Individually Rolled
Yield: 1 serving

1/2 cup skim ricotta cheese
Pinch nutmeg
Pinch pepper
1 oz. (1/4 cup) skim mozzarella cheese, small dice
1 teaspoon parmesan cheese
1/2-1 egg white
* 2 each fresh tri-colored pasta sheets; cooked 1/2 way, drained and
   patted dry
1 oz. (1/2 cup) mushrooms, sliced, blanched and dried well
1/2 oz. smoked turkey or chicken, sliced thin
2 oz. (1/3 cup) blanched spinach, all liquid squeezed out
4 oz. (1/2 cup) red sauce, heated (see above recipe)
Parchment paper
Basil leaf

In bowl, mix nutmeg and pepper with ricotta. Add mozzarella, then
parmesan and mix well; add egg white and mix.

Preheat oven to 350 F.
To assemble: On pasta sheets, layer cheese mixture, mushrooms, spinach
and smoked turkey or chicken. Roll and then wrap each roll tightly in
parchment paper. Bake in casserole, with a little water, until hot throughout, about 10 minutes.
Cover bottom of plate with red sauce and place the two lasagna rolls on
top. Garnish with a basil leaf.

* Can use plain, fresh or dry, lasagna sheets.

Nutritional info. per serving
Calories	554	
Protein	36	g
Carbohydrate	60	g
Fat	32	%
Sodium	617	mg
Cholesterol	56	mg
Fiber	3	g

Cafe American Style
Lord & Taylor Aventura Mall (305)932-2777

Robert Jackson spent 11 years in Atlanta, before Lord & Taylor transferred him here. He is a native Floridian!
Robert's mentor - his mother.

♥ American Waldorf Salad
Yield: 8 servings - approx. 2 1/2 oz. dressing per person

Dressing:
1 cup Japanese rice vinegar
1 cup nonfat plain yogurt
1 1/2 cups lite mayonnaise
1 tablespoon Dijon mustard
1/2 cup honey
1/4 cup lite soy sauce
1/8 cup vegetable oil
3/4 cup water/cornstarch mixture (optional, see food preparation tips)

In bowl, mix vinegar, nonfat yogurt, mayonnaise and mustard until smooth. Add honey and soy sauce; slowly mix in vegetable oil and water/cornstarch mixture until blended.

Mixture:
2 lbs. cooked skinless chicken meat, cubed
Lettuce
1 cup cantaloupe, cubed
1 cup apple, cubed
4 teaspoons walnuts

Pour some of the dressing on chicken meat to coat. Serve on a bed of lettuce, topped with cantaloupe and apples; sprinkle walnuts over. Serve with remaining dressing.

Nutritional info. per serving

Calories	334	
Protein	38	g
Carbohydrate	16	g
Fat	35	%
Sodium	409	mg
Cholesterol	104	mg
Fiber	1	g

♥ Chicken Marbella
Yield: 4 servings

4 - 5-6 oz. chicken breast, skinless
1/2 tablespoon garlic, minced
1/4 cup olive oil
1/4 cup red wine vinegar
1/4 cup capers (with a small amount of juice)
3 Spanish olives
1/8 cup (2 tablespoons) fresh oregano
1/2 cup pitted prunes
1/2 cup dried apricots (can use mixed dried fruit)
3 bay leaves
1/8 cup (2 tablespoons) fresh Italian parsley
Pepper

Mix all ingredients in bowl and marinate chicken overnight in baking dish.

Preheat oven to 350 F.

1/2 cup white wine
1/2 cup brown sugar

Add white wine and sprinkle brown sugar over mixture. Bake in oven for 40-50 minutes.

Nutritional info. per serving

Calories	528	
Protein	37	g
Carbohydrate	52	g
Fat	30	%
Sodium	187	mg
Cholesterol	96	mg
Fiber	3	g

Chef's serving suggestion: Serve with brown rice.

Chef Allen's

19088 N.E. 29 Ave., Aventura (305)935-2900

*Allen Susser, Chef/Owner, graduated from F.I.U.'s School of Hospitality Management, after work-
ing in the Bristol Hotel in Paris. He has worked at Le Cirque in New York and Turnberry Isle Yacht
and Country Club in North Miami Beach. Allen also teaches culinary and management skills at
F.I.U. His philosophy is to have a "team effort" in cooking!
Most memorable meal - when he cooked for Paul Bocuse ("one of the most significant French
chefs of the decade)."
His mentor - Alan Salhaic, Chef at Le Cirque.*

♥ Angel Hair Pasta with Grilled Vegetables, Tomato and Basil
Yield: 4 servings

1 medium zucchini, cut in diagonal wedges
1/2 lb. asparagus, peeled
1 medium vidalia onion (when available), or another sweet onion, sliced
    into wedges
2 medium tomatoes,cut into thick wedges
10 shiitake mushrooms, stems removed
1 tablespoon thyme
Pepper to taste
1 lb. angel hair pasta
1/2 bunch basil, julienned
4 oz. (1/2 cup) olive oil
5 oz. chicken or vegetable stock (optional)
1 teaspoon crushed red pepper or to taste

    Season the vegetables with thyme and pepper, and spray with olive oil
cooking spray; grill on a hot grill.

Cook angel hair al dente according to package directions. Drain and toss in basil, olive oil (and stock if desired) and crushed red pepper. Chop the grilled vegetables roughly and add to the pasta. Serve immediately.

Nutritional info. per serving

Calories	746	
Protein	21	g
Carbohydrate	104	g
Fat	35	%
Sodium	140	mg
Cholesterol	-	
Fiber	3	g

♥ Vegetable Couscous
Yield: 4 servings

2 tablespoons olive oil
1 medium carrot, julienned
1 zucchini, cut 1/4" slices
6 shallots, julienned
1/4 lb. baby squash (yellow summer), cut in half
1 cup couscous
2 1/2 cups chicken broth
Pinch saffron
1/4 teaspoon crushed red pepper
Fresh black pepper

Heat olive oil in large pan and saute shallots, carrots, zucchini and baby squash for 2 minutes over medium heat. Add couscous and chicken broth; simmer for 3 minutes. Add saffron and crushed red pepper; continue simmering for 5 minutes. Add more broth if needed; the mixture should remain brothy. Season with pepper.

Nutritional info. per serving

Calories	297	
Protein	11	g
Carbohydrate	45	g
Fat	25	%
Sodium	501	mg
Cholesterol	1	mg
Fiber	2	g

♥ Field Greens with Tea Smoked Scallops
Stuffed with Pistachio Pesto
Yield: 3 servings

Greens - any combination of these or others in the market:

mache	dandelion greens	curly endive
red oak leaf	baby red romaine	endive
bibb	red spinach	fennel
radicchio	kale	arugula

Season the greens to taste with:

1 teaspoon extra virgin olive oil
Fresh lemon juice
Black pepper
Balsamic vinegar, if desired

12 oz. sea scallops
1 oz. orange pekoe tea, dry leaves (split open tea bag)
3 tablespoons dark corn syrup
1 tablespoon lite soy sauce
4 oz. (1/2 cup) Sauvignon Blanc wine
1/2 teaspoon black pepper
4 tablespoons garlic
1 1/2 oz. pistachio nuts
1 oz. (6 tablespoons) grated parmesan cheese
1 oz. (16) sundried tomatoes, rehydrated
1 tablespoon olive oil
1/2 teaspoon herb vinegar such as tarragon vinegar
2 tablespoons fresh basil

1 pita bread pocket (or grain of your choice)

Marinate the sea scallops in the tea, corn syrup, soy, Sauvignon Blanc, black pepper and 3 tablespoons of garlic for almost 1 hour.

For the pesto: Puree together the pistachio nuts, parmesan, sundried tomatoes, olive oil, 1 tablespoon garlic, vinegar and basil.

Drain and dry the scallops. Cut a small pocket on the side. Put the pesto in a small pastry bag (or use tiny spoon)and stuff the scallop plump. Let them set in the refrigerator for 1 hour.

On a wood burning grill, after the heat has died down, smoke the scallops slowly. Cover for approx. 5 minutes. Serve warm on the seasoned greens with 1/3 pita (or grain of choice) per serving.

Nutritional info. per serving

Calories	471	
Protein	36	g
Carbohydrate	37	g
Fat	34	%
Sodium	813	mg
Cholesterol	68	mg
Fiber	3	g

Ristorante Il Tulipano
11052 Biscayne Boulevard, North Miami (305)893-4811

Owners - Filippo and Caroll Il Grande.

♥ Carabinieri Salsa Verde con Risotto Estivo
Yield: 4 servings

Risotto Estivo:
3 cups chicken broth
2 cups short grained Arborio rice (or other imported Italian rice)
1 cup finely chopped onion
2 tablespoons virgin olive oil
1 cup chopped curly leaf spinach
4-6 each asparagus, cut into approx. 1 " pieces
Pepper to taste
1/4 cup (4 tablespoons) grated parmesan cheese

1 lb. jumbo Mediterranean shrimp, peeled and deveined, leaving
    head and tail intact
Pepper to taste
4-6 bamboo skewers

Salsa verde:
4 tablespoons olive oil
1 bunch fresh parsley (flat leaf preferred), washed, trimmed

    Heat the chicken stock in a medium saucepan to a boil. Add rice and onions, stir, and reduce heat to simmer. Simmer, uncovered for 15 minutes, or until the rice is soft and the liquid is completely absorbed.
    While the rice is cooking, in a separate saucepan heat the oil over medium heat and saute the spinach and asparagus for a few minutes. Add vegetables to rice mixture. Season with pepper, toss with parmesan cheese and cover rice until ready to serve.

    Preheat oven to 350 F.
    Lightly season shrimp with pepper and thread onto skewers, approx. 2-3 per skewer.

Prepare salsa verde: Place salsa ingredients into a food processor fitted with steel blade attachment and process until parsley is finely chopped and ingredients are well blended.

To cook shrimp: Cook in oven 5-8 minutes, or broil or grill approx. 4" from heat, 3-5 minutes on each side.

To serve: Spoon cooked risotto onto warm plates. Remove shrimp from skewers and arrange the shrimp on each plate. Pour the salsa verde over shrimp.

Nutritional info. per serving:

Calories	710	
Protein	37	g
Carbohydrate	81	g
Fat	33	%
Sodium	862	mg
Cholesterol	177	mg*
Fiber	3	g

* If you are watching your cholesterol, decrease the amount of shrimp called for in the recipe.

♥ Vitella Con Manico alla Bruschetta
Yield: 4 servings

Dressing:
1 tablespoon virgin olive oil
1/4 cup balsamic vinegar
1/4 teaspoon mustard
2 tablespoons chopped flat leaf Italian parsley
1 each garlic clove, minced
Pepper to taste

1 lb. veal loin medallions, pounded thin
2 tablespoons Skim Milk
1/4 cup liquid egg substitute
1/4 cup Italian style breadcrumbs
1 tablespoon olive oil
2 cloves garlic, peeled

Topping:
1 1/2 cups radicchio, chopped into small pieces
1/2 cup arugula, chopped into small pieces
1 medium tomato, peeled, seeded and diced (about 1/2 cup)

2 cups cooked pasta (or grain of your choice)

In a small bowl whisk all dressing ingredients together until well blended.

Dip veal pieces in milk then egg. Roll in breadcrumbs, shake off excess.

Heat 1 tablespoon oil in non-stick skillet over medium high heat. Lightly saute garlic, then veal pieces, about 1 minute on each side or until golden brown. Pat pieces on paper towels and hold on dinner plates.

Quickly toss together in skillet the radicchio, arugula and the tomatoes until heated through. Place a small amount on top of veal portions and drizzle prepared dressing over the top.

Serve with 1/2 cup cooked pasta (or grain of choice) per serving.

Nutritional info. per serving:

Calories	345	
Protein	30	g
Carbohydrate	29	g
Fat	31	%
Sodium	460	mg
Cholesterol	91	mg
Fiber	2	g

The Unicorn Restaurant and Unicorn Village Market

3565 N.E. 207 St., Aventura at the Waterways (305)933-1543/3663

Steven M. Petusevsky is the Director of Creative Food Development. A graduate of the C.I.A., Steve instructed there and at several other culinary schools. He has used his culinary skills in other areas of the U.S., as well as in Europe!
His most memorable meal - while at the Intercontinental Hotel in Germany, there was a grand buffet for 1,000 people in honor of the King of Jordan, who was on horseback!

♥ Tropical Seafood Chowder
Yield: 7 servings

1 tablespoon canola oil
4 oz. carrots, diced
4 oz. celery, diced
4 oz. onions, diced
4 oz. sweet potatoes, diced
2 each chayote squash, peeled and diced
1 tablespoon garlic clove, minced
1 tablespoon ginger, minced
1/2 teaspoon allspice, ground
1 teaspoon chili flakes, crushed
1- 28 oz. can crushed tomatoes with juice
1 quart fish stock or clam juice
1/2 bunch kale, chopped
1 lb. firm fish trimmings (dolphin, grouper)
4-6 oz. scallops (optional)
4-6 oz. shrimp (optional)
Lime juice to taste
Pepper
Chopped parsley
1 oz. dry sherry (optional)

Heat oil in stock pot; add all diced vegetables and saute with garlic and spices approx. 4-5 minutes. Add crushed tomatoes and juice, fish stock or clam juice and bring to a boil, lower to simmer. Simmer, covered, an additional 15-20 minutes, and add chopped kale. Add seafood and simmer 5-8 minutes, until seafood is cooked through.

Season with lime juice and pepper.

Garnish with chopped parsley. Add dry sherry, if desired.

Nutritional info. per serving

Calories	205	
Protein	25	g
Carbohydrate	17	g
Fat	16	%
Sodium	623	mg
Cholesterol	74	mg
Fiber	3	g

♥ Tuscan Vegetable Saute
Yield: 3 servings

1 teaspoon olive oil
2 oz. green pepper, diced
2 oz. red pepper, diced
2 oz. purple onion, diced
2 oz. celery, diced
4 oz. zucchini, diced
2 oz. chick peas, cooked
10 black olives, pitted
2 teaspoons fresh garlic, minced
1/2 teaspoon dry oregano
4-5 leaves fresh basil, minced
1/2 teaspoon rosemary, crushed
1 large tomato, diced
1 cup escarole, diced
Cayenne pepper, to taste
3 cups cooked pasta (or brown rice)

Heat olive oil until hot in a large saute pan. Add peppers, onion, celery, zucchini, chick peas, olives, garlic and seasonings. Saute for 5-7 minutes until vegetables are almost tender; add vegetable oil cooking spray if needed. Add fresh tomato and escarole, continue to cook for approx. 2 minutes longer. Season to taste with pepper. Serve over 1 cup cooked pasta (or brown rice) per serving.

Nutritional info. per serving

Calories	282	
Protein	11	g
Carbohydrate	52	g
Fat	17	%
Sodium	179	mg
Cholesterol	-	
Fiber	6	g

♥ Unicorn Village Turkey Loaf
Yield: 7 servings

1 teaspoon canola oil
1/2 cup celery, diced
1/2 cup onions, diced
1/2 cup carrots, diced
1/2 cup mixed red and green pepper, diced
1 tablespoon dry oregano
1 teaspoon dry basil
1 tablespoon minced garlic
1 teaspoon white pepper
2 lbs. ground turkey
1 cup rolled oats
1/2 cup bread crumbs
7 small-medium potatoes, baked

Preheat oven to 375 F.
In nonstick pan, heat oil and saute vegetables with herbs; add vegetable oil cooking spray if needed. Reserve and cool.

Mix ground turkey, seasonings and reserved vegetables with oats and bread crumbs. Incorporate all ingredients well. Form into loaves and bake in baking pan in oven for approx. 45-55 minutes until cooked through and golden brown on top.

Serve with 1 potato per serving.

Nutritional info. per serving

Calories	476	
Protein	37	g
Carbohydrate	43	g
Fat	33	%
Sodium	200	mg
Cholesterol	95	mg
Fiber	3	g

♥ Serve with tomato sauce of choice or a mixture of ketchup, brown sugar and dry mustard.

Turnberry Isle Yacht and Country Club
19735 Turnberry Way, Aventura (305)932-6200

Mark A. Vinchesi, Spa Director.

♥ Pasta with Roasted Pepper Sauce
Yield: 8 servings

2 large sweet red peppers, roasted and diced
2 large sweet green peppers, roasted and diced
1 lb. ripe plum tomatoes, chopped
2 tablespoons olive oil
1 garlic clove
1 onion, minced
1/3 cup chopped fresh Italian parsley leaves
1 lb. thin pasta or penne; cooked al dente

In processor, blend tomatoes and peppers to a puree.
In a large pan heat oil with garlic and saute onions until translucent. Add the rest of the ingredients; cook for 5-6 minutes. Add pasta and toss.

Nutritional info. per serving

Calories	265	
Protein	9	g
Carbohydrate	49	g
Fat	16	%
Sodium	10	mg
Cholesterol	-	
Fiber	2	g

The following was developed by Robbin Haas and Cheryl Hartsough, and was the winning recipe in the beef category at the 1991 Broward County Dietetic Association Culinary Hearts Cook-off. F. Robbin Haas, Executive Chef, has cooked as far west as Los Angeles with stops in Dallas, Chicago, Cincinnati and most recently Palm Beach at The Ocean Grand Hotel before joining Turnberry Isle.
Cheryl Hartsough, R.D., is the Director of Nutrition at the Spa at Turnberry Isle. Cheryl travels throughout the country as a member of the Gatorade Speakers Network as an expert on Sports Nutrition.

♥ Grilled Smokey Tenderloin of Beef
Passion Fruit Barbeque Sauce
Quinoa Lentil Salad with Fire Roasted Vegetables

For the Beef:
Yield: 4 servings
4 - 4 oz. beef tenderloin steak, all visible fat removed
2 teaspoons smoked paprika
1/4 teaspoon ground cinnamon
1 teaspoon chopped fresh thyme
1 teaspoon freshly ground black pepper
1/2 cup Cabernet Sauvignon Wine
1 tablespoon light soy sauce

Combine paprika, thyme, cinnamon and black pepper; rub well into beef.

Combine wine and soy sauce and pour over beef in non-corrosive pan. Let marinate for 2 hours.

Grill over hot coal or wood fire - 4 minutes for medium-rare, 6 minutes for medium and 8 minutes for well done.

For the Barbeque Sauce:
Yield: 16 - 1 oz.(2 tablespoons) servings after strained
1 each sweet red + yellow pepper - seeded and quartered
1 small onion, diced large
2 garlic cloves, chopped
1 medium tomato, diced large
1 jalapeno, diced
3 tablespoons minced ginger
1/2 cup Vermouth
1 cup orange juice
1 cup passion fruit juice
1 cinnamon stick
1/4 teaspoon allspice
1/2 cup apple cider vinegar
1/4 cup unsulphured molasses

Combine first 7 ingredients; place in heavy bottom saucepan and cover over low heat for 20-25 minutes. Stir occasionally.

Remove cover and add remaining ingredients. Cook uncovered over medium heat for 20-25 minutes.

Remove cinnamon stick, let cool and puree in blender. Pass through metal strainer; sauce should be consistency of warm honey. If sauce is too thin, return to heat and reduce; if sauce is too thick, thin with orange juice.

Set aside and keep warm or refrigerate until needed.

For the Quinoa and Lentil Salad:
Yield: 8 - 3/4 cup servings
1 cup dry green lentils
1/2 cup (2 1/2 oz. dry) quinoa
3 cups chicken stock or broth, fat skimmed
1 each sweet red and yellow pepper, seeded and cut in half
1 zucchini, sliced lengthwise
1 small red onion, diced
3 tablespoons chopped cilantro
Juice of 2 limes
1 teaspoon black pepper

Heat 2 cups chicken stock and cook lentils until soft (about 30 minutes). Drain and cool.

Heat 1 cup chicken stock and cook quinoa according to package directions. Drain and cool.

Spray a wood or charcoal grill with a vegetable oil cooking spray and grill vegetables lightly. Cool and dice vegetables.

Combine all ingredients and mix - checking seasoning. For extra taste, add small amount of barbeque sauce.

Nutritional info. per serving
Calories	382	
Protein	34	g
Carbohydrate	35	g
Fat	27	%
Sodium	486	mg
Cholesterol	70	mg
Fiber	6	g

♥ Try using the barbeque sauce on chicken (or other meats), and save the strained pureed vegetables from the barbeque sauce to use as a relish.

Dominique's Famous French Restaurant
The Alexander All-Suite Luxury Hotel & Private Residences
5225 Collins Avenue, Miami Beach (305)865-6500

Executive Chef Aristides "Ted" Mendez graduated from the French certified training school "Le Pot Au Feu" in Paris. He has worked with such renowned chefs as Pascal Oudin, Suki Sugura and George Massarf.
He considers both Oudin and Massarf his mentors.
His funniest meal was during the 1988 Taste of the Nation to Benefit the Homeless, where he worked with local media and served Chicken Liver Mousse with 3D Crawfish Sauce...3D glasses not included!

Alligator and Buffalo tongue are two of the many exotic dishes Dominique D'Ermo is famous for serving at his restaurants in Washington, D.C., Palm Beach and Miami Beach, Florida.

♥ Grilled Salmon with Fresh Dill and Coriander Seed Vinaigrette
Yield: 1 serving

1 - 6 oz. Salmon fillet
1/6 bunch fresh dillweed or 1 teaspoon dry
1 tablespoon olive oil
1 oz. (1 average) shallots, chopped
1/4 oz. (1-2 cloves) garlic, chopped
1 teaspoon coriander seed
6 oz. (3/4 cup) white wine
2 oz. (1/4 cup) red wine vinegar
8 oz. (1 cup) fish stock or clam broth
3 oz. tomato juice
1/2 cup cooked white rice (or grain of your choice)

Preheat oven broiler.
Rub fish with dillweed.
In a small saucepan, heat olive oil over medium heat. Add shallots, garlic and coriander and saute until lightly browned. Add white wine and deglaze the pan. Add vinegar, fish stock and tomato juice. Reduce by 1/3, whisking the mixture.

Meanwhile, broil fish, approx. 5 minutes per side, turning once.

Serve broiled fish portion with sauce and 1/2 cup cooked white rice (or grain of choice).

Nutritional info. per serving:

Calories	674	
Protein	40	g
Carbohydrate	46	g
Fat	35	%
Sodium	893	mg
Cholesterol	94	mg
Fiber	5	g

Chef's serving suggestion: Serve with vegetables.

♥ Raspberry Souffle
Yield: 4 servings

Vegetable oil cooking spray and sugar to line mold
1 cup skim milk
2 egg yolks
1/4 cup sugar
1/4 cup flour
6 oz. frozen raspberries, thawed
2 oz. (1/4 cup) Chambord (Raspberry liqueur)
4 egg whites, room temperature
Pinch cream of tartar
1 pint (2 cups) fresh raspberries

Preheat oven to 350 F.

Spray 1 1/2 qt. souffle dish with deep sides with a vegetable oil cooking spray and dust with 1-2 tablespoons sugar.

Bring milk to a boil in a 1 qt. saucepan.

In a separate bowl combine yolks, flour and sugar. Add hot milk, slowly to egg yolk mixture, whisking, then return to low heat, whisking until stiff and thick. Remove from heat.

Chill mixture, covered with a sheet of waxed paper, 2-3 hours. After chilling, combine mixture in food processor with frozen raspberries and Chambord until smooth.

In large mixing bowl, whip egg whites until frothy. Add cream of tartar and continue beating until stiff but not dry. Carefully fold in 1/2 pint (1 cup) of the fresh raspberries and the processed mixture.

Pour souffle mixture into prepared dish and bake 25 minutes or until almost set and lightly browned. Serve immediately with fresh raspberries.

Nutritional info. per serving:

Calories	266	
Protein	8	g
Carbohydrate	47	g
Fat	12	%
Sodium	88	mg
Cholesterol	108	mg
Fiber	6	g

Epicure Market

1656 Alton Rd., Miami Beach (305)672-1861

Hector Morales, Executive Chef, is a graduate of Broward Community College and has taken an advanced baking course at the C.I.A.
Most memorable meals - Winter 1991: it was his honor to present a brunch for Elizabeth Taylor and guests at the Biltmore Country Club.
- A dinner party for Baryshnikov, after his performance at a private estate.
Hector's mentor - his father, Chef Cruz Morales, his "longtime friend and advisor!"

♥ Vegetable Cutlets
Yield: 16 - 8 oz. cutlets

1/4 lb. margarine
4 oz. (6) shallots, minced
1 1/2 oz. garlic, minced
1/2 bunch sweet basil, minced
1 teaspoon thyme
1/4 teaspoon white pepper
3/4 lb. cauliflower, cut in small florets
3/4 lb. broccoli, cut in small florets
3/4 lb. parsnips, peeled and diced
3/4 lb. yellow squash, diced
3/4 lb. zuchinni squash, diced
6 oz. frozen kernel corn
2 1/2 lbs. potatoes, peeled
1/2 lb. soda crackers, crumbled
1-2 egg whites mixed with 2-3 tablespoons water

Preheat oven to 350 F.
   Melt margarine in very large saute pan (can use stockpot), add shallots, garlic, basil, thyme and white pepper; saute until shallots are soft. Add all vegetables and saute until vegetables are half cooked (cover and stir-steam if desired). Remove from fire and drain vegetables in colander, reserve juice (if any).

In large pot, cook potatoes in boiling water until soft, drain and put in mixing bowl. Add one cup of vegetable juice (if any reserved), potato water or stock, whip, add crumbled crackers and mix well. Combine potato mixture with vegetables, mix until incorporated. Form into 8 oz. patties. Brush the patties with egg whites; bake on baking sheet in oven for about 25 minutes until patties are light golden in color.

Serving suggestion: Top with marinara sauce (2 tablespoons per person) and skim mozzarella cheese (1 oz. per person) and heat until cheese is melted.

Nutritional info. per serving

	Plain		With Sauce & Cheese	
Calories	228		310	
Protein	5	g	13	g
Carbohydrate	37	g	40	g
Fat	29	%	34	%
Sodium	99	mg	418	mg
Cholesterol	-		16	mg
Fiber	4	g	5	g

Pritikin Longevity Center
5875 Collins Avenue, Miami Beach (305)327-4914

The Pritikin Longevity Centers, founded in 1976 by Nathan Pritikin, feature medically-supervised diet/exercise programs. The Pritikin program is a multi-faceted approach to lifestyle change combining health and nutrition education, exercise and stress management. The Pritikin Lifetime Eating Plan emphasizes a diet high in natural complex carbohydrates, including over 40 g of fiber per day, and low in fat.
This recipe was developed by Barbara Lewin, R.D., Nutrition Director, and Tom Baggot, Cooking School Director, for the 1990 Broward County Dietetic Association Culinary Hearts Cook-Off.

♥ Arroz Con Pollo
Yield: 5 servings

1 1/2 teaspoons garlic powder
1 tablespoon low sodium soy sauce
2 oz. (1/4 cup) chicken stock (1) (preferably Pritikin)
20 oz. chicken breast, cut into strips
1 lemon, halved
16 oz. (2 cups) additional chicken stock (2), as needed
1/4 cup chopped onion
2 tablespoons minced garlic
1/4 cup chopped green pepper
1 bayleaf
1/2 cup dry sherry
4 oz. Tomato sauce, no salt added or Pritikin Mexican Sauce
2 tablespoons low sodium soy sauce
1 cup raw brown rice, cooked according to package directions
   (3 cups cooked)
1/2 cup chopped pimentos
1/2 cup frozen green peas
1/4 teaspoon saffron
1 teaspoon Italian seasoning blend*
1/8 teaspoon cumin
1/8 teaspoon pepper
1 tablespoon lemon juice

Garnish:
5 artichoke hearts, canned or frozen then steamed, halved
10 asparagus spears, fresh or frozen, steamed
Additional pimento (optional)

Mix together garlic powder, soy sauce and chicken stock (1). Marinate chicken pieces for 1 hour.

Preheat oven to 375 F.
Place chicken in a single layer in a 1" deep baking pan and pour marinade over. Bake at 375 F. for 30 minutes.

Heat skillet or electric wok over medium high heat. Add 3/4 cup of chicken stock (2). When stock bubbles, add onion, garlic, green pepper and bayleaf; saute for one minute until soft.

Add chicken pieces and 2 oz. (1/4 cup) of the sherry. Stir in tomato sauce and soy sauce and cook for 2 minutes.

Stir in cooked rice, pimentos, green peas, remaining sherry and saffron. Add chicken stock as needed. Stir in Italian blend, cumin, pepper and lemon juice. Stir until liquid has evaporated, but rice is still moist.

Portion arroz con pollo on serving plates. Garnish with artichoke hearts, asparagus spears and additional pimento, if desired.

Nutritional info. per serving:

Calories	347	
Protein	33	g
Carbohydrates	42	g
Fat	7	%
Sodium	603	mg
Cholesterol	65	mg
Fiber	6	g

* Or homemade mixture of basil, oregano, rosemary and thyme.

Stars & Stripes Cafe and A Mano

The Betsy Ross Hotel 1440 Ocean Dr., Miami Beach (305)531-3310

Norman Van Aken, Executive Chef and author of Feast of Sunlight cookbook.

♥ Escabeche
Yield: 6 servings

Marinade:
18 oz. boneless, skinless fresh fish (choose a fine, delicate variety)
1 teaspoon freshly ground cumin seed, toasted
1 teaspoon ground black pepper, toasted
1/2 teaspoon cayenne pepper
1 teaspoon sugar
2 jalapenos, stems and seeds removed, slivered
3 garlic cloves, thinly sliced
1/2 red onion, thinly sliced
1/2 bunch cilantro, torn
1/2 bunch mint leaves, torn
3 oz. cold tequila
1 tablespoon virgin olive oil

1 teaspoon peanut oil

For Fruit:
1/2 cup diced pineapple
1/2 cup diced mango
1/2 cup diced papaya
1/2 cup diced red onion
1 jalapeno, minced

Dressing:
2 oz. Spanish sherry wine vinegar
2 oz. fresh lime juice
2 oz. fresh orange juice
3 tablespoons virgin olive oil

Plantains:
2 very ripe plantains
1/4 cup flour
1 teaspoon ground cinnamon
1/2 tablespoon olive oil
1/2 tablespoon margarine

To prepare fish: Lay in a flat non-corrosive dish. Rub with cumin, black pepper, cayenne and sugar. Allow to "cure" 30 minutes. Mix jalapeno, garlic, red onion, cilantro, mint, tequila and olive oil. Pour this marinade over the spice rubbed fish and allow to marinate for at least 30 minutes, turning fish once or twice. Heat a non-stick or well seasoned black cast iron pan and add peanut or other light oil capable of withstanding high heat. When pan is smoking hot, lift the fish fillets out of the marinade and sear the fish briefly on both sides. Return to marinade and let cool. Refrigerate covered if you wish to prepare ahead up to this point.

To prepare fruit and the dressing: Mix together all the ingredients in the "fruit" list in a bowl and reserve. Whisk together the ingredients in the "dressing" list and reserve.

To finish the dish: Remove fish from the marinade and pull into bite size pieces, allowing marinade to drip off. Place fish on a clean plate.

Remove the prepared dressing and fruit-jalapeno mix from the refrigerator. Assemble your plates.

Peel plantains and cut them on a strong bias into slices about 1/4" thick. Mix together the flour and ground cinnamon; dredge the plantains in this mixture.

Heat a non-stick or well seasoned pan and add the olive oil and margarine, heat. When the margarine begins to foam, add the plantain slices and cook on each side until golden brown. Drain on paper towel.

Spoon the fruit mixture into a peasant type (earthenware) bowl ("cups" of radicchio would also make a sensational presentation). Top the fruit with the shredded fish and spoon the dressing over the fish and fruit. Surround with the cooked plantains and serve.

Nutritional info. per serving

Calories	379	
Protein	23	g
Carbohydrate	35	g
Fat	31	%
Sodium	166	mg
Cholesterol	58	mg
Fiber	2	g

The Forge Restaurant
432 Arthur Godfrey Road,Miami Beach (305)538-8533

Executive Chef Kal Abdalla was born and raised on a small island in the Mediterranean, which has greatly influenced his cooking style.
In his 7 years at The Forge he has cooked for such celebrities as Kurt Russell, Goldie Hawn and Jimmy the Greek.

♥ Red Snapper with Yogurt and Garbanzo Beans
Yield: 1 serving

6 oz. red snapper fillet
1/2 teaspoon olive oil
1/4 teaspoon dried basil or up to 1 teaspoon fresh, chopped
1 teaspoon fresh chopped parsley
Black pepper to taste
1 tablespoon olive oil
1/2 cup cooked garbanzo beans
1/4 cup plain lowfat yogurt
1 oz. Pita bread pocket

Brush red snapper with 1/2 teaspoon olive oil and grill over hot coals or broil until done.

Mix together basil, parsley and pepper with 1 tablespoon olive oil.

In a small sauce pot, heat garbanzo beans thoroughly, stirring occasionally.

To serve, place garbanzo beans on plate and top with grilled fish. Place 2 tablespoons plain yogurt on either side of the fish and drizzle seasoned oil over the top. Serve with pita.

Nutritional info. per serving:

Calories	560	
Protein	48	g
Carbohydrate	42	g
Fat	35	%
Sodium	320	mg
Cholesterol	66	mg
Fiber	6	g

♥ Penne with Asparagus
Yield: 1 serving

1 tablespoon olive oil
2 tablespoons onion, finely chopped
1 garlic clove, crushed
1 teaspoon fresh basil, chopped or 1/4 teaspoon dried
1/4 teaspoon fresh thyme or 1/8 teaspoon dried
1 cup fresh tomatoes, peeled and chopped (1 large)
Pepper to taste
2 oz. dry penne (or other tubular) pasta
4 oz. fresh or frozen asparagus spears
2 tablespoons grated parmesan cheese

Heat olive oil in medium saucepan; saute onion and garlic over medium heat until onion is translucent, 3-5 minutes. Add basil, thyme, chopped tomatoes and pepper, and saute 4-5 minutes.

Meanwhile, cook pasta according to package directions; drain well and hold on serving plate. Top with sauce.

Steam asparagus spears and place on top of penne and sauce. Top with parmesan cheese and serve.

Nutritional info. per serving:

Calories	525	
Protein	20	g
Carbohydrate	74	g
Fat	30	%
Sodium	465	mg
Cholesterol	8	mg
Fiber	8	mg

The Bankers Club
One Biscayne Tower 14th Floor, Miami (305)374-1448

Steven Salley, Executive Chef, is a 1985 graduate of the C.I.A., who began working as a sous chef at the Bankers Club and worked his way up to being Executive Chef.
His most memorable meal is preparing a Chaine des Rotisseurs dinner.
Steven's mentor - Chef Allen Susser, owner and operator of Chef Allen's in North Miami Beach.

♥ Chicken or Capon Vegetable Medallions with Tequila Lime Salsa
Yield: 4 servings

4 - 6 oz. Capon or chicken breasts, skinless, boneless and pounded thin

Stuffing:
2 tablespoons olive oil
4 oz. zucchini, finely chopped
4 oz. yellow squash, finely chopped
4 oz. red pepper, finely chopped
1/2 teaspoon fresh basil leaves, chopped
4 oz. onion, finely chopped
1/2 cup or more bread crumbs, unseasoned
2 egg whites, beaten lightly

Salsa:
2 tablespoons olive oil
1/2 cup chopped onions
1/2 cup chopped celery
1/4 cup chopped shallots
1 tablespoon fresh lime zest
1/4 cup fresh lime juice
1/2 cup dry white wine
1 oz. (2 tablespoons) Tequila
1 cup peeled and chopped tomatoes
2 tablespoons cornstarch mixed with 1/4 cup cold water
Black, white and red pepper to taste

Preheat oven to 350 F.

Heat oil in large saute pan and saute all stuffing ingredients together, except bread crumbs and egg whites, over medium heat until onions are translucent, 3-5 minutes.

Remove pan from heat and add bread crumbs and egg whites to bind, adding more bread crumbs, if needed.

Spread stuffing among flattened meat portions and roll each up, tucking ends in as you roll. Place on foil lined baking sheet seam side down and cover pan with foil.

Bake for approximately 15-20 minutes.

Meanwhile, prepare salsa: Heat oil in saute pan and saute onions, celery and shallots until translucent. Add lime zest and juice, wine, tequila and tomatoes and reduce slightly.   Mix in cornstarch/water mixture and heat to boiling point to thicken. Season as desired with pepper.

Remove meat portions from baking sheet and slice into 1" thick medallions. Arrange on hot serving plate and top with salsa.

Nutritional info.per serving:

Calories	500	
Protein	46	g
Carbohydrate	30	g
Fat	31	%
Sodium	341	mg
Cholesterol	99	mg
Fiber	4	g

Regines

Top of Grand Bay Hotel 2669 S. Bayshore Dr., Coconut Grove (305)858-9600

Lisa Pethybridge, Executive Chef, is a graduate of The C.I.A. She has previously worked at The Ritz Carlton in Chicago, and The Fountainbleu Hilton, Bonaventure and Sheraton Design Center here in Florida.
Most memorable meal - one of them was cooking for Linda Evans!
Lisa's mentor - Helmut Tevini with whom she has worked the past 5 years.

Shrimp and Scallop Seviche
Yield: 3 servings

4 oz. shrimp
4 oz. scallops

Marinade:
Juice of 4 oranges
Juice of 4 limes
Dash of cumin
1 teaspoon chopped garlic
2 bunches cilantro, chopped
3 splashes Tabasco
2 tablespoons ketchup
1 1/2 tablespoons sugar
Pepper to taste
Orange and lime sections

In saucepan, blanch shrimp and scallops for 1 minute in Court Bouillon. Shock in ice bath and drain. Prepare marinade and marinate shrimp and scallops for at least 15 minutes.

Arrange orange and lime sections as garnish. Spoon marinade over top.

Nutritional info. per serving

Calories	144	
Protein	13	g
Carbohydrate	22	g
Fat	6	%
Sodium	247	mg
Cholesterol	70	mg
Fiber	1	g

The Grand Cafe
Grand Bay Hotel 2669 S. Bayshore Dr., Coconut Grove (305)858-9600

Katsuo "Suki" Sugiura, born in Tokyo, Japan, was trained in classic French Cuisine. He left to work and study in the kitchens of fine European hotels in Helsinki, Finland; Oslo, Norway; Berlin, West Germany; Le Havre, France; and Buckinghamshire, England before coming to the United States. In this country, he has worked in New York, Chicago and Beverly Hills. Suki was the Executive Chef at the Remington Hotel in Houston, the Vanderbilt Plaza in Nashville, the Biltmore Hotel in Miami, The Grand Bay Hotel in Miami and the Director of Culinary at Trump Taj Mahal in Atlantic City before coming back to Grand Bay Hotels as Corporate Chef.

Tomato Ginger Vinaigrette For Red Snapper
Yield: 6 servings

1 tablespoon Pommery mustard
1/2 cup fruit vinegar
1/4 cup safflower oil
1 shallot, chopped
2 large tomatoes, peeled, seeded and chopped
1 oz. fresh ginger root, finely grated
Pepper to taste
24 oz. cooked Red Snapper (2 lbs. raw)
3 cups cooked brown rice (or grain of your choice)

In large bowl, mix mustard and vinegar together thoroughly. Gradually add oil while whisking. Stir in shallot, tomatoes, ginger and pepper.

Serve with 4 oz. cooked red snapper and 1/2 cup cooked brown rice (or grain of choice) per serving.

Nutritional info. per serving

Calories	352	
Protein	33	g
Carbohydrate	26	g
Fat	31	%
Sodium	105	mg
Cholesterol	53	mg
Fiber	2	g

Sauternes Granite with Kiwi Coulis
Yield: 6 servings

4 very ripe kiwi fruit
2 cups Sauternes wine (or other sweet dessert wine)
6 oz. water
6 large strawberries, sliced (garnish)

Blend kiwi fruit and pass through a fine sieve to make coulis. Mix Sauternes and water and either freeze in ice cream making machine or transfer to a freezer, stirring frequently until frozen into crystals (granite).

Pour a little coulis onto a plate and arrange two scoops of granite on top. Garnish with sliced strawberries.

Nutritional info. per serving

Calories	161	
Protein	1	g
Carbohydrate	19	g
Fat	2	%
Sodium	11	mg
Cholesterol	-	
Fiber	2	g

Lentil Soup with Fennel and Spring Vegetables
Yield: 6 servings

1 tablespoon safflower oil
1/4 cup carrots, roughly chopped
1/4 cup celery, roughly chopped
1/4 onion, chopped
1 teaspoon garlic, minced
1 1/2 quarts homemade chicken stock (or broth)
2/3 cup dry lentils
1 bay leaf
1/2 tablespoon fennel seed in cheesecloth bag
1/2 cup spinach, blanched, roughly chopped
White pepper
18 Natural Rye Krisp crackers (or grain of your choice)

Heat oil in stock pot and saute carrots and celery. Add onions and garlic and cook until soft. Add chicken stock, lentils, bay leaf and fennel seed pouch. Bring to a slow boil and simmer covered until lentils are soft (about 20 minutes). Add spinach and white pepper to taste.

Remove fennel seed pouch prior to serving.

Serve with 3 crackers (or grain of choice) per serving.

Nutritional info. per serving

Calories	100	
Protein	7	g
Carbohydrate	10	g
Fat	35	%
Sodium	843	mg
Cholesterol	1	mg
Fiber	2	g

Aragon Cafe

The Colonnade Hotel 180 Aragon Ave., Coral Gables (305)441-2600

Pascal Oudin, Executive Chef, directs all food operations at the hotel including Aragon Cafe, Doc Dammers Saloon, hotel banquets and room service. He was born and educated in France, and received the prestigious "Paul Lacombe Award" as France's best apprentice chef in 1977! He has worked "with the greatest names in french cooking." Previously he was in Washington, D.C., Virginia and at The Alexander Hotel (Dominiques) on Miami Beach.
Most memorable meal - a dinner in Washington, D.C. for The Royal Family of Monte Carlo in honor of The Foundation of Princess Grace.
His mentor - Alain Ducasse, Executive Chef, Hotel de Paris, Monte Carlo.

♥ Cold Seafood Sausage with Tomato Basil Vinaigrette
Yield: 6 servings

3/4 lb. fresh halibut fillets, cut into 1/2" squares
3/4 lb. sole fillets, cut into 1/2" squares
Zest of 1 lemon, minced
1 garlic clove, minced
1/2 teaspoon white pepper
1 tablespoon olive oil
1 teaspoon heavy cream (or evaporated milk)
3 3/4 tablespoons (1/4 cup) evaporated skim milk
1 cup packed fresh spinach leaves (3 oz.), well rinsed and
    coarsely chopped
Sausage casings, soaked for 14 hours in cold water with a dash of vinegar
Dill sprigs or basil leaves for garnish

3 pita bread pockets (or grain of your choice)

   Place halibut in mixing bowl and set aside.
   Place sole in the bowl of food processor fitted with steel blade. Add the lemon zest and garlic and process. Add pepper and process to blend. With motor running, add the olive oil, cream and the evaporated skim milk through the feed tube. Add sole puree and chopped spinach leaves to the reserved halibut and stir well to combine.

Note: To prepare without a food processor, puree the sole in a food mill, and beat the remaining ingredients.

With a sausage machine, or pastry bag, stuff mixture into the casings, tying off at intervals of about 4 inches. Twist and tie between the sausages with white kitchen twine. Refrigerate for 30 minutes. Grill the sausage, then refrigerate until ready to serve. If casing is not available, wrap in clear plastic wrap forming sausage shape. Refrigerate, then poach 5-7 minutes in Court Bouillon; refrigerate.

Tomato Basil Vinaigrette
Yield: 12 servings
5 tomatoes, peeled and seeded
1 garlic clove, minced
1 egg yolk
6 tablespoons red wine vinegar
1/2 teaspoon white pepper
1/4 cup olive oil
3/4 cup water/cornstarch mixture (optional, see preparation tips)
4 fresh basil leaves, chopped (about 2 tablespoons)

Core and quarter 4 tomatoes, place in bowl of food processor fitted with steel blade (or in a blender). Add garlic, egg yolk, vinegar and pepper, and puree. With motor running, add olive oil and enough water/cornstarch mixture in a slow stream to emulsify, and give desired consistency. Strain through a sieve. Chop the remaining tomato, and blend into the sauce with chopped basil.

To serve, spoon the vinaigrette onto chilled salad plates, and place sausages on each plate. Garnish with fresh herbs, and serve with 1/2 pita (or grain of choice) per serving.

Nutritional info. per serving
Calories	289	
Protein	33	g
Carbohydrate	15	g
Fat	33	%
Sodium	231	mg
Cholesterol	81	mg
Fiber	1	g

Note: You could serve 12 smaller portions - divide nutritional info. in half.

Caffe Abbracci

318 Aragon Ave., Coral Gables (305)441-0700

Nino Pernetti, owner.

♥ Gnocchi al Pomodoro
Yield: 10 servings

2 lb. spring potatoes
1 lb. (4 cups) all purpose flour
1 egg

In large pot, boil potatoes with skin in water until cooked; peel and mash the potatoes. Mix potatoes with the flour and egg thoroughly in a large bowl. When pasta is firm, roll into long sausages, the size of a finger - if necessary sprinkle flour on top, and cut into 1" pieces. Cook in boiling water in large pot 5-10 minutes until cooked.

Nutritional info. per serving

Calories	276	
Protein	8	g
Carbohydrate	58	g
Fat	4	%
Sodium	12	mg
Cholesterol	21	mg
Fiber	2	g

♥♥ Experiment with various spices and vegetables to make different flavors of gnocchi, i.e. saffron, pepper, mushrooms (chopped finely)....

Serve with your favorite tomato sauce and add parmesan to taste.

Caffe Baci

2522 Ponce de Leon Blvd., Coral Gables (305)442-0600

Nino Pernetti, Owner.

♥ Pasta Primavera
Yield: 4 servings

1 lb. spaghetti; cooked according to package directions
2 tablespoons olive oil
2 cups broccoli, florets
2 cups carrots, sliced
2 cups zucchini, sliced
2 cups mushrooms, chopped
4 garlic cloves, minced
Approx. 1 cup chicken stock
4 tablespoons parmesan cheese

Heat 1 tablespoon of olive oil and vegetable oil cooking spray in large pan and saute vegetables with garlic until tender. Add the remainder of oil and stock to cooked vegetables and heat. Mix pasta with vegetables and stock, toss. Sprinkle with parmesan cheese and serve.

Nutritional info. per serving

Calories	466	
Protein	17	g
Carbohydrate	77	g
Fat	22	%
Sodium	347	mg
Cholesterol	5	mg
Fiber	9	g

♥♥ Add spices to your liking, i.e. pepper, nutmeg. Also, experiment with different vegetables, cutting them in different sizes and shapes for variety (you may want to pre-blanch the longer cooking vegetables)!

Casa Rolandi

1930 Ponce de Leon Blvd., Coral Gables (305)444-2187

Alfredo Alvarez, Executive Corporate Chef, learned from European Chefs, including Angelo Giramini. He was also the Executive Chef on The Michaelangelo and Leonardo DaVinci Italian cruise line, and opened Alfredo's of Rome at Epcot Center.
Alfredo's mentor - his father, also a chef.

♥ Salmon Alfredo
Yield: 2 servings

2 teaspoons oil
1- 10-12 oz. salmon fillet
1 teaspoon garlic
1 leaf fresh rosemary
4 leaves fresh sage
1/2 cup fish broth (clam juice)
1/2 cup white wine
Pepper to taste
5 oz. radicchio, chopped
3 oz. endive, chopped
4 oz. grapes, chopped
2 small-medium potatoes, steamed

Preheat oven to 400 F.
Heat oil in large pan and saute salmon with garlic, rosemary and sage briefly on each side. Add clam juice and wine to pan, season with pepper. Add radicchio, endive and grapes and bake in baking pan (or leave in saute pan if ovenproof) for 15 minutes. Serve with 1 small-medium potato per serving.

Nutritional info. per serving

Calories	439	
Protein	36	g
Carbohydrate	37	g
Fat	30	%
Sodium	171	mg
Cholesterol	56	mg
Fiber	4	g

JJ's American Diner

5850 Sunset Drive in South Miami (305)665-5499
2320 Galiano in Coral Gables (305)448-6886
12000 North Kendall Drive (305)598-0307

♥ Bran Muffins
Yield: 18 muffins

1 3/4 cups all-purpose flour
1/2 cup bran flour
1/2 cup sugar
1/2 teaspoon salt
4 teaspoons baking powder
2 whole eggs
5 tablespoons vegetable oil
1/4 cup molasses
1 medium apple (about 3 oz.), grated
1 cup water
1/2 cup raisins

Preheat oven to 400 F.
Sift dry ingredients together in large mixing bowl.
In a separate bowl, beat eggs until frothy. Whip in vegetable oil. Stir in molasses, grated apple, water and raisins. Fold wet ingredients into dry and stir just until well blended.
Fill muffin cups (1/2 full) that have been sprayed with a vegetable oil cooking spray. Bake approx. 20 minutes or until toothpick inserted in center is almost dry. Cool muffins 5-10 minutes before turning out.

Nutritional info. per serving:

Calories	137	
Protein	2	g
Carbohydrate	22	g
Fat	29	%
Sodium	142	mg
Cholesterol	24	mg
Fiber	1	g

♥ Carrot-Zucchini Spice Muffins
Yield: 24 large muffins

3 1/4 cups all-purpose flour
2 cups sugar
1 1/2 teaspoons baking soda
4 teaspoons baking powder
1 teaspoon salt
1/2 teaspoon cinnamon or more to taste
1/8 teaspoon nutmeg
1/8 teaspoon allspice
3/4 cup vegetable oil
2 whole eggs + 1 egg white
2 cups hand-grated carrots (about 4-5 total)
1 1/4 cups hand-grated zucchini (about 1 large)
1 teaspoon vanilla extract

Preheat oven to 400 F.
Sift all dry ingredients together in large bowl.
Whip vegetable oil and eggs + egg white together in a separate bowl. Stir in carrots, zucchini, and vanilla.
Fold wet ingredients into dry and stir just until blended.
Fill large muffin cups that have been sprayed with a vegetable oil cooking spray 1/2 full. Bake approx. 20 -25 minutes or until toothpick inserted in center is almost dry. Cool muffins 5-10 minutes before turning out.

Nutritional info. per serving:

Calories	200	
Protein	3	g
Carbohydrate	31	g
Fat	33	%
Sodium	209	mg
Cholesterol	18	mg
Fiber	1	g

♥♥ Try adding cranberries and raisins for a fruit/veggie-mix muffin!

Justa Pasta

216 Palermo Ave., Coral Gables (305)446-3644

Ignacio Suarez has been in the food business since age 17. He likes to be creative and cook his "own things," with influences from French, Italian, Mexican, Spanish and Oriental cuisines.

♥ Cajun Tuna with Capellini
Yield: 1 serving

1/4 lb. angel hair pasta; cooked al dente according to package directions
1 tablespoon olive oil
1/2 cup mushrooms, sliced
1/4 cup diced onions
1/4 cup broccoli florets
1/4 cup sliced carrots
3 oz. tuna
Blackening or Cajun spice, to taste
1 tomato, peeled, seeded and diced
1/4 cup chicken stock

Heat olive oil in large saute pan and saute vegetables (add vegetable oil cooking spray if needed) until tender; add tuna and spice. Add tomato and chicken stock, and heat.

Toss with angel hair pasta.

Nutritional info. per serving

Calories	733	
Protein	43	g
Carbohydrate	101	g
Fat	23	%
Sodium	564	mg
Cholesterol	35	mg
Fiber	4	g

♥ Capellini Cake (Omelette)
Yield: 1 serving

1/4 lb. angel hair pasta; cooked al dente according to package directions
1/4 cup chicken stock

1/4 cup cauliflower florets
1/4 cup broccoli florets
1/4 cup sliced carrots
1/4 cup snow peas
1/4 cup onions, diced
2 garlic cloves, minced
Pepper, basil, to taste
1 tablespoon olive oil

Spray large saute pan with vegetable oil cooking spray, add stock and heat; add vegetables with garlic, basil and pepper, and cook until tender.

In teflon (non-stick) pan, heat 1/2 tablespoon olive oil and vegetable oil cooking spray; "fry" 1/2 of cooked pasta until brown and crispy. You will be making an omelette with pasta as the outside: Spread 3/4 vegetables on pasta, top with other 1/2 of pasta and flip like an omelette. Add remaining olive oil and vegetable oil cooking spray, heat, and "fry" until this side is brown and crispy.

Serve with remainder of sauteed vegetables on top.

Nutritional info. per serving

Calories	607	
Protein	20	g
Carbohydrate	99	g
Fat	23	%
Sodium	223	mg
Cholesterol	-	
Fiber	3	g

♥ Try adding 1 oz. of skim mozzarella, and tomato sauce, on top of vegetables for variety ... use your favorite vegetables!

La Bussola
270 Giralda Ave., Coral Gables (305)445-8783

Claudio Giordano, the owner, is responsible for all the recipes at the restaurant. He has previously worked at The London Hilton and Munich International. While we were writing the recipes, Gloria Estefan came in for lunch!

♥ Black Linguini with Calamari and Roasted Peppers
Yield: 4 servings

1 lb. black linguini (squid ink); cooked al dente according to package directions
2 tablespoons garlic, finely minced
2 tablespoons finely minced anchovies
2 teaspoons capers
10 calamata olives, pitted and cut in half
1 pinch dried red pepper flakes, crushed
1 red bell pepper, roasted (cut in strips finger size)
Pepper to taste
1/3 lb. fresh calamari, cut in rings
1 cup fresh peeled, seeded and cubed tomatoes
1/4 cup extra virgin olive oil
1 tablespoon finely chopped Italian parsley

In large pan, sprayed with vegetable oil cooking spray, saute all ingredients except linguini, calamari, tomatoes, oil and parsley for 3 minutes. Add calamari and tomatoes and cook for another 3 minutes; add olive oil. Add pasta to sauce. Saute everything for 30 seconds more. Add parsley, mix and serve.

Nutritional info. per serving

Calories	531	
Protein	18	g
Carbohydrate	77	g
Fat	29	%
Sodium	504	mg
Cholesterol	109	mg
Fiber	4	g

Yuca Restaurant
148 Giralda, Coral Gables (305)444-4448

Chef Douglas Rodriguez, originally from Miami, is a graduate of the Johnson and Wales Culinary Program in Providence, Rhode Island. Born of Cuban parents, he cites his mother as his mentor, and that every night at the restaurant is a new experience.

♥ Malanga and Boniato Gnocchi with Tomato Basil Sauce
Yield: 4 servings

Tomato-Basil Sauce:
1 tablespoon virgin olive oil
1 1/2 tablespoons finely chopped fresh basil
2 cloves garlic, finely chopped
4 oz. (1/2 cup) canned plum tomatoes, drained and crushed
1 bay leaf
1/2 teaspoon sugar

Heat olive oil in medium saucepan over medium heat and saute basil and garlic 1 minute. Add tomatoes, bay leaf and sugar and simmer 20 minutes.
Keep sauce warm, covered, until ready to serve.

Gnocchi:
1 lb. malanga, peeled and cut into cubes
3/4 lb. white boniato, peeled and cut into cubes
2 tablespoons parmesan cheese, grated
1 egg
2 tablespoons margarine, melted
Up to 1 lb. (about 4 cups) all-purpose flour

In a medium saucepan, boil the boniato and malanga cubes until tender. Drain and while still warm, not hot, process until smooth in a food processor.
Add remaining ingredients, except flour, and process again. Remove mixture to a floured board and work in flour with hands, little by little, until the consistency of dough is reached.

303

Bring a large stockpot of water to a simmer. Roll the gnocchi mixture into long sausage shapes, approx. 3/4 " in diameter. Cut off 1 " pieces and drop them into the hot water. Simmer the gnocchi gently about 3 minutes or until they rise to the surface. Remove with a slotted spoon and drain on paper towels. Serve with Tomato-Basil Sauce.

Nutritional info. per serving:

Calories	740	
Protein	21	g
Carbohydrate	133	g
Fat	16	%
Sodium	366	mg
Cholesterol	60	mg
Fiber	8	g

♥ Gloria's Traditional Black Bean Soup
Yield: 8 servings

1 lb. dried black beans (or 6 cups canned)
3 quarts water (if using dried beans or 2 quarts for canned)
2 bay leaves
1/4 cup virgin olive oil
1 small onion (about 4 oz.), diced
1 large red pepper, coarsely diced
1 large green pepper, coarsely diced
3 small shallots, diced
1 clove garlic, minced
1 tablespoon cumin, ground
2 tablespoons dried leaf oregano
2 tablespoons chopped fresh oregano
2 tablespoons chopped parsley
1 1/2 tablespoons sugar

Garnish:
4 green onions (scallions), finely chopped
8 tablespoons light sour cream or plain yogurt

Rinse dried beans well and soak in water in a large heavy pot overnight. The next day, add bay leaf to the beans and water and bring to a boil. Simmer, uncovered over low heat for three to four hours until tender and beans begin to split open. Stir occasionally and add more water, if necessary. If using canned beans, heat beans with 2 quarts water in large pot.

In a separate heavy bottomed skillet, heat olive oil over medium heat and saute the onions, peppers and shallots until the onions are translucent. Add garlic, cumin, oregano and parsley and saute 30 seconds more; add sugar. Puree mixture thoroughly in food processor or blender. Add to cooked beans and cook 20-30 minutes more. Adjust seasoning and add water to thin soup, if desired.

Garnish portions with chopped green onion and a dollop of light sour cream or yogurt.

Nutritional info. per serving:

Calories	275	
Protein	12	g
Carbohydrate	39	g
Fat	28	%
Sodium	57	mg
Cholesterol	2	mg
Fiber	13	g

Capriccio
12313 S. Dixie Highway, Miami (305)255-3422

Francisco Portobanco, Executive Chef, was an apprentice to Vasco Cecchi (his mentor), the "top culinary chef from Montecatini, Italy."
His most memorable meal - cooking with no electricity on a gas stove with candles.

♥ Linguini Al Pomodoro Fresco E Rugola (Linguine with fresh Tomatoes and Arugula)
Yield: 4 servings

1/4 cup extra virgin olive oil
3 or more garlic cloves, minced
6 plum tomatoes, seeded and chopped
3 tablespoons chopped fresh basil
1 bunch of arugula
Pepper
1 lb. linguini; cooked al dente
1/4 cup chicken broth (stock), if desired
4 oz. Buffalo mozzarella (skim), diced
1 tablespoon grated parmesan cheese

Heat 1 teaspoon of oil in large skillet over medium heat; add garlic and saute until brown. Stir in tomatoes, basil and arugula and season with pepper (add vegetable oil cooking spray if needed). Toss with cooked linguini in skillet. Add remainder of oil (and chicken stock if desired). Add mozzarella cheese and saute for 1 minute until partially melted. Add parmesan cheese to taste.

Nutritional info. per serving

Calories	626	
Protein	24	g
Carbohydrate	89	g
Fat	30	%
Sodium	281	mg
Cholesterol	17	mg
Fiber	7	g

Norman Brothers Produce
7621 S.W. 87 Ave., Miami (305)274-9363

Craig Basiliere, Executive Chef/Director of Catering, has a Culinary Arts Degree from Johnson and Wales, and a B.S. from the FIU School of Hospitality Management.

♥ Turkey Stuffed Cabbage in Wine Sauce
Yield: 2 servings

1/4 cup onions or shallots, minced
9 oz. ground turkey
1 egg white, beaten
3 tablespoons seasoned bread crumbs
1 teaspoon tamari soy sauce
1/8 teaspoon ground white pepper and nutmeg
2 garlic cloves, pressed
4 medium green cabbage leaves, blanched
1/2 cup tomato sauce
1/4 cup chicken stock
1 teaspoon onion powder
2 tablespoons dry red wine (optional)

1 cup cooked brown rice

In non-stick skillet sprayed with vegetable oil cooking spray cook shallots/onions until soft. In medium bowl combine cooked shallots with ground turkey, egg white, bread crumbs, tamari, pepper, nutmeg and garlic, and mix well.

Remove about 1" from core end of each blanched cabbage leaf. Place 1/4 of mixture in center of leaf and roll tightly, tucking in sides to enclose filling. In same skillet arrange filled leaves, seamside down.

In small bowl combine remaining ingredients; pour over cabbage rolls, bring to a boil and cook for 10 minutes. Reduce heat to low, cover and let simmer until cabbage is tender (about 25 minutes).

Serve with 1/2 cup cooked brown rice per serving.

Nutritional info. per serving

Calories	458	
Protein	35	g
Carbohydrate	45	g
Fat	29	%
Sodium	889	mg
Cholesterol	83	mg
Fiber	7	g

Snooks Bayside Club

MM 99.9, Key Largo (305)451-3857

Patricia A. Mathias, Executive Chef, always loved to cook but until the age of 30, did everything except restaurant work, including being a teacher, bookkeeper and secretary.
Most memorable meal - her mother's leg of lamb.
Patricia's mentor - Andre Mueller, Chef/Owner of Marker 88. He gave her "her first job in a kitchen after much pleading - a grueling instructor who demanded perfection and taught her well!"

Pat's sister, Karen Punturo, is the Pastry Chef who makes pasta and bakes fresh breads and desserts. Karen went to college for nursing in South Carolina, but got "hands on" culinary experience at night.
Her mentor - Jim Smeal, a baker in Charleston.

♥ Shrimp Pesto (Pasta)
Yield: 4 servings

Pesto:
1/2 cup basil, sliced in strips
1/4 cup Asiago cheese (or parmesan)
1/4 cup pine nuts, coarsely chopped
2 tablespoons chopped garlic
1 tablespoon olive oil (to bind)
Black pepper to taste

   Mix together pesto ingredients in processor.

12 oz. dry fettucini; cooked according to package directions
1 tablespoon olive oil
12 oz. shrimp, peeled and deveined
1/4 cup white wine
2 tablespoons lemon juice
White pepper to taste
2 tomatoes, peeled, and diced
4 scallions, cut diagonally

Heat olive oil in large pan and saute shrimp with white wine, lemon juice and pepper. Cook on 1 side; turn shrimp then add tomatoes and green onions (scallions). Toss with pasta, then add pesto. Heat and serve.

Nutritional info. per serving

Calories	503	
Protein	28	g
Carbohydrate	67	g
Fat	25	%
Sodium	262	mg
Cholesterol	116	mg
Fiber	4	g

♥ Strawberry Rhubarb Pie
Yield: 8 servings

1 cup sugar
3 cups rhubarb, chopped
3 cups strawberries, sliced
1/2 cup dry tapioca
1- 9 inch pie crust- made with polyunsaturated vegetable oil
5 1/2 oz. phyllo dough. Slice each strip lengthwise in half; fold each half into thirds.
1/2 cup margarine, melted

Preheat oven to 375 F.
Mix sugar, rhubarb, strawberries and tapioca together for filling. Place in pie crust. Brush each phyllo strip with margarine (both sides) and place on top of pie: standing up in concentric circles covering entire top!

Bake in oven covered with foil for 1 hour. Remove foil the last 10 minutes. Leave pie in pan.

Nutritional info. per serving

Calories	387	
Protein	4	g
Carbohydrate	61	g
Fat	35	%
Sodium	305	mg
Cholesterol	-	
Fiber	1	g

♥ To decrease fat and calories, eliminate margarine, and spray phyllo strips with a vegetable oil cooking spray.

Note: 1. You can use raspberries instead of strawberries. 2. If you substitute another type of berry to replace rhubarb, lower sugar in recipe and cut margarine (if used) in half to keep fat percentage below 35%.

Marker 88
MM 88
Overlooking Florida Bay on Plantation Key (305)852-5503/9315

Andre Mueller, Chef de Cuisine/Owner.

♥ Fish Rangoon
Yield: 4 servings

Fish:
1-1/2 lbs. fillets of yellowtail, snapper, grouper, or similar firm white fish,
  all bones and skin removed
1 teaspoon Worcestershire sauce
2 tablespoons lemon juice
1/4 teaspoon white pepper
1/4 cup flour
1 egg + 1 egg white
2 tablespoons vegetable oil
1/4 teaspoon ground cinnamon
3 tablespoons currant jelly

Sauce:
2 tablespoons margarine
1/2 cup diced each: bananas, pineapple, mangos and papayas (if mango or
  papaya are not available, peaches may be used)
1 tablespoon chopped parsley
2 tablespoons lemon juice

Preheat oven to 350 F.
Season boneless fillets with Worcestershire sauce, lemon juice and white
pepper. Dip in flour, then in egg wash.
Heat skillet with vegetable oil and vegetable oil cooking spray. Place fillets in skillet and saute on both sides; then finish cooking in oven - in skillet, if ovenproof, or baking pan.

When fillets are done, remove them to a serving platter. Sprinkle with ground cinnamon and spread currant jelly over them. Keep warm.
For sauce: In skillet quickly melt margarine; add fruit, parsley and lemon juice. Shake skillet until heated through. Do not cook or heat too long. Top each serving of fish with some of the sauce and serve.

Nutritional info. per serving

Calories	405	
Protein	39	g
Carbohydrate	29	g
Fat	33	%
Sodium	202	mg
Cholesterol	115	mg
Fiber	2	g

♥ Fish Sauces

Serve each sauce over 4 - 4 oz. portions of cooked fish that have been seasoned with pepper, lemon juice and your favorite spices, along with 1 medium-large boiled potato (or grain of choice) per serving.

When fish is just about finished cooking, start the sauce. For each sauce: In skillet, melt margarine, and saute longer cooking ingredients, such as mushrooms, apples etc., first, then add the rest of fruits and vegetables, parsley, lemon juice, etc. Shake skillet or stir until ingredients are cooked and heated through. Do not cook or heat too long!

♥ Senator
Yield: 4 servings

2 tablespoons margarine
2 1/2 cups sliced fresh mushrooms
1/3 cup sliced blanched almonds (roasted in oven before adding to sauce)
2 tablespoons chopped parsley
Approx. 3-4 tablespoons lemon juice
1/3 cup scallions, diced

Calories	415	
Protein	37	g
Carbohydrate	39	g
Fat	27	%
Sodium	123	mg
Cholesterol	53	mg
Fiber	4	g

♥ Port of Spain
Yield: 4 servings

2 tablespoons margarine
3/4 cup diced apples
3/4 cup diced banana
1/2 cup diced tomatoes
1 pimento, diced
2 tablespoons chopped parsley
Approx. 3-4 tablespoons lemon juice
1/3 cup sliced scallions

Nutritional info. per serving*

Calories	396	
Protein	35	g
Carbohydrate	47	g
Fat	17	%
Sodium	122	mg
Cholesterol	53	mg
Fiber	4	g

♥ Seminole
Yield: 4 servings

2 tablespoons margarine
8 oz. fresh baby bay scallops
1 cup diced tomatoes
1 cup mushrooms, diced
1 cup sliced scallions
Approx. 3-4 tablespoons lemon juice

Do not overcook scallops.

Nutritional info. per serving*

Calories	409	
Protein	44	g
Carbohydrate	39	g
Fat	18	%
Sodium	214	mg
Cholesterol	72	mg
Fiber	3	g

* Nutritional analysis for each sauce recipe includes sauce, fish and potato.

The Atlantic's Edge
Cheeca Lodge MM 82, The Keys (305)664-4651

Dawn Sieber, Executive Chef, comes from a family of doctors. She likes to tease her father that she was born with a knife of a different kind in her hand! Dawn, who graduated first in her class from Baltimore's International Culinary Arts Institute, oversees all foodservice operations at Cheeca Lodge, including the award winning The Atlantic's Edge. Dawn is an active member of the A.C.F..

♥ Florida Lobster Salad

Strawberry Vinaigrette
Yield: dressing for 6 salads
Strawberry mixture:
1/2 cup strawberries, crushed
1 tablespoon sugar
1/2 cup white wine vinegar

1 Florida orange
1 tablespoon Dijon mustard
1/6 cup hazelnut oil
1/6 cup vegetable oil
2/3 cup water/cornstarch mixture (optional, see preparation tips)
1 teaspoon honey
Pepper to taste

Let strawberries, sugar and vinegar sit for at least 15 minutes to 24 hours in a bowl.
In another bowl, squeeze orange, use juice and pulp but no pith, and mix in mustard; splash in 1-2 tablespoons of the strawberry mixture. Whisk in hazelnut and vegetable oils, water/ cornstarch mixture, as desired, and 1/2 cup of strawberry mixture. Add honey and pepper.

Yield: 1 Salad Serving
2 cups mixed greens
5-6 oz. raw lobster meat
1/2 key lime
4 quartered strawberries
1 Florida orange, cut into segments
1 teaspoon hazelnuts, toasted and chopped
1/2 pita bread pocket (or grain of your choice)

Endive spears and watercress

In pan, poach lobster half covered with water and juice of 1/2 key lime for 6 minutes. Plunge in ice bath and put in refrigerator; cut lobster meat into medallions.

To toast hazelnuts, place on a flat sheet pan (cookie sheet) in a hot dry 350 F oven for 10-15 minutes. When brown starts pulling away, remove and let cool. Place cloth on top and roll your hands over to pull skin off.

Toss greens with 2 tablespoons of the vinaigrette and place on a plate. Place medallions of lobster over the top and surround with quartered strawberries and orange sections. Top with hazelnuts.

Garnish with endive spears and watercress, and serve with 1/2 pita (or grain of choice).

Nutritional info. per serving

Calories	432	
Protein	29	g
Carbohydrate	47	g
Fat	31	%
Sodium	582	mg
Cholesterol	81	mg
Fiber	8	g

♥ Fresh Chicken Steamer
Yield: 1 serving

5-6 oz. raw chicken breast, skinless and thinly sliced
1 stem bok choy
1 oz. wild mushrooms, shiitake, sliced
1/4 head broccoli, florets
1/3 red pepper, cut in rings
2 oz. snow peas
Lemon, basil and pepper to taste

Use a Bamboo or regular steamer. "Paint a picture":
Place green leafy part of bok choy under chicken (so it won't stick). Sprinkle vegetables and spices around; steam.

Sesame Sauce

Yield: 10 portions

1/4 cup lite soy sauce
1/4 tablespoon lime juice
1/4 tablespoon honey
1/2 tablespoon dry mustard
1/4 cup rice wine vinegar (use up to 1/2 cup if you like vinegar taste)
1/3 cup sesame oil
1/3 cup vegetable oil
1 cup water/cornstarch mixture (optional, see preparation tips)

Place all ingredients in blender and mix. Pour over steamed chicken and vegetables; serve.

Nutritional info. per serving

Calories	476	
Protein	42	g
Carbohydrate	38	g
Fat	35	%
Sodium	364	mg
Cholesterol	96	mg
Fiber	4	g

Louie's Backyard
700 Waddell Avenue, Key West (305)294-1061

Chef Doug Shook.

♥ Peanut-Marinated Chicken with Asian Vegetables in a Garlic-Ginger Vinaigrette
Yield: 4 servings

For the Peanut Marinade:
2 tablespoons sesame seeds
1/2 cup chicken broth or stock
1/3 cup creamy peanut butter
1/4 cup red wine vinegar
2 tablespoons lite soy sauce
1 tablespoon sugar
1 tablespoon dry sherry
1 1/2 teaspoons Chinese chili paste
1/2 cup chopped green onions (scallions)
2 tablespoons freshly grated ginger (or 1/2 teaspoon ginger powder)
   or to taste
1 large garlic clove, minced

4 - 6 oz. chicken breasts, skinless, boneless, pounded thin

1 1/3 cups raw Basmati or other short-grained rice; cooked according
   to package directions

Toast the sesame seeds until golden in a small, ungreased skillet (note: seeds can also be toasted on foil or baking sheet in hot 400 F. oven for about 5 minutes - do not let them burn!). Transfer seeds to a shallow bowl. Add the remaining marinade ingredients and stir well. Pour out half the marinade into a separate bowl and reserve, covered.

Add chicken breast portions to marinade in bowl. Cover and refrigerate at least 1 hour. Meanwhile, prepare rice and Garlic-Ginger Vinaigrette.

Vinaigrette:
1/4 cup red wine vinegar
2 tablespoons lite soy sauce
2 tablespoons dark sesame oil
1 garlic clove, minced
2 teaspoons fresh grated ginger
1/2 teaspoon sugar

Whisk all vinaigrette ingredients together in mixing bowl and hold aside.

Heat charcoal grill or broiler. Cook chicken 6-8 inches from heat approx. 5-7 minutes each side, basting with remaining marinade. Meanwhile, prepare Asian vegetables.

Vegetables:
2 tablespoons peanut oil
1 medium green pepper or a mixture of red, green and yellow peppers, julienned (about 1 cup)
1/4 cucumber, julienned (about 1/4 cup)
1 medium carrot, julienned (about 1/4 cup)
1/2 cup shredded Napa cabbage
1/2 cup julienned Bok Choy
1/2 cup shredded red cabbage
1/4 cup julienned daikon radish
1/2 cup asparagus, cut into 1" pieces
1/4 lb. snow peas, julienned

Heat peanut oil in large skillet or a wok and stir fry the vegetables until they are very hot but still crisp. Cover and steam 1-2 minutes, if desired. Add 1/4 cup of the vinaigrette and heat to boiling.

Cut cooked chicken breast portions into strips and arrange on serving plates. Spoon hot vegetables and vinaigrette around chicken. Serve with hot rice.

Nutritional info. per serving:

Calories	757	
Protein	55	g
Carbohydrates	68	g
Fat	35	%
Sodium	905	mg
Cholesterol	98	mg
Fiber	5	g

♥ Roasted Tomato Soup with Avocado Ice
Yield : 1 qt. soup (4 portions)

Tomato Soup:
4 red ripe tomatoes (approx. 1 lb. total)
4 branches fresh thyme (or 1/4 teaspoon dried leaves)
1 teaspoon chopped garlic (approx. 1 large clove)
Freshly ground pepper to taste
Cayenne pepper

Preheat oven to 400 F.
Remove the core from the tomatoes, cut them in half and place them in a shallow pan. Scatter the thyme and garlic over the tomatoes and sprinkle with pepper.

Place the pan in hot oven for 30-45 minutes until the tomatoes have begun to shrink in their skins and exude their juice. Remove the pan from the oven and allow the tomatoes to cool.

When the tomatoes are cool, remove the thyme branches and pour the contents of the pan into a food processor fitted with a steel blade, or a blender. Puree and strain the mixture. Chill thoroughly, then season with black pepper and cayenne pepper.

Avocado Ice:
1 large ripe avocado (about 6 oz. pulp)
Juice of 1 lemon
2 tablespoons sugar
1 1/4 cups cold water

Peel and split the avocado and puree with the lemon juice. Whisk the sugar into the water and combine with the avocado. Process until smooth in a blender or food processor.

Place the mixture in an ice cream freezer and freeze according to manufacturer's directions.

To serve:
1/2 cup fresh basil, cut into fine ribbons (chiffonade)
4 pieces Whole grain bread or Pita bread pockets, toasted and cut into triangle quarters

Place one cup of the chilled soup in a wide rimmed soup bowl. Put a 3-oz. scoop of the ice in the center. Scatter the basil ribbons over the soup. Serve with 1 slice toast points per serving.

Nutritional info. per serving:

Calories	183	
Protein	4	g
Carbohydrate	28	g
Fat	35	%
Sodium	132	mg
Cholesterol	-	
Fiber	7	g

Associations and Abbreviations Featured in Today's Specials

American Culinary Federation: A.C.F.
The American Culinary Federation is a professional, educational and fraternal association of chefs and cooks dedicated to the advancement of the culinary profession.
Headquartered in St. Augustine, the A.C.F. offers a means for culinarians to gain experience, training, education and fellowship with their colleagues. The A.C.F. is also a member of the World Association of Cooks Societies, the international federation of chefs and cooks.

American Dietetic Association: A.D.A.
A professional organization whose purpose is the promotion of optimal health and nutritional status of the population. Most ADA members are Registered Dietitians (R.D.). who have completed at least a Bachelors degree, internship or equivalent experience and a qualifying exam. Continuing Education is required to maintain the R.D. status. This certification process encourages high standards of performance to protect the health, safety and welfare of the public! An R.D. is a reliable source of information on diet, food and nutrition.

Chaine des Rotisseurs:
An international gourmet society for professionals and non-professionals whose goal is to bring together people interested in food and wine and fine dining.

Culinary Institute of America: C.I.A.
A leading culinary training program located in Hyde Park, New York.

Florida International University: F.I.U.
Florida International University School of Hospitality Management offers comprehensive degree programs in hotel and restaurant management for Bachelor of Science degrees in Hospitality Management and Master of Science degrees in hotel and foodservice management.

Florida Restaurant Association: FRA
Since its founding in 1946, the Florida Restaurant Association has led the foodservice industry forward in the promotion of excellence and professionalism. It keeps its members informed on governmental issues, industry trends and other foodservice related activities.

References

Charley, Helen, Food Science, John Wiley & Sons, Second Edition, 1982

Lang, Jenifer H., Larousse Gastronomique, Crown Publishers, Inc., 1988

Rombauer, Irma S. and Becker, Marion R., Joy of Cooking, Bobbs-Merrill Company, Inc., 1975

Schneider, Elizabeth, Uncommon Fruits and Vegetables, Harper & Row, 1986

The Culinary Institute of America, The New Professional Chef, Fifth Edition, Van Nostrand Reinhold, 1991.

Whitney, Eleanor N., Hamilton, Eva M., et al, Understanding Nutrition, Fifth Edition, West Publishing Company, 1990

Order Form

To: Nutritional Marketing Services, Inc.

1131 N.W. 99 Ave.   or   260 Hibiscus Ave.
Plantation, Florida   Lauderdale-by-the-Sea,
33322   Florida 33308

Please send me _____ copies of "Today's Specials" cookbook at $18.35 per copy ($14.95 plus .90 tax and $2.50 for shipping and handling). Out-of-state residents $17.45 per copy.

Enclosed is my check for $_____.

Name _____

Street _____

City _____ State _____ Zip _____

_____ This is a gift. Please send directly to:

Name_____

Street _____

City _____ State _____ Zip _____

Additional Information to Order

I would like to be on a mailing list for any
supplemental or new publications _____ yes

I would like to have my recipe(s) * analyzed at
$4.00 @/$13.00 for 4.   _____

Include recipe(s) with order form and indicate
if you would like us to make them "heart healthy."

I would like to have my (or spouse or child's)
diet nutritionally * analyzed at $12.00 @.   _____

Write down everything you (or others; keep
separate forms) eat and drink for 3 days,
including amounts (measurements) of foods and
liquids. Include this information with order form.

I would like a list of proven Behavior Modification
techniques to help with weight loss and control-
                              $5.00.   _____
Please send SASE.
Name _____
Street _____
City _____ State _____ Zip ___

Enclosed is my check for $

*Nutritional analysis includes information on 30 + nutrients,
including data on protein, carbohydrate, fat, cholesterol, sodium and
fiber.

Tropical Produce Availability and Nutritional Chart

	Season	Source	Serving Size	Calories	Protein gr	Carbo- hydrate	Fat gr	Sodium mg	Potassium mg	Vit A I.U.	Vit C mg
ATEMOYA	Aug.-Oct.	South Florida	1/3 cup	94	1.4	24	.64	2.2	314	10	9
AVOCADO	July-March	South Florida	1/2 cup (cb)	96	1.0	6.6	8.25	3	453	220	10.5
BONIATO	All year	South Florida	1/2 cup	90	1	20	tr	7	612	0	12
BREADFRUIT	Apr.-Nov.	Haiti/Dom.Rep.	1/2 cup	115	1.1	30	.2	0	548	45	32
CALABAZA	All year	Costa Rica	1/2 cup	32	.7	8.2	tr	3	246	5460	15
CARAMBOLA	Mid Aug.-Mar.	South Florida	1/2 cup	22	.3	6	tr	0	115	338	15
CASSAVA	All year	Costa Rica	2/3 cup	120	3	27	tr	8	764	10	48
CHAYOTE	All year	Costa Rica	1/2 cup	16	1.0	3.5	tr	3	98	37	7
CILANTRO	Dec.-Apr.	South Florida	1/4 cup	1	tr	.1	tr	1	22	111	tr
COCONUT	All year	Dom.Rep./Honduras	1/2 cup (sh)	139	1.4	3.75	14.1	9	103	0	1
GUAVA	Nov.-Mar./June-Aug.	South Florida	1/2 cup	42	tr	10	tr	0	234	654	150
KUMQUAT	Mid Oct.-Mar.	South Florida	1 fruit	12	.2	3.2	tr	1	44	110	7
LIME	All year	South Florida	1 lime	19	.5	6.4	.1	1	69	10	25
LYCHEE	June-Mid July	South Florida	10 fruits	58	.8	14.8	.3	3	153	n/a	38
MALANGA	All year	Costa Rica/So. Fla.	1/2 cup	137	2.2	32	tr	n/a	n/a	0	8
MAMEY	June-Aug.	South Florida	1/2 fruit	223	2.2	55	2.2	65.5	206	1010	61
MANGO	May-Aug.	So.Fla./Haiti	1/2 cup (sl)	54	.6	14	.35	6	156	3960	29
PAPAYA	All year	So.Fla./Bahamas	1/2 cup (cb)	55	.8	14.0	.1	4	328	2450	78
PASSION FRUIT	All year	South Florida	1 fruit	16	.4	3.9	.1	5	63	130	5
PUMMELO	Oct.-Feb.	South Florida	1/2 cup (sec)	35	tr	9	tr	0	205	0	57
TAMARIND	Grows wild	Caribbean	1 fruit	5	tr	20	tr	0	2	0	0
TARO	All year	South Florida	1/2 cup	56	tr	14	tr	6	307	0	2
WATERCRESS	All year	South Florida	1 cup (ch)	24	2.8	3.8	.4	65	353	6130	99

(cb) Cubes, (ch) Chopped, (sec) Sections, (sh) Shredded, (sl) Slices

SOURCES
Composition of Fruits and Fruit Juices, Agriculture Handbook 8-9. U.S.D.A. Human Nutrition Information Service, 1982.
Composition of Vegetables and Vegetable Products, Agriculture Handbook 8-11. U.S.D.A. Human Nutrition Information Service, 1984.
Composition of Seeds and Nuts, Agriculture Handbook 8-12. U.S.D.A. Human Nutrition Information Service, 1984.
Food Composition Table for Use in Africa. FAO, 1968.
Food Composition Table for Use In Latin America. INCAP, 1961.

BEEF

The Skinniest Six

ROUND TIP
157 calories
5.9 gms total fat*
(2.1 gms sat. fat)

TOP LOIN
176 calories
8.0 gms total fat*
(3.1 gms sat. fat)

TOP ROUND
153 calories
4.2 gms total fat*
(1.4 gms sat. fat)

EYE OF ROUND
143 calories
4.2 gms total fat*
(1.5 gms sat. fat)

TENDERLOIN
179 calories
8.5 gms total fat*
(3.2 gms sat. fat)

TOP SIRLOIN
165 calories
6.1 gms total fat*
(2.4 gms sat. fat)

Quick, Easy, Delicious

Florida Beef Council
P.O. Box 421929
Kissimmee, FL 34742
(407) 846-4557

NUTRITIONAL VALUE OF FRESH FLORIDA TOMATOES

According to the USDA, fresh tomatoes are the third most popular vegetable in the U.S. (after potatoes and lettuce). Florida tomatoes not only add color and fresh flavor to a variety of dishes but also are a valuable source of nutrition.

One medium tomato (5.3 ounces):
- contains only 35 calories
- supplies 40% of the U.S. recommended daily allowance (U.S. RDA) of vitamin C and 20% of vitamin A, some of which is in the form of beta-carotene associated with a reduced risk of certain cancers.
- is a good source of dietary fiber, containing about as much as a slice of whole wheat bread.
- provides potassium, iron, phosphorous and also contains some B vitamins.
- is low in sodium and, like all produce, contains no cholesterol.

BASIC TOMATO PREPARATION

To Peel: Peeling fresh tomatoes is not necessary, unless the fruit is to be cooked. Heat causes skins to slip away from the flesh, so it is best to peel a tomato before adding it to a heated dish. To peel fresh tomatoes, submerge them in a bowl of boiling water for about 30 seconds. Transfer to cold water and the skins will slip off.

To Seed: Scrape seeds away from the flesh with a pointed utensil, such as a grapefruit spoon, being careful not to puncture skin. NOTE: Tomato seeds contain significant nutritional qualities and few recipes are affected by seeds. Avoid seeding if possible.

To Slice: Using a serrated knife, slice tomatoes lengthwise, rather than crosswise, to retain juice.

To Stuff: Cut off stem end and scoop out seeds and pulp with sharp utensil, such as a grapefruit spoon, being careful not to puncture skin. Sprinkle the cavity lightly with salt and turn upside down on a paper towel to drain.

To Stew: Place peeled whole or cut-up tomatoes in a saucepan without water. Season with salt, pepper and a pinch of sugar; add diced onion or green pepper, if desired. Simmer, tightly covered, over low heat until done, 10 to 15 minutes, stirring occasionally.

To Broil: Remove core, halve crosswise or slice. Dot with butter, sprinkle with salt, pepper or other seasonings. Broil until tomatoes are tender and topping is lightly browned.

To Bake: Half crosswise, dot with butter and season as desired. Bake in hot oven (425°F.) 10 to 15 minutes.

To Microwave: Prepare as directed above for baking and microwave on High (100% Power) 3 to 4 minutes for four halves; 5 to 6 minutes for six to eight halves.

Tomato Equivalents
- 3-4 medium tomatoes weigh about 1 pound
- 1 pound of fresh tomatoes, peeled and seeded will produce about 1½ cups pulp.

FLORIDA TOMATO COMMITTEE
P.O. Box 140635, Orlando, FL 32814-0635